BRYAN ADAMS

BRYAN ADAMS

Everything He Does

Sorelle Saidman

SIDGWICK
&JACKSON

First published 1993 by Random House of Canada Ltd, Toronto

This edition published 1994 by Sidgwick and Jackson
an imprint of Macmillan General Books
Cavaye Place London SW10 9PG
and Basingstoke

Associated companies throughout the world

ISBN 0 283 06246 0

1 3 5 7 9 8 6 4 2

A CIP catalogue record for this book is available from
the British Library

Printed and bound in Great Britain by
Mackays of Chatham PLC, Chatham, Kent

Grateful acknowledgement is made to EMI Music Publishing Canada
to reprint lyrics from the following songs:

"Until I Find You" by Bryan Guy Adams and Budd Marr
"Song for a Star" by Bryan Guy Adams and Dan Gaudin
Both songs © 1977 Beechwood Music of Canada Limited, c/o EMI
Blackwood Music Canada Ltd. All rights reserved. International
copyright secured. Reprinted by permission.

PHOTO CREDITS:
Cover photograph: Raj Rama
Photographs 5–8, 12–15, 17, 18, 24, 25 by Raj Rama
Photograph 9 by Bev Davies
Photograph 10 courtesy of Keith Norbury/Goldstream News Gazette
Photograph 11 courtesy by Paul McGrath/North Shore News
Photograph 16 by Lawrence Kirsch
Photographs 19–23 courtesy of Alistair Palmer
Photograph 26 by Kevin Statham

Dedicated to Bruce Allen
and, of course, to Bryan Adams

In memory of Brian Too Loud MacLeod (1952–1992)
and the real ticketmaster, Gary Switlo (1946–1992)

CONTENTS

Acknowledgements   viii
Introduction   xi
1 A Donkey of a Song   1
2 Rebel on a Rampage   9
3 Sweeney Todd: In the Nick of Time   23
4 Adams/Vallance: First Dance   37
5 The Colonel and the General   51
6 Bryan Adams Hasn't Heard of You, Either   65
7 First Cuts   83
8 Heaven and Hell: Reckless to the End   103
9 Reckless on the Road: Tears, Tours and
    Oh Chute, Why Me?   120
10 Live Aid, Amnesty, Royalty and Victory   141
11 Into the Fire   158
12 Into the Void   177
13 Everything He Does   200
14 So far . . . so good   216
    Appendix   221

Acknowledgements

Special thanks to Barbara-Lynn Pollard and Terry Tarapacki (they did all the work); to Mom, Dada, the family who, as usual, gave me 100% support; and to Nancy Flight and Jeff Bateman, good friends, excellent advisors and even better editors.

Extra special thanks to Chu Chu, Hans Maas and Louise Allen. (You don't know how special you are.)

I'd like to gratefully acknowledge the contributions of such media stalwarts as Ellie O'Day (her articles and interviews make up a substantial piece of the early career material), Les Wiseman, Keith Sharp and John Mackie. Much of their input is attributed, but some of it is not. I'd also like to acknowledge major contributions from Tom Harrison, Larry LeBlanc, Bill Deverell and Terry David Mulligan.

The bandmembers were not interviewed for this book—the contributions from Pat Steward, Dave Taylor, Keith Scott, John Hannah and Mickey Curry are all taken from previous interview.

Likewise, previous interviews with Jim Vallance were incorporated into the manuscript in addition to recent material addressing the break-up of his songwriting partnership with Adams.

Others making contributions, some minor, some

substantial, include: Sherri Decembrini-Bergmann, Grant Gislason, Michael Godin, Mike Harling, Crystal Harbidge, James Monaco (featured less than he deserves), Alistair Palmer and Martin Shaer; and Michael Adjenstadt, Michael Becker, John Bell, Michael Bilkoski, John Booth, Casey Boyle, David Brian, Susan Broach, Drew Burns, Lloyd Burritt, Ken Caravetta, Andrew Carral, Blake Elliott, Alison Glass, Len Goddard, Graham Hicks, Rob Hoskin, Paul iverson, Eric Kagna, Michael Kamen, Lawrence Kirsch, Marty Kramer, Daryl Kromm, Stuart Lester, Dee Lippingwell, Chu Chu Maas, Craig McDowall, Lindsay Mitchell, Morgan Creek, Steve Newton, Keith Norbury, Mark Nyberg, Gerry O'Day, Jame Omara, Bill Ott, Skip Prest, Raj Rama, Dave Reimer, Rick Saikaley, Barry Samuels, Larry Semkew, Kevin Statham, Anna Skokan, Brian Wadsworth, Steve Weakes, Ron Wright and dozens of others who prefer to remain anonymous.

The following media sources have provided attributed material: *Music Express*, Sandy Robertson, *Saturday Night* magazine, *Boston Globe, Seventeen, Smash Hits, Kerrang!, Rock* magazine, *Record* magazine, *Toronto Star, Rolling Stone* magazine, *Billboard, Cashbox, Record World, West World* magazine, *Winnipeg Free Press, Winnipeg Sun, Calgary Herald, Sunshine News, Georgia Straight, Playboy, Edmonton Sun, Sunday Express, Ottawa Citizen, Faces* magazine, *Hit Parader, Maclean's, Pittsburg Press, Bop, Vancouver Sun, Vancouver Magazine, Sounds, Album Network, Radio and Records, Record Mirror, Graffiti, Toronto Sun, Look In, Daily Star, Los Angeles Times, Rockline, New Musical Express, Canadian Business, Creem, Q* magazine, *New York Times, Gavin Report, Music Paper, Atlanta Journal, Canadian Musician, Canadian Press, The Globe and Mail, Canadian Composer, Modern Drummer, Victoria Times-Colonist* and Dublin's *Hot Press*.

Valuable information was also provided by The Record, *Performance* magazine, MuchMusic, Radio One, CFOX, BCTV, CBC-TV and UTV.

Research was provided by Mike Harling in England, Michael Adjenstadt in Israel and Louise Allen in Toronto, with much thanks to Keith Sharp and the staff at Music Express/Impact. Additional assistance for Terry and Barbara in Vancouver was provided by Sherri Decembrini-Bergmann, Sherri Chisholm, and Chandra Halko.

Thanks to the fans (the Adams experts), Erica Gipp, Carina Sjunnesson, Romana Krasny, Victoria Vitkay, Keiko Kurata, Inigo Ramirez-Escudero, Sharon Leeson, Maria Efthymiatou, S. Macagni, Mona Nilsson, Brian Hall Gert-Jan and Monique Zomer and to anyone I missed.

On a personal note, thanks to Doug, Sarah, Craig, Michelle, Magda, Liam, Paul, Deb (for being so nice), Jason, Ron, Bud, Derek Nyberg, Denise, Perry Goldsmith, Roger Shiffer, Lou, Jennifer and all at BATP (thanks anyway), Colin Smith, Ted Hamelin, Linda, Sandy Flett, Bob H, Sharon (SLS), Chris W, Alan Alvarez, Bubbles and Putty for retrieving the faxes.

And thanks again, Mom!

Introduction

January 1992 was a slow month. January is normally a slow month, but this one was slower than usual. The company I was doing a lot of work for had landed a national Bryan Adams tour; it was a windfall for everybody but me. Why pay for publicity when the artist's in-house publicity department is right across the hall?

Besides, Adams spent most of his career figuring out how NOT to get publicity. People joked that the sign over the publicity office door should read SECURITY. It was manned by one beleaguered Kimberly Blake—an extremely pleasant person who genuinely hates saying no, but who has learned to do so a hundred ways over the years, each time with much empathy.

Meanwhile, the editor of a local Vancouver monthly, Sherri Decembrini, had put in a request for an interview, which of course had been denied. She had put her pen to paper (having not yet mastered the computer), hard-pressed to come up with a story with nothing to base it on but a CD and a record company biography. I came to her rescue. I was well able to come up with a feature on Adams sans interview. I had been doing it for years.

I started renting office space from Adams' manager, Bruce Allen (a man well worth a book of his own), in 1980, and around the same time, I began writing a "backstage" music column for the weekly Georgia Straight. This combination gave me the opportunity to follow the career of Bryan Adams pretty closely.

He was a guilty pleasure—in the world of the then-alternative press, it was cool to like "punk" or "new wave." Mainstream was a dirty word, especially in reference to a guy who had previously had a disco hit. But I couldn't help but like him. "Remember," "Lonely Nights," and (especially) "One Good Reason" were among my favourite songs of the era.

I was only across the hall, but I didn't see much of Adams—even then he wasn't all that accessible. He was on the road a lot, and I was somewhat cocooned in my office. In any case, I didn't think he noticed me too much, although in later years, I realized he must have. He notices everything.

I'd do the occassional telephone interview with him, but for the most part I talked to his management, his record company and his booking agent.

Two years later, I relinquished my office space to Loverboy co-manager Lou Blair and moved into the Georgia Straight offices to take on increased duties with the paper.

Two years after that, Crystal Harbidge, Allen's second-in-command, approached me about publishing a fan club newsletter for the now-budding Bryan Adams, whose third album was taking off in a big way. Within a few months, I was back in the 68 Water Street complex pretty much full time, producing newsletters and writing tour programs, and reporting to Craig McDowall, the merchandiser for Adams and Loverboy.

The next three-and-a-half years were spent wrestling information from and about Bryan Adams for the newsletters, tour programs and my weekly column. I would go to Kimberly Blake, Kim would go to Bruce, Bruce would go to Bryan, and eventually Bryan would phone me. But mostly I relied on a network of press, friends, fans, and record company and management personnel.

In the early press interviews, Adams was quite forthcoming,

but as time progressed, he become more and more wary (and weary) of the media. He was never friendly, but neither was he rude or arrogant. He was just very uninformative. If you could find some other topic that appealed to him, he loved to give his opinion—he could be downright garrulous—but he didn't like to talk about himself.

He told his fans more than he told the media, but questions about his personal life were usually dismissed with a "we don't want to talk about that." His editing of my copy included cutting most mentions of his friends and family and all references to his first band, Sweeney Todd.

My job was a challenge.

This project was born when the media uproar over Adams' lack of access in early 1992 presented a similar challenge; one I was well-equipped to handle. It had become a media game as to who could come up with the most information on Adams, in spite of his lack of cooperation, and I wanted to play. If it meant that Adams would never invite me over for tea, well, he never had before.

I was already writing the local magazine article for Ms Decembrini; I just kept going. I put the call out to all my media contacts. I gathered dozens of interview tapes from the print media; scores of radio and TV interviews; and hundreds, if not thousands, of press clippings. A call to his fans brought in stacks of more tapes and clippings from around the world.Tracking down his friends, former co-workers and schoolmates also provided me with some more interesting insights.

If there were to be a credited co-author, it would have to be my computer. It took the help of a memory chip to piece together this picture of Bryan Adams. Everything he said, as well as everything that was said about him, was pumped into that 386-DX40. A search on a subject would reveal the story as told to twenty different sources. Although there were times when Adams gave twenty different responses to the same question, generally the pieces would fit together like a jigsaw puzzle, an ever-developing portrait.

Like most people, I can't say I know Bryan Adams, but I can sure say I know a lot about him—pretty much everything he says and "everything he does." And that reveals a lot about the man.

Sorelle Saidman

October 1993

1

A Donkey of a Song

It was the spring of 1991. Bryan Adams's manager had his feet up in the studio of a Vancouver radio station during a commercial break in his weekly talk radio show. Bruce Allen had just fielded yet another inquiry as to the release date of the new Adams album. "It'll be out when it's out," he snapped, disconnecting the hapless caller.

It was a testy time. Adams hadn't had a new album in four years. The topic was taboo.

"You know what I want?" said Allen morosely. "I want this next album to be huge, then I can tell them all to fuck off!"

If Allen was uptight, so, too, was Adams. It had been tough on the ego since his last album, *Into the Fire*, ran a shorter-than-hoped-for course after its release in March 1987. The years between had been filled with dissension, apprehension, mounting pressure and disappointments—dissension because Adams and Jim Vallance, his songwriting partner of ten years, had divorced in 1989; apprehension because Adams was working with a new cowriter and producer, Robert John (Mutt) Lange; pressure because A & M Records had been counting on making the next Bryan Adams album its top priority of the year; and disappointment because the year-release dates still remained undetermined. These dates had been reset at least twice annually since early 1989.

The longer the album took, the more critical its success became. Momentum is everything for rock stars. The press and public have short memories for past glories.

For Adams, the important thing was respect, and when it came to getting respect, there was nothing like a hit record.

Coming into 1991, the pressure was explosive. Aside from the obvious deadlines, there was the question of the Juno Awards. Bruce Allen had fought long and hard to bring the national awards show—traditionally held in Toronto—to Vancouver, and he got his wish that year. With the West Coast focus, not to mention Allen's involvement, all eyes were on Adams.

It was expected Adams would, at best, do a full show for the accompanying Juno concert series (copromoted by Allen), and sing and hand out a trophy at the awards. At worst—or so organizers thought—he wouldn't appear with his band, but would sit in with someone else at the concert series and just present an award. The organizers got the bad news just a week before the event. Bruce Allen couldn't deliver his own client.

Adams was staying put in England, where he had been writing, recording and living pretty much full–time since he started working with Lange in mid–1989. They were into the final stages of the new album, and he refused to abandon it for even a few days, especially if it meant he would have to put himself within firing range of questions about the record. Allen was not a happy man—the situation was rumoured to have caused a series of closed–door screaming matches—but publicly he stood up for his boy.

"What's he supposed to do?" asked Allen. "He's not going to get up and do his old songs again, and he sure as hell won't do his new stuff."

Worse yet for the manager, he had booked a June tour of Europe opening for peer group ZZ Top. Adams had to be finished with the record before going out on tour—once on the road, he would be out of time. It was a frightening period for the volatile, often caustic Allen. He was "the man astride the tiger," and Allen was losing his grip. It didn't help that the mouthy Adams had made his own set of enemies in the industry, and that he wasn't exactly a media darling, either. Many were anticipating a downfall and were predicting the end of a decade of Adams's success.

Still, Adams and Lange stood their ground on their intention to release the best record they could, and to that end they fastidiously perfected every note of the twelve songs they had written for the album.

"It will be out when it's good enough" was Adams's answer to the queries. The real question was whether it would ever be good enough for Lange and Adams.

Then Adams received a gift. He was sent a tape and a message from his old friend David Kershenbaum, formerly his closest ally at A & M Records. Kershenbaum was now copresident of a new label, Morgan Creek Records, an affiliate of Morgan Creek Films, a large Hollywood movie company. He needed lyrics for a song to be included on Morgan Creek's first release—the soundtrack to *Robin Hood: Prince of Thieves*.

The film was the most heralded of the season—it starred *Dances with Wolves* megastar and multi–Academy Award winner Kevin Costner—and it was certainly going to be a box–office smash. The company also wanted a hit record. Pop songs on soundtracks had done well on the charts over the past few years, as Adams well knew—he had had a #1 hit in 1985 with the song "Heaven," from a much less successful movie, *A Night in Heaven*.

The composer of the *Robin Hood* score, Michael Kamen, was not as enthusiastic about creating a hit song. He was a New Yorker living in England, but he was a Hollywood veteran, with the scores of movies like *Brazil*, *Lethal Weapon* and *Die Hard* to his credit. He knew what to expect.

"It's just business," explained Kamen, "but the movie industry will try to get a song, the more commercial the better, attached to the movie without any regard for the substance of the score, the composer of the score, the director, the characters, the story or the title—it doesn't matter.

"I was very, very plain with Kershenbaum—'I don't want

you going out to Guns N' Roses and various and sundry
people looking for the disco version of the *Robin Hood*
theme, or the club version, or the concert-hall version. I want
the song to come from the film.'"

Kamen sent the company samples of three recurring themes
in the score. The unanimous choice was a love ballad, Maid
Marian's song. His first call was to Kate Bush, asking her to
write the words and sing on the record. She agreed, but
pulled out of the project when the company asked her to do
it as a duet with another singer.

Next on the list was Annie Lennox, but, said Kamen, "She
wanted to sing it in Old English, and that didn't work." Lisa
Stansfield was suggested and subsequently met with Kamen.
She was the front-runner as the singer, but the deal was nixed
by her management and her record label.

Meanwhile, in a bid to get the lyrics written in the face of
the looming deadline, Kershenbaum had sent the song to
Bryan Adams and to singer and ex–Chicago front man Peter
Cetera. Both were asked to courier their ideas to the company.

The packages received by Adams and Cetera contained a
demo of the melody, with harplike chords emulating a medi-
eval instrument while Kamen hummed into a microphone.
According to Kamen, they arrived with two messages—both
writers were asked to use a specific lyrical theme from a line
in the movie, and to write their songs with a duet in mind.

Cetera wrote his lyrics, and also chose to submit a full
demo of the song as a duet with Julia Fordham. Adams sang
his own lyric—cowritten with writing partner and coproducer
Mutt Lange—over Kamen's demo tape and submitted it to
Morgan Creek.

At that time, Adams had no intention of singing the song—
he was simply writing a lyric—but he soon decided that he
also wanted to be the performer: "I knew it was an international melody, the kind of melody your mom would like, so
we thought it would do well," he told *Music Express* editor
Keith Sharp.

Peter Cetera was just as anxious. "Look," Cetera told

Kamen, "this is the wedding song of the nineties. I want to do this song."

"In all honesty," said Kamen, "Cetera's [treatment] was too pretty. I write very sweet melodies, and sometimes they need someone to deliver them with enough authority to make sure that you don't fall asleep. Bryan's voice is more suited because of its rough edge... His voice is so loaded with integrity there is no way he could be bullshitting you.... And it was absolutely clear that [Adams's] lyric made more sense. It tugged at your heart immediately."

"The challenge was first of all, do we have time to work on this, and can we make it into a song?" Adams told MuchMusic host Terry David Mulligan. "So I asked for the script—I read the script and made some notes..." Adams said he zeroed in on the love story between Robin Hood and Maid Marian. In the film, Robin asks her to help him defeat the evil sheriff of Nottingham. "Will you do it for your king?" he asks. "No," she answers. "I'll do it for you."

"I thought this is what this song should be about—complete and utter devotion," said Adams. "So we wrote a lyric that no guy would ever say, but he might sing."

The lyric was "(Everything I Do) I Do It for You."

Kamen's story varied greatly from Adams's memory of the event. According to Kamen, he gave the directive from the start to use the theme "I'll do it for you": "I pointed it out to Bryan, to Kershenbaum—I pointed it out to everybody— that's what the lyric should be."

They did, however, agree on the perils of dealing with Hollywood. Said Kamen: "In the record business you take yourself into the studio and shut the doors for five years and nobody will know anything until you decide that they will have it. In the film business, you're in a fish tank. Hollywood is filled with people who are experts at every job except their own. Someone has something to say about everything."

The film required a huge orchestral score—110 pieces— which didn't leave Kamen too much time to be involved. Still, he did get his two cents' worth in, as did more than the usual run of movie personnel, and record-label reps, and even a major American radio consultant. Not that any of it had any effect.

The duet directive was one of the first points of contention. Adams flatly refused. Said Adams in a *Music Express* article: "I told Michael 'You worry about the score, I'll worry about the song—but I do it my way, or give it to Peter Cetera.'"

Adams stood his ground in other debates: Kamen wanted the title closer to the "do it for you" theme; somebody at the record company wanted to call it "I Die For You"; another debate ensued over the parentheses. Suggestions were put forth about the tempo and even the musicians (the piano player came from the Morgan Creek Records roster).

In an interview in *Saturday Night* magazine, Adams told writer William Deverell that Kamen had imagined it as "a very light, lilting 'Greensleeves' thing, twelfth–century score. Lutes and flutes. Add a real piano or a real guitar? What, drums? Out of the question," said Adams. "When we turned it into a rock ballad, he just lost his mind..."

Responded Kamen: "I did object to the piano...I spent a long time establishing my version of twelfth-century reality, then the song comes in with a piano. To my ear—and only to my ear, apparently—it was a glaring anachronism."

Adams also told Deverell that he and Lange "compromised" by not taking musical credit: "[Kamen] was incredibly precious about who else was going to be involved in the writing process," said Adams, "to the point he actually nixed Mutt and me out the of the music credits, even though we wrote half the music to the song. He came up with the original melody, we created the middle eights, a structure, bridges."

This was the real war—the assignment of the writing credits led to more fight scenes than in the movie. Adams insisted that he, Lange and Kamen each take a third of the song. Kamen wouldn't hear of it.

"I didn't take the song to Bryan Adams," he said, fuming. "I gave it to David Kershenbaum and I said get me a lyric. I knew when I got a lyricist I was giving up fifty percent of the song. That's normal. And I was not going to give up another iota. That's the long and the short. The beginning and the end.

"Bryan said when he collaborates with somebody he does an equal split. And it's a great policy, except that I didn't collaborate. I wasn't there. I never met him until it was done. I never agreed to collaborate. I just wanted somebody to put a lyric on my song—and he did and it was great."

Kamen readily conceded that Adams and Lange had substantial input into the structure and feel of the song, and that the performance and production were paramount in its success.

"I love what they did," he said, "and it was very much original, very much their own. It's a lovely piano bridge, a big part of the song. I love the piano break, the guitar solo, the extended ending. But, sadly, that's an arrangement, so it's not a copyrighted piece of material.... They made a middle eight which is new material but based on my original material. They based all of their additions on what was already there."

The war was intense. Adams was determined to get a bigger cut of the action, and he and Bruce Allen charged in with both feet. Weapons included lawyers, publishers, threats, cajoling, and delivery deadlines pressed to the max.

Much of the assault was verbal, describes Kamen: "Adams said things like 'I've made a racehorse out of your donkey.' He said one of his publishers told him that. Another one was 'We made a four–course salmon dinner out of a lox and bagel.'"

Kamen wouldn't budge. "They caught the wrong guy off guard. I'm not a battler. I'm really not. I won, but that was because as far as I was concerned, there wasn't even a battle.... After a certain point it's much better to sit back and watch the bodies of your enemies slip under the bridge."

Ironically, the entire scenario took place over a three–and–a–half-week time frame. It had taken Adams four years to write and record twelve tunes for his new album; in spite of the politics, it took less than ten days to write and record lucky thirteen—"(Everything I Do) I Do It For You."

The song turned into the biggest hit record of all time for a single artist—second overall only to the all–star "We Are the World"—and it topped the charts in twenty-one countries in the process, breaking the previous record for the longest consecutive run ever at the #1 chart position.

Just before the movie was released, relates Kamen, he was back home in London when he was sent an anonymous message: "Somebody rang the doorbell, and I opened the door and there was a live donkey outside my flat."

Of course, the meaning was clear. "We turned a donkey into a racehorse."

2

Rebel on a Rampage

It was November 5, 1959—Guy Fawkes Day—and a cold snap had iced the streets of Kingston, Ontario; traffic was at a standstill. Captain Conrad J. Adams was away on manoeuvres, and his wife, Jane Adams, was in labour. A cab wouldn't come to the house, so she walked nearly a mile and a half to the hospital. Just hours later, a screaming Bryan Adams made his world debut.

It was somewhat prophetic that the boy was given the middle name of Guy. Guy Fawkes was a seventeenth-century English rebel who unsuccessfully attempted to blow up Parliament, and King James I with it. It would soon become painfully apparent that young Adams shared an attitude with his rebellious namesake, much to his father's displeasure.

Conrad was a soldier, a "stiff upper lip" Brit who had grown up in a working-class neighbourhood in Plymouth, England. Like his grandfather and brother before him, he had trained at the prominent Sandhurst military academy, intent on becoming an officer. He was a short man, but he liked to walk tall. The army was in his blood; he was obsessed with authority and discipline. *Insubordination* and *disobedience* were the dirtiest words in his dictionary.

Elizabeth Jane, who, like Conrad, was born around 1930, had come from a comfortable Lyme Regis family that also had roots in the military. She worked as a schoolteacher and later as a librarian. A slight, feisty redhead, she was as humorous and free-spirited as Conrad was humourless and rigid. In Conrad's world, she was a bad army wife—she wouldn't follow orders. The marriage was doomed from the start.

After serving with the British army for several years, Conrad switched to the Canadian military while still in London. He emigrated with Jane to Ontario in the early fifties to pursue a career as a military diplomat.

Little brother Bruce came along a year after Bryan. The family moved to Ottawa when the boys were toddlers, then overseas when Bryan was six. The first stop was Vienna.

Bryan hated it. He had been uprooted from a comfortably familiar Canadian life, transported across the ocean and told to learn a foreign language. "It sounds impressive," he recalled in an interview with the Boston *Globe*, "but it really wasn't at that age. When you're only five or six, you don't understand when someone tells you: 'Well, we're going to Austria. There's great skiing there.... And by the way, you have to learn to speak German.'"

Worse still, there was opera. Conrad was fanatical when it came to "serious" music—he had requested the posting for that reason. He was in his element in Vienna, one of the world centres of the art form. Bryan originally liked the opera and classical records his father played on the stereo, but his rebellious streak put an end to that at an early age. Music became a source of family disharmony when Bryan was barely out of kindergarten. On various occasions he would be suited up and dragged off to the opera hall, protesting every step of the way.

"I really thought the opera was a load of bullshit," said Bryan. "I've grown to appreciate it now, but at the time, though, I absolutely hated it. It was a major point of contention in my childhood."

The next stop, when Bryan was about seven, was Portugal, which was more to his liking. The family lived there from 1967 to 1971, for the most part in the small town of Bierre, near Lisbon. They kept their British ties—Bryan and Bruce would often spend holidays with relatives in Devon and Reading, and they mostly attended private British or American schools.

Bryan portrays his childhood as rowdy. He says his teeth are still a little crooked because he lost one when it was kicked out in a fight with a Portuguese classmate at school in Lisbon and replaced with a crooked crown. Bryan admitted to starting the fight. "I asked for it," he confessed. "I was a real mouthy kid, and that's what usually got me in trouble."

He says he asked for it once too often at that school. Bryan's nemesis was a Scottish headmaster who was very free with his cane, marking an X on the unfortunate child's hand before striking the blow. Bryan incurred his wrath one day by booting a soccer ball through his study window. When the irate headmaster stormed out to reprimand the young Adams, he was greeted with an argument and a curse instead of an apology. Bryan, as usual, didn't know when to keep his mouth shut. The X was slapped on his hand, and the feared cane soon followed, as did expulsion from the school. It had been the last in a long list of infractions.

But the punishment Bryan found at school was not nearly as harsh as on the home front. Conrad, by now promoted to the rank of major, had a passion for discipline, and he was far less tolerant than the schoolmasters. He ran his home like an army camp, in a strict military style. His authority was absolute.

Bruce and Bryan were the privates and Conrad the high-ranking officer, always to be addressed as "sir." Infractions of the rules meant KP, solitary confinement, a cuff across the head or even angrily launched missiles in the form of shoes and other objects. Major Adams was also a deadly shot with verbal abuse. Bryan was constantly berated and criticized.

Bryan wanted to be home—he didn't fancy school at all—but he also didn't fancy having to deal with his father. "I'd get the strap at home," said Adams. "I'd be pissed off and belligerent when I got to school, so I'd mouth off and get the strap at school. Then I'd be in trouble at home again."

He sought refuge in soccer and music. The latter took

precedence once he discovered the Beatles. His first clear
memory of the band is on a ferry crossing from Spain to
England when he was about six years old. He was instantly
hooked. He can't remember when he started buying singles,
but his first album purchase was the Beatles' *Sgt. Pepper's
Lonely Hearts Club Band* in 1967.

He would lie in bed at night with a transistor radio under
his pillow tuned to the rock stations of Europe. He soaked up
every note of favourite songs, like "Hey Jude," "Bridge over
Troubled Waters," "Willy and the Poor Boys," "Pinball
Wizard" and "The Thrill Is Gone." He'd trade records with
his mates at school.

When Bruce and Bryan were children, their favourite toys
had been their musical instruments—a toy marching drum, a
Mickey Mouse guitar, a tin horn. Bryan was still very young
when his parents, in hope of channelling his energy, reluc-
tantly agreed to buy him a set of drums. It was a cheap toy set,
and the boisterous Bryan smashed it to irreparable smither-
eens within a few days of the purchase. He wanted another
set, and a few battles were fought over the issue.

Conrad and Jane were not about to resubject themselves to
that insufferable pounding. Besides, it was clear that the
affordable models would just be broken again in short order.
Jane strongly felt that compensation was owing. A piano was
the first choice, but that option was too expensive. They
settled on an acoustic guitar.

"I was annoyed at first," Adams told *Seventeen*, "but I
soon took a liking to it."

The older he got, the more defiant he became. Music
provided a vehicle for both rebellion and escapism. The bulk
of the major battles between Conrad and Bryan were fought
over rock and roll. Thus, the more Bryan used music as a
release, the more he needed it as an escape. There was just
one stereo in the house, and it was the site of many household
wars as father and son fought to play their very different
records. Bryan would always try to get home first to play
what he wanted as loud as he wanted. His father's arrival
would put a quick end to that, and Conrad would often end up

angrily cuffing a mouthy Bryan.

By the time Bryan was eleven, the family was back living in Ottawa, and playing his guitar had become the focus of Bryan's life. He discovered that his other love, soccer, was not the major part of the curriculum and culture in Canada that it was in Europe, but he still managed to play, establishing a close rapport with his soccer coach.

Bryan made his first recording in his Ottawa basement, a version of "Jumpin' Jack Flash" that he put on tape with a school friend. Bryan was not yet much of a singer. "It's terrible, but I might put it out as a B-side one of these days, it's so funny," he later told *Smash Hits*.

Unfortunately, the major thought it was anything but. He remembered coming home from the office to be greeted by the most dreadful racket coming from the basement. He went downstairs to discover Bryan and a few friends in full performance, complete with vividly annoying strobe lights. They had taken all of Conrad's electrical equipment and built a light show to go along with their thrashing drums and screeching guitars. Conrad angrily threw the lot of them out of the house.

On another occasion, reported the London *Sun*, when Bryan refused to turn down a blaring radio, Conrad smashed it to bits.

"My father went insane," said Bryan of the period to journalist Sandy Robertson. "He said I was a bloody hippy, y'know? I just did what John Lennon told me to do, grow my hair and play guitar." Later he told *Kerrang!* that "[Conrad] tried to deter me [from music] in every way."

The major would have preferred that his son listen to anyone but John Lennon; he hated the decadent era spawned by the Fab Four. Ever the British officer, he couldn't stand uncreased pants and scuffed shoes, much less long hair and dirty sneakers. Mostly, though, he had been totally outraged when Lennon returned his coveted Member of the British Empire honours, bestowed upon the Beatle by the queen herself.

In whatever form, "the rock and roll thing" begat battles

between father and son. But the ultimate war was about military boarding school. Bryan point-blank refused to go, and Jane stood behind him. Since Bryan's father, grandfather, uncle and cousins had all graduated from Sandhurst, he would be the first in the family not to do the same. It was a slap in the face to family tradition and to Conrad's authority. Jane, meanwhile, had been standing between father and son with increasing frequency and firmly stood up to her raving husband on the issue. "That's when the friction really became evil," said Adams to *Kerrang!*

The stay in Ottawa had turned out to be a short one, as Jane, Bryan and Bruce once again followed Conrad overseas, this time to a position at the Canadian embassy in Tel Aviv, Israel. It was in Tel Aviv, Adams says, that he was introduced to sex and drugs, commonplace for many North American thirteen-year-olds, and also to war, something that few of his Canadian classmates had experienced. "They're influences you never forget," he told *Rock* magazine's Daina Darzin. "Here [in North America] in school, they have fire drills. There, you're sitting in class and all of a sudden an air raid siren goes off, and everyone's got to blitz into the bomb shelter in thirty seconds flat."

Bryan had other ways of living dangerously in Israel. He and Bruce captured live scorpions, threw bags over them and tossed them into a metal tank to watch them fight. One variety was black, the other yellow, and the yellows always won. And, naturally, Bryan always ended up managing the yellow fighters. "We were boys on the rampage," he said with a laugh.

He was living dangerously at home, too, deliberately disobeying Conrad, angrily mouthing off, and defiantly cranking up his electric guitar, bought the previous year by Bryan and an uncle (Jane's brother) in Reading, half paid for out of Bryan's earnings from a paper route. The guitar, banned by Conrad but allowed by Jane, was a constant thorn. According to the *Sun* in London, Bryan developed a skin condition as a result of all the stress. At school, too, he displayed a terrible temper. He argued at the drop of a hat and lashed out at the first hint of discipline. After he was expelled, his principal suggested counselling. Jane agreed, and Bryan was duly dispatched to an analyst.

Although Jane told the *Sun* that the visits had been helping until Conrad put an end to them, Bryan told the U.S. magazine *Record*'s Larry Fissinger that he thought they had been a huge waste of time. Said Bryan: "The person wasn't really interested in me, so fuck 'em."

As the situation at home became increasingly physical, Jane, with the help of the embassy staff, packed up the two boys and left. Conrad was ignominiously escorted to London, to be kept under the watchful eyes of his superiors. Jane and the boys soon returned to Ottawa.

Bryan came back to Canada a self-described "opinionated little boy with long hair." He was profoundly disturbed by the breakup of his family. His guilt was overwhelming; after all, he had been at the centre of most of the disputes.

Conrad also returned to Ottawa. He would call Jane on the phone, abusive and threatening, or show up on her doorstep. Although she had promised the boys that their nomadic life was over, she once again packed their things, this time heading west to Vancouver, making sure she didn't leave a trail for her husband to follow. Bryan didn't mind.

"Ottawa was cold and boring. When my mom said, 'Let's move to Vancouver,' I went, 'Oh, great!'" He was fourteen.

The major would not see his son again for ten years. "That was the mother's fault, she chose it to be that way," Conrad told the *Toronto Star*.

Jane and the two boys eventually settled on Vancouver's North Shore, an area encompassing the boroughs of North and West Vancouver, where Bryan still maintains a residence. "I didn't really like having to relocate all the time," he said, "because it's difficult making new friendships. It was nice to finally settle down and just not travel for a while."

The best thing about the divorce, Adams said, was that he could play his guitar without anyone "moaning at him." Jane was making up for the strictness of the past by giving him virtually unlimited access to the sharpest point of previous contentions, rock and roll. The worst thing was that with Conrad gone, Bryan, Bruce and Jane were no longer supported by his paycheque. The family was suddenly poor—and this would make a strong impression on Bryan and greatly influence his adult life. Jane went to work, sometimes holding down two or three jobs at once.

Reflected Adams, "I may have been better equipped to cope with more day-to-day problems than anyone else was because of an upbringing that ranged from proper British schools to the street. We went from being reasonably well-off to being completely poor within a matter of months. I've seen both sides of the coin."

Later he told one reporter that his habit of giving generously to a variety of charities was born of that period. "I do it every now and then because I remember when my family was starting out and had a lot of trouble getting going and those kinds of organizations helped us out."

Bryan was enrolled in grade nine at Sutherland Secondary in 1974. He was quiet and painfully shy and didn't talk to classmates about his travels. He later said that in those days he was occasionally prone to outrageous outbursts, especially when faced with incompetence or authority—or both. "I'd be sitting in class listening to some teacher giving me wrong information about some place that I had been. I couldn't handle that," snorted Adams. "I'd tell the teacher to fuck off."

Classmates disagreed: "He was very, very quiet," recalled one student. "I never heard him say anything, much less anything outrageous. And he didn't exactly appear to excel in class."

Adams admitted to being a little slow at math, good at science, especially keen on English and other languages and, naturally, a whiz at geography. He said his British schooling had put him a grade and a half ahead of his Canadian classmates in his own age group. But it didn't matter—he wasn't paying much attention.

"I was ahead in terms of education—y'know how British

schools are, uniforms and hard work. You're in school longer and, for some reason, you jump faster.

"I was in shock when I found out about American schools and Canadian schools and how loose they were. [Back in Canada] I walked in and it was wild. Kids throwing paper airplanes, spitballs at each other, skipping classes. It was a party for me, it gave me excuses to slack off. It was allowed here. They gave me a licence to go nuts, so I did."

His report card read: "Bryan is a very attentive student— when he attends." He didn't bother going to classes he didn't like; if he liked the teacher, he'd go. "I'm the same way today. If I get the feeling that someone doesn't give a shit, then I can't pay attention to them. I'm not interested."

He was also of the opinion that nothing the schools were teaching had anything to do with his intended pursuit in life. He was going to be a rock and roll guitar player. At this point in his adolescence, however, he seemed better suited for life as a convict in Sing Sing, or at least juvenile detention.

The family's new neighbourhood, Lynn Valley, was full of trees, hills and canyons; it had a mountain on one side, the ocean on the other and a pleasant urban sprawl in between. Close by were train yards, shipyards, warehouses and docks. For teenage boys, it was tailor-made for adventure—and trouble. It was a nice middle-class area with lots of upper-middle-class houses, but for some reason Lynn Valley had spawned a gang that was historically feared throughout Greater Vancouver. A few years before Bryan's arrival, the neighbourhood kids had made citywide headlines by smashing virtually every merchant's window in the area on Halloween. Teachers remember starting almost every new year with a massive cleanup of vandalized school facilities. Broken bottles and the smell of beer were the norm every Monday during the school year.

When he wasn't playing guitar, Bryan ran with the Lynn Valley toughs. The typical gang dress was jeans, sweatshirts, and plaid jackets with the arms cut off. The gang kids would play chicken with trains, sneak on board freighters, break into warehouses, and throw rocks through windows and eggs at passing cars. Along with drinking, vandalism, trespassing and petty thievery, the usual recreational gang activities included smoking pot and dropping acid.

Adams readily admitted to trying his share of drugs—his nickname, said one source, was Roach. "I was never a junkie," Adams told *Rock* magazine, "but you have to blow it—you have to fall flat on your face and then come back and say, 'That was tough. I've learned. I won't do that again.' I got in trouble with the police and that was a rude awakening. That was it. I'd seen the bottom of the pit and it was time to scrape myself out of it."

Jane was pulling her hair out, but she stood by him.

"My mom tried," said Adams, "but it was tough to control me, because I was an uncontrollable boy with a lot of energy that I wanted to vent. Nobody could make me do anything I didn't want to do, and I couldn't figure out what it was that I did want to do.

"I always intended to make a mark for myself. I didn't know exactly where I was going to end up. I knew it was music, though. Then I started putting that energy into things that mattered and not into stupidity."

Although he ran with a pack and made acquaintances easily, Bryan didn't make close friends as readily, a fact that remains true today. "I think that I'm reasonably personable," confirmed Adams, "but I don't think that I'm that easy to get to know, and I really don't know that many people. I have one or two really good friends that I have known for years, and they'll always be there."

His best friend was—and is—neighbourhood bandmate Chris Ainscough, called Beanbag by Adams. Later on he became friends with keyboardist Steven Weakes. With Jane working two and sometimes three jobs, Bryan spent a lot of time with Steven and his other pals in a series of thrown-together groups. The bands occasionally rehearsed in Steven's parents' basement. According to Steven's mother, Rita, the waiflike Bryan always stood out; he was the one with the strongest personality. He would talk the fastest, the loudest and the most often. And he always got his own way.

Girlfriends were a little harder to come by. Back in those early days, they weren't flocking to join his fan club. "Girls didn't like me at all," related Adams. "I was too busy playing soccer after school, and at night I used to run around with the gang and terrorize the neighbourhood. And I wasn't exactly Mr. Handsome in those days, either. I had my hair down past my shoulders and I just didn't really care."

He changed schools in 1976, moving to Argyle High in the same neighbourhood for grade eleven. By this time, Bryan's "rock guitar player" pursuits had pretty much superseded all other extracurricular activities, even soccer and basic neighbourhood destruction. His interest in music was fuelled and shaped at Argyle. The high school offered four music courses, including choir, band, traditional music composition and music composition using the manipulation of sounds on tape—a process called musique concrète. Bryan chose the latter and joined a small class of a dozen students instructed by Lloyd Burritt, a teacher he liked and respected.

In Burritt's class, Bryan learned how to use tape, to edit and splice. Working with tape and a razor blade, this was song construction in a very physical sense. It was good practice for Bryan's future as a songwriter and recording artist.

Burritt was also a practitioner of transcendental meditation, and he would occasionally turn his class into a TM experience, which greatly appealed to Bryan.

"In one class," Adams told *Kerrang!*, "we'd just turn off the lights and sit in a room listening to a record—that'd be the whole class! But it was weird, the way he taught it was so interesting, so fun and you waddled out having had such a good time.... I enjoyed those classes; I spent hours with him. And I learned how to appreciate individual instruments, even a voice, but most of all I learned to appreciate each instrument in its natural environment."

Burritt's memories of Bryan are of a very shy, quiet and respectful boy. "He was always very, very introverted, around us at school, anyway," said Burritt. "He was never a great musician at that time," he added, "but he was a great 'rock star' with long hair to his waist and flamboyant outfits," including red tights, belts with buckles, pirate shirts and high boots. Noting that Bryan's dress did not match his demeanour, Burritt, who is now a drama teacher, commented, "I guess he was a shy little boy saying, 'Here I am, look at me.'

"You'd get to know the kids by asking them what they were planning on doing after graduation, and Bryan would say, 'Well, I'm going to be a rock star.' It brought to mind asking a kid, 'What are you going to be when you grow up?' and getting 'I'm going to be a fireman.' But this was 'I'm going to be a rock star.' There were no ifs, ands or buts. He knew what he wanted. I said, 'Yes, okay, then you'd better learn some background,' so we started with the Beatles and worked into the Moody Blues, then Pink Floyd."

"Bryan really wasn't a very good musician," admitted Burritt. "I could see he wasn't focused on learning skills. Instrumental technique didn't turn him on. He was interested in communicating."

While waiting to hit big as a rock guitar player, and in order to buy better guitars, amps and other effects, Bryan would take on part-time work three or four hours a day after school. Since Jane's various jobs barely maintained the family's shoestring budget, Bryan was on his own for anything more than the bare necessities.

He would do "whatever was necessary." He would go to the local employment office and apply for anything up on the board. He pulled plywood forms from construction concrete, delivered mail in an office and worked as a clerk in a pet-supply shop. His most celebrated job was one of his first— he worked as a dishwasher for $2.50 an hour at the Toma-hawk Barbecue in North Vancouver.

He remembered it well: "I worked there until I had enough money to buy my first amplifier. I got pretty sick of using my Philips stereo as an amp. It was after school from six o'clock to twelve. I was a good dishwasher."

Here the fifteen-year-old was cruelly teased by his bosses and coworkers about his complexion, his hair and his mode of dress. Bryan did not take this abuse silently. "I'll show you!" he'd shout. "Fuck you!"

His determination grew stronger. He and his white Stratocaster were inseparable. He played it constantly, at home and at school. He even serenaded the kids at other schools. Students at neighbouring Carson Graham High remember the kid with the long hair and acne showing up alone during the lunch hour, setting up his amp in the courtyard and playing Jimi Hendrix licks to the crowd that gathered.

"It was his attitude that carried it off," recalled Mark Nyberg, a Carson Graham student at the time. "It was cocky, but a nice cocky, sort of a 'Hey, guys, come out and play!' kinda thing."

A few months later, Adams and some buddies, including Steven Weakes, auditioned Nyberg in their incessant search for a singer. "I couldn't sing with them," said Nyberg. "They were way too loud."

Around the same period, Bryan became a common sight at Vancouver bar band tryouts, hauling his guitar, his wall of amplifiers and his attitude from audition to audition. He was invariably told to get lost; he was too loud and too cocky.

One such audition was with current bassist Dave Taylor. "He was a bull in a china shop," said Taylor. "He was all acne and amplifiers. He showed up with this whole roomful of gear; he was running all over the place plugging in stuff. And he was just a terrible guitar player; he knew three chords on ten." Taylor told him to get lost.

Tired of the endless search for a singer, and equally tired of being greeted at every audition by a half-dozen or more better guitar players—and well aware of the sex appeal of a front man—Bryan made a career move.

Confirmed Adams: "I wasn't a good enough guitar player, and it was really hard to find singers. I had managed to sing backup vocals for all the people who came to audition for all the different basement groups I played in, and finally, when I was sixteen, I just got tired of trying to find someone, so I thought, 'Shit, I'll be the singer.' That was the answer to everything. That was what I wanted to do with my life."

Brian Wadsworth remembered Bryan Adams walking into his office at Bruce Allen Talent Promotion, the city's largest booking agency, looking for work. "He had this long shag haircut, bell-bottom jeans, and a face like a pizza. He was just a little kid. I laughed at him. I guess he had checked us out when he was looking for work as a guitar player, but now he was looking as a singer. He pulled out this tape of him singing over top of other people's songs—the Top 40 hits of the day—stuff like Rod Stewart or whatever. He was all right, but he was nothing special.

"He was really persistent. He'd call the office at least three times a week and say, 'Got any work for me? Know anybody?' I think I was the only one in the office who would talk to him. I'd tell him who was looking, and he'd go and check them out."

Now auditioning as a vocalist, Bryan landed the front duties in a B-level bar band called Shock. "We really tried to be heavy, but we really weren't heavy at all," said Adams of his first "professional" group. Over the years, his own basement repertoire had grown progressively tougher, from the Beatles to White Punks on Dope to AC/DC. Shock played Top 40 standards, interspersing them with lesser-known material by Rod Stewart, Humble Pie and Deep Purple.

The gigs weren't much—Shock was far down the pecking order in the bar band community—but Bryan was onstage singing, and for the first time he was really performing. And, more importantly, people—especially girls—were taking notice. He had found his niche.

3

Sweeney Todd:
In the Nick of Time

Summer 1976. Vancouver rock band Sweeney Todd had a #1 record on the charts—and a problem. "Roxy Roller" was a hit song in Canada, but it was written and performed by the androgynous, fair-haired Nick Gilder, and Gilder had gone south. His replacement's nickname was Clunk. Things just weren't working out.

"Shortly after we got to #1 with 'Roxy,'" related producer Martin Shaer, "Nick was singing into every mirror, wearing shades in the house, doing his hair—you know, that kind of stuff. He got really affected. He didn't think the rest of the band could keep up with him."

The British-born Gilder had founded Sweeney Todd a few years earlier with his cowriter, guitarist Jim McCulloch. The band stabilized with drummer John Booth, bassist Budd Marr and keyboardist Dan Gaudin. A mix of glam, glitter and pop, they were a cross-pollination of acts like David Bowie, Queen and Sweet. In the early days they appeared in costumes and face glitter, but the act was eventually toned down to scarves and eye make-up.

Timber One, the production company that employed Shaer, who was newly arrived from England and touted as the hot new producer in town, also owned a studio and thus was able to back the recording of an album. The company leased the resulting tracks to London Records to distribute and market in Canada.

The band's self-titled debut album was released in 1975, and by early 1976 "Roxy Roller" had climbed to the #1 position on the national chart. But for Gilder a Canadian hit wasn't enough; he wanted international success. He caught the eye of Chrysalis Records, a U.K. label readying itself to make a move on the United States. The company wanted Nick alone, not the rest of the band.

"I had a choice between a band and no U.S. deal, or a U.S. deal and no band," Gilder lamented to reporters. After waffling a while, he took the south fork and went with Chrysalis, cowriter McCulloch in tow.

Timber One, meanwhile, had gotten into financial trouble, and had handed over Sweeney Todd's contract to Shaer's own company in lieu of moneys owed him as a producer. Shaer thus became the band's manager, cowriter, producer and record company. He owned the band lock, stock and barrel.

"We were on a straight salary," recalled Booth. "We'd make $150 a week whether we played, recorded or whatever. We were on London Records, but the deal was with Shaer's company, Top Hat, not the band, so we never saw one dime in royalties. As the manager, he'd get the money from all the gigs, too. He was constantly harping on what a good deal he gave us and how much money out of his own pocket he was spending."

Chrysalis ended up buying Gilder and McCulloch from Shaer, kicking in extra for the ownership of the original master tapes and the right to release the existing "Roxy Roller" to the rest of the world under the name Nick Gilder. The remainder of Sweeney Todd recruited Skip Prest to play guitar and Clarke (Clunk) Perry to take over the lead singer's duties. Shaer didn't waste any time before recording the new vocalist over the existing tracks of "Roxy Roller." The move was in direct violation of his deal with Chrysalis.

Perry didn't work out. "It wasn't anything against him," explained Prest. "His voice didn't have the sweetness we needed, and he just didn't suit the image. We were trying to replace Nick Gilder with a guy that looked like Charles Bronson."

Enter Bryan Adams.

As Shaer tells it today—in storybook form—he was sitting in his office, hunched over his desk, when a kid in a Dick Tracy trench coat, the collar turned up, breezed into the room. "He looked like a rock star," recalled Shaer. "He had these long, reddish-blond locks, and this attitude. ... He just hit you right between the bloody eyes."

The kid introduced himself as "Bryan Guy Adams, the guy you're looking for, the one to replace Nick Gilder in Sweeney Todd." Shaer said he was immediately impressed with the cocky, self-confident teenager and arranged an audition that day.

The story was different in 1977, when Shaer told *Music Express* magazine that Adams had approached him in a bar in Surrey, a Vancouver suburb, when Sweeney Todd was playing there. "He said he was sixteen and could do four times the job our current singer was doing, and I said, 'Oh yeah, I'll see you later.' He said, 'No, I'm serious, I'm the guy for Sweeney Todd.' I said, 'What band are you playing with?' and he said, 'I'm not.' I said, 'What bands have you played with?' and he said, 'None,' and I said, 'You've got no experience!' He said, 'I'm still better than the [singer] you've got.'"

Shaer said Adams became so persistent that he finally gave in and invited him to the next day's rehearsal.

Guitarist Skip Prest remembered it differently: "I went to see my friend Ray's band, Shock. We were looking for a singer and I had heard that Shock's was pretty good. They were playing at a bar in Surrey, the Scottsdale. When I walked in, I think they were doing 'Can't Get Enough of Your Love' by Bad Company. Bryan sounded a lot like Paul Rodgers; he was a great mimicker. And he had the rock performance down pat. He was all dressed up in fancy clothes and high shoes.

"He really sang well. I asked him next break if he'd be interested in trying out with Sweeney Todd. He was pretty excited—he was a sixteen-year-old kid being offered a chance to front a recording band with a hit single on the charts. He showed up at our sound check for our next gig, the next day or the day after, and sang a few tunes."

And Bryan's version?

"Sweeney who?" he'd ask. He wanted his whole involvement with the band forgotten. "Don't dig up the old grave, for God's sake," he ordered.

To his credit, Adams adhered to the "if you can't say something nice..." philosophy. On the rare occasion early in his career when he did talk about what had happened, he didn't mention names.

"I don't like talking about Sweeney Todd," Adams told then-cub reporter Monika Deol, "because it was such a small part of my career—it was for such a short period of time."

Actually, he lasted nearly a year and a half with the band, beginning with that sound check.

"The group was put together and run by one guy," he said in another 1980 interview. "It was a fabrication. It was totally unnatural. In the studio, I came in, sang and split, and that was all there was to it. Nothing sincere, nothing really musical about the whole trip; it was really forced."

From the first few notes, it was obvious that Bryan Guy Adams would get the job. "I couldn't believe it," said Shaer. "He sang the songs better than Nick." He sang in the right register, he had the Nick Gilder simper down pat, and he knew all the lyrics. Whether he was a fan or had just studied for the test, he passed with flying colours. For Shaer and the band, the slight, fair-haired Adams was a gift from the gods.

Sweeney Todd had a tour of eastern Canada lined up for the fall. School was now a thing of the past for Adams. He had started playing with Shock during grade eleven and found that it was pretty much impossible to play a bar until 2:00 a.m. and still make a 9:00 a.m. class. Adams said the decision to forgo his education was not made lightly. In the British school system, dropping out was an absolute sin.

"Over there," he points out, "if you drop out, what are you going to do? The unemployment is scandalous. You'd never want to drop out. And besides, you'd want to continue because you're with your mates, and that's more important than anything else."

Adams was determined to make it in rock and roll, and this was his big chance. It was an opportunity for instant success through a more-than-half-decent outlet—the band had a hit record and was performing in front of large crowds.

Jane, for her part, was supportive of Bryan's new career, if not enthusiastic. She knew she couldn't stop him from joining the band and touring even if she wanted to, and she was enough of a free spirit to appreciate his yearnings. He got her blessings, and some advice: "She told me okay, if that's what I wanted to do," recalled Adams, "but she said if you're going to do it, make sure you really do it."

Bryan, although still a minor, signed a personal services contract with Marty Shaer. He went into the studio with Shaer to record a new vocal track for "Roxy Roller," replacing one cut by Clarke Perry—again in violation of the Chrysalis agreement. Adams and the band then embarked on a five-week tour of Ontario and Quebec. Spirits were high all around.

Any discomfort about riding on Gilder's coattails was lost in the youthful exuberance with which Adams attacked his new gig. "Adams," recalled Prest, "was this wired sixteen-year-old kid in the back of the bus. We were always yelling at him. It was always 'Ah, shaddup!' It was all in good fun, though."

"He could be quite the pain," confirmed John Booth. "We'd be lying in bed on a Saturday morning after a night of gigging and partying, and Bryan would come kicking at the door. He'd barge in, open the shades, turn on the TV and start watching cartoons. He was this young kid. Times like that, we wanted to kill him."

"He was tremendously mature," added Grant Gislason, Prest's eventual replacement. "He was just spunky."

Adams was having the time of his life. He was travelling— his favourite pastime—for the first time since settling in Vancouver, but instead of his father "moaning," girls were screaming, fans were applauding, and promoters and agents were paying attention. He was getting what he wanted most— appreciation and respect.

In performance, Adams was the ghost of Nick Gilder. He moulded himself to the role, though it was a pretty close fit to begin with—he sang with the same high, sweet, clear tone, and projected the same semiglam English pop persona, though without Gilder's heavy English affectations.

"He was always the one trying to keep Sweeney Todd sounding like Sweeney Todd," said Prest. "Whenever any- one would stray off that path, he would be the one to remind everyone that 'Hey, man, we're Sweeney Todd. We have to keep sounding like Sweeney Todd.'"

On stage, Adams played the rock star while singing the songs, but his between-song banter was pretty low-key, at first almost nonexistent. The other members, all good stage performers—especially drummer Booth—took up the slack. The staging and special effects helped.

The main event on that first tour was a huge outdoor show for over ten thousand kids in Toronto's Nathan Phillips Square, complete with a gold album presentation on stage, a backstage schmooze, and all the media trappings.

"At the moment," reported the Toronto *Sun*, "he shows the inaccuracy and strain of raising his range to that of Gilder, but where he is comfortable, his voice is quite exciting. And just as important, he is equally exciting to watch in a pranc- ing bisexual way reminiscent of Mick Jagger."

Adams quickly gained confidence. "On stage he carries himself like a rock star to the manor born," wrote Tom Harrison for *Music Express* a few months later, "a little affected and self-conscious as yet as he develops his own individual style, though for now his youthful good looks are enough to cover for him."

He was in the limelight. Already stung by Nick Gilder's abandonment, the core band members were not too im- pressed to find the sixteen-year-old newcomer the focus of all the media interviews, with Skip Prest next in line for attention.

"Bryan and I had trouble fitting in from the start," said Prest. "We were always being compared to Jim and Nick. The band didn't have a great camaraderie—management didn't promote that. It was fairly disassembled all the time. There wasn't a lot of continuity—it had a lot to do with the business being scrambled. No one knew what was going on from day to day."

The single as recorded by Perry had already been shipped to points in the States, and the new version with Adams had just as quickly been shipped to Europe. The song was breaking out in places like Detroit, West Germany, Spain, Australia and New Zealand. Very soon afterwards, Chrysalis released the original "Roxy Roller" under the name Nick Gilder, as agreed. It began taking off in France and the United States. The song was also recorded by Suzi Quatro in England.

In the long run, no fewer than five versions of "Roxy Roller" flooded the marketplace—three by Sweeney Todd, one by Nick Gilder, and the cover by Quatro. They all cancelled each other out, but in any case the Perry and Adams versions for Sweeney Todd were shut down by lawsuits and injunctions. The records were stopped dead in their tracks.

"Things had been so great," reminisced a wistful Skip Prest. "We had hit *Billboard* right away. We were ready for a world tour. They stopped us cold. One minute we were on top the charts, on top of the world. The next minute, all the shit went down and it was rock bottom. They were calling us Sweeney Fraud."

According to all sources, Adams, at least to outward appearances, was unfazed. "Sweeney Todd was still his ticket, and he was too driven and too focused to let anything interfere with that," said one observer.

At the time, he also had other things to think about. He had met a girl named Angela Hudson, who was visiting from Toronto. Angela (never "Angie") was spunky, flirtatious and fun-loving, and he fell in love. She was a year or two older than Bryan, who was about to turn seventeen, and at around five foot six, she was close to his height. She was attractive, with curled blondish hair, blueish-green eyes and a youthful face and figure—she was invariably asked for ID at the bars. They were together every possible minute; he even took her on tour. She took up residence in Vancouver and for a time moved in with Bryan, Jane and brother Bruce.

Sweeney Todd forged ahead, anxious to make the world forget "Roxy Roller" by replacing it with their own #1 hit. They began recording bits and pieces of a second album, slated for release in January, but the date was quickly shifted to May.

They continued to play live, mostly headlining, but in January 1977 the band got a last-minute call to open a show for Dr. Hook in front of a large crowd in Vancouver. A review in the next week's paper said they "looked as if they were playing for themselves," and they might as well have been. The Dr. Hook crowd of grungy rockers had no use for the dolled-up boys with the flowing scarves and platform shoes, although the press did find Adams full of potential, just in need of some "individual style."

It was his first brush with the "opening act" syndrome, the standard practice of making the lead act sound better by making the support act sound the pits. Fresh performers like the young Adams would revel in their first such offer with thoughts of "blowing them off the stage," but with only half the lights and sound and no staging or special effects, it was rarely to be.

The band continued to work on the new album, *If Wishes Were Horses*, in fits and starts, interrupted by tours, club dates and assorted one-nighters. They were hampered by a shortage of material, money and studio time and delayed by bad scheduling and other problems.

The backstage battle between Gilder and Sweeney Todd heated up with the nomination of "Roxy Roller" for a Juno Award as Single of the Year. When the ceremonies rolled around in early March in Toronto, Shaer and Adams attended and accepted the award when the song won, while Nick Gilder sat in L.A. Bryan thanked "Nick and Jimmy."

Said Shaer: "I took Bryan up on stage with me because I

didn't want to pass up an opportunity like that to show everyone that this is the new vocalist replacing Nick."

Gilder and others in the industry accused him of trying to pass Adams off as Gilder. "It's rather upsetting they gave it to Bryan," Gilder told Keith Sharp of *Music Express.* "It's typical of the music industry. They tried to hide the fact that I left the group. They tried to pass Bryan off as me, which is sick."

Adams, meanwhile, was still undaunted by the politics. He was not about to pass up an opportunity to promote himself to a thousand or more of the country's music industry elite. "Whatever it took," said Prest.

"That drive to have himself recognized in the future is who he was," said another observer. "There's no doubt in my mind that Bryan would have taken advantage of every opportunity presented to him that night."

Shaer said Adams took to the Junos schmooze like a duck to water. "You've got to realize just how arrogant this guy was," he insists. "After we got the award at the Junos in Toronto, we went to a party at Arnold Gosewich's suite—he was the chairman of CBS. The Snidermans were there, Sam and Eleanor from Sam's, the biggest retailer in the country. I have a photo somewhere of Bryan with his arm around Eleanor. He was hobnobbing with real high-up-type people like he'd been doing it all his bloody life. A seventeen-year-old little snotty-nose kid, acting like he's been on top for years! It was quite impressive, actually. You could tell he was going places."

Shaer said his convictions about Adams's potential as a rock star were intensified when the singer-guitarist added a new dimension to his talents—songwriting.

"I heard Bryan singing this tune on his acoustic guitar in the hallway," said Shaer, "and it was a great little song— 'Until I Find You.' I told him we had to put it on the album. Budd Marr worked on it a bit, and we did it. I think that was his first original song ever.

The lyrics were youthfully awkward, with phrases like "I won't quit/I'll go down with my ship" and "Please take the time/To open your eyes and shine."

Adams submitted two other songs for the album. "Pushing and Shoving," referred to the groupies milling in front of the stage and told one subject that he could love her if she were a Rolls-Royce, but that she handled like a Model T. The most fascinating, though, was "Song for a Star." It was obviously written for Nick Gilder. It was a *mano a mano* challenge that found the inexperienced and arrogant teenage Adams offering advice to Gilder about the vagaries of stardom, warning him to "take a lesson before you fall," and telling the tale in graphic terms—"You can be a star if you can climb/Just make sure you're in the nick of time."

Gilder responded to the barb with a rock of his own. Shortly after the release of *If Wishes Were Horses*, he debuted his own solo album, *You Know Who You Are*. The cover showed Gilder pointing at the camera while being lectured by a puppet reportedly depicting Bryan Guy Adams.

If Wishes Were Horses eventually came out in mid-August of 1977. The front cover featured an airbrushed half-woman, half-horse image; the back pictured the long-haired Adams (with a pageboy haircut) in an old top hat and tails, looking like a classy young Dickens street hustler. Singing the whimsical title song (written by Shaer), Adams sounded more like Shirley Temple than Rod Stewart. His clear, high, childlike voice is unrecognizable as that of today's Bryan Adams.

In the months preceding the album's release, an already tense situation grew tenser. The band was awash in backbiting, politics and bad feelings. "Everyone was tired, everyone was upset because everything was falling apart all the time," remembered Prest with a grimace. "A lot of the gigs were falling through before we got there, technicians were being fired on the road, things like that. It was generally a mess."

With Prest on a fast burnout, Adams pushed to get Victoria, British Columbia, guitarist Grant Gislason in the band. Not only was he a talented guitar player, the man had better-than-average business acumen, and he owned a truck and some sound gear. The band wanted to lose Shaer, and Gislason paved the way. Shaer was used to sever the few remaining ties with Skip Prest. Then, with Gislason on board, the band severed ties with Shaer.

There was little resistance. Noted one source: "There were obviously irreconcilable differences, plus there was no money to pursue, so why pursue it? Once it got into the legal questions, the agreement had been breached in so many ways—there had never been any accounting—and Martin Shaer was more than happy just to have everything go away."

Gislason was appalled at the business side of his new band, and he did what he could for a few months, then lobbied for some help. He suggested club owner Ron Wright, a fellow Victorian.

Wright recalled his first meeting with the group: "They were playing my club, the Bacchanalia, and over the course of a couple of days it came out that they literally had no moneythey didn't have enough to get home. We started talking about where the money was going, and the conversation just progressed from there."

The divorce of Sweeney Todd and Marty Shaer effectively meant the end of their record deal with London; it had been made through a lease arrangement with Shaer's company, and the label had little interest in promoting the band. *If Wishes Were Horses* was going nowhere.

Bryan's enthusiasm waned. He was still a school-age kid and, though more responsible than most, according to the band, he was prone to diversions. The problem increased considerably with the arrival of Angela.

"We were hoping that this would be the thing that would settle Bryan down," said one member, "but it got worse because she was such a distraction for him."

"It became an irritant," confirmed another observer. "He was so flipped over this chick. It was his first girlfriend. It was worse on the road. He'd be so homesick for her. She had to be there all the time, or he was calling her all the time. At this point, Bryan just didn't handle the road well. He hated it, and he made everybody miserable because of it."

"I wasn't getting off on playing the club circuit over and

over again," he said in an interview. "And I was getting very tired of what was going on in the group, you know, intellectually...I just couldn't relate to it."

Sweeney Todd rode into the fall on the fresh enthusiasm provided by Gislason, but the crunch came pretty quickly. Gislason had connected with Bruce Allen Talent Promotion, which, with Wright, booked the band on a tour that covered forty-some shows in fifty-some days, including a number of backup dates for Trooper, as well as some clubs and school dances as headliners.

"Bryan had gotten so mouthy and insecure that we knew the tour was going to be hell," said a bandmate.

Hell might have an easier climate. The dates included a couple of weeks in Toronto, and Adams, with Angela in tow, spent little time with the band. While Ron Wright was knocking on doors looking for a new deal for Sweeney Todd, Adams made the rounds of the record companies, telling the record reps he was looking for a bite as a solo artist. Neither of them got so much as a nibble. And when the rest of the band found out what Adams had been doing—and that he had done it before, on earlier trips—things got even nastier.

"By the time we left Toronto," confirmed Wright, "the band wouldn't talk to him, even to the point of asking him to pass the salt."

The situation was confirmed by *Music Express*'s Keith Sharp: "The first time I met Bryan, Sweeney Todd was touring Alberta, and at that time our offices were at the front part of a sound and light company [in Calgary]. These bands would come in and they would rent the system and then party when they brought the gear back. We used to go to these parties to protect our own stuff.

"Sweeney Todd comes in, and there's this kid with this long Prince Valiant hairdo nursing a glass of pop or whatever, and I honestly didn't even picture him as being part of the band. He was so away from it all. We got to talking, and he's Bryan Guy Adams, the singer. He felt so out of the band thing, plus it really wasn't his trip hanging out with groupies, so he just hid away in a corner. I felt so sorry for him."

The usual opening-act syndrome on the tour was heightened for Sweeney Todd by the gruelling schedule, miserable weather and frequent disagreements among themselves and with Trooper. Not long after playing Calgary, the band found itself travelling in a major snowstorm in a not-overly-comfortable Winnebago.

"We were driving into Lethbridge," recalled Wright. "The RCMP come on the radio and order everybody off the road in lower Alberta because all the roads had just turned to a sheet of ice. We kept going, because we had a gig to do, and if we didn't do it, we didn't get paid, and getting paid was important.

"So we're driving down this hill trying to avoid a couple of semis that are jackknifed halfway down, and we doughnut ourselves down into the ditch, and went right up on two wheels and almost tipped over. A loose speaker came flyin' out and rang Bryan's bell. We thought it had killed him. So we ended up getting back on the road, we pull into the arena, and we get there and the tour manager gives us shit for being late and that started a whole battle.

"There was one show that [Trooper] told us not to have an encore, but the fucking kids wouldn't let us off the stage—" Wright laughed "—so we had two encores. All hell broke loose that time. I think we got into a fist fight that night.

"One performance a flashpot was set off underneath John Booth's drum stool right in the middle of 'Roxy Roller.' He couldn't see, breathe or hear. The Trooper crew sat backstage and laughed, but I don't think we had much of a sense of humour at that point."

Adams finally said he had had enough. "I'm going home," he told the band in December, with a couple of weeks left on the tour. Wright talked him out of it, but agreed that Bryan would finish the tour and then go his own way.

Over the next week or so, Adams continued to talk about walking out. "That's it," he'd say. "I'm going home today." It finally happened with just two dates left to go, including a New Year's Eve gig in Duncan, British Columbia. Adams called Jane from Medicine Hat, Alberta, and had her wire him a ticket to Vancouver. He told Wright, and another argument ensued—Wright was so mad he had Adams up against the wall, with his fist poised. This time the singer remained unswayed. Bryan was on the next plane home.

Gislason points out that Adams's motive was probably self-preservation. "He was leaving the band—he was worried about a pie in the face, or worse," he said. "With all the stupid stuff normally done on the last night of a tour, combined with him leaving, combined with him being a cocky kid who had pulled a lot of his own tricks, something for sure would have been done to him."

Nevertheless, the move was viewed as a deliberate slap in the face to the band, the management and the agency, Bruce Allen Talent. Adams was now persona non grata.

4

Adams/Vallance: First Dance

January 1978. While browsing through the guitar section of the Long and McQuade music store on Vancouver's Fourth Avenue, Bryan Adams chanced across a friend and fellow musician, Ali Monroe. She was with a studious-looking gent, a bespectacled, prematurely balding young redhead who looked out of place against a backdrop of Fender Stratocasters and Flying Vs.

The introductions were made, and Bryan Adams shook hands with Jim Vallance. The two didn't know it at the time, but it was a momentous occasion.

"I've heard you sing," Vallance told Adams. "I like your voice."

"Jim wrote most of the last Prism album," said Monroe, citing one of the most popular—and least conservative—Vancouver hard rock recording acts of the day.

Adams shook his head. "That was Rodney Higgs."

"Jim *is* Rodney Higgs" was the response. Vallance explained that he hadn't wanted his parents and his highbrow-music friends to know he was working in rock and roll, and anyway, he wasn't one for the limelight. Thus the nom de plume.

Vallance and Adams exchanged numbers and agreed to get together the next day. They each had their motives—Vallance thought Adams would make the perfect demo singer for his songs; Adams thought Vallance could give him a stronger in with the jingle crowd. While recording the ill-fated *If Wishes Were Horses* album, Bryan had hung around the other sessions at Little Mountain Sound, watching some of the city's top players write and record commercials. "I got really excited by the tightness and professionalism that went on," he recalled. "I really wanted to play with some good musicians."

He also viewed the ads as a creative outlet for his writing, something he wanted to do more of. "I got involved in it because writing commercials is almost like writing a song," he said in 1980. "Every song tries to say something and get a point across, actually. It's good training."

In addition, commercials could pay the rent. Adams was broke and needed an income.

They met at Jim's house, not far from Bryan's. Vallance had his eight-track ministudio set up in the basement. It wasn't ideal—it was dark and chilly, it smelled like his cats, and it occasionally flooded in heavy rain—but it served its purpose.

Discovering their mutual fondness for tea and the Beatles—not necessarily in that order—the two hit if off within minutes. Adams had shown up with a tape of two songs he had written. Vallance later told *Rolling Stone* that he tried to be tactful, but in fact "Bryan was an unruly young fellow, and the song ideas were just unstructured and undisciplined."

"I had good ideas," countered Adams. "It was a matter of assembling them. In the beginning, it was a matter of finding someone who would pull back on the reins: 'There's a good idea —let's harness it.' I had been feeling my way around, I had written with other guys. Finding someone who had good musical and lyrical sense, as well, was hard."

The two discarded the material they had been working on independently and started from scratch. That afternoon they wrote a song called "Don't Turn Me Away," which eventually appeared on the B-side of their first hit—the second song they started that day, "Let Me Take You Dancing."

Agent Brian Wadsworth remembered getting a call from

Vallance: "I knew Jim pretty well. I had been seeing him a lot with Jet, a bar band he had been drumming with. He called me up that day and told me I should come over right away—he had some songs he wanted to play me. I went over, and it turns out he had linked up with Bryan Adams, the kid from Sweeney Todd. That was a giggle. I listened to the stuff and told him I thought there was something there. Jim was definitely pretty happy with it."

Still looking for reactions, Vallance and Adams took a drive, picked up a couple of hitchhikers, popped the tape in the car deck and grilled their captive audience for feedback. At the end of the day, Adams was elated with the material they had produced. Vallance offered him fifty cents for bus fare home—and he took it, even though he could have floated there on cloud nine.

The relationship that quickly developed was a close one, based more on mutual respect and admiration than on similar interests or similar points of view. Their common ground was Lennon and McCartney, and a poster of the two former Beatles on the studio wall became their inspiration.

"We are different people," acknowledged Vallance. "Bryan always had his set of friends, and I had mine. On a day off, I'd stay home and play with my computer, whereas Bryan would go skiing or to a hockey game."

With all the work time spent together, socializing was redundant, but still, said Adams, they were friends.

"I'm just another asshole to him, see, and he's just another asshole to me," he told *Record* magazine's Larry Fissinger. "I was the teenage kid with spots and long hair, and he was the hippie with flairs and clogs. Supposedly Elton [John] has a sign above his bar that says I'd Be Nothing without Bernie [Taupin]. I feel the same way about Jim."

Jim Vallance was born in 1952 in the small town of Chilliwack, an hour out of Vancouver, but was raised in small, remote communities like Terrace and Vanderhoof in northwestern British Columbia. He began piano lessons at the age of seven and spent his early youth studying serious music. He was eleven when the Beatles hit North America and music took on a whole new meaning for him.

For his thirteenth Christmas, he was given a cheap reel-to-reel tape recorder. It was basically just a toy, but the clever lad figured out how to cover the erase head with Scotch tape and do overdubs. He was hooked on recording. He got a two-track at sixteen, and in 1972 he got one of the first TEAC reel-to-reel four-tracks in Vancouver—a machine that, he said, changed his life by allowing him to record decent-sounding multitrack demos.

After graduating from high school in 1970, he entered the music program at the University of British Columbia and studied the cello, among other endeavours. Looking at a rather bleak economic forecast in the field of serious music, and considering his love of the Beatles and rock and roll, he quietly switched to pop. With a trumpet player named Bruce Fairbairn at the helm, Vallance and several other UBC alumni launched a band project called Sunshyne. Vallance, who could play virtually every instrument in the group, ended up on the drums.

They performed the obligatory horn-band standards of the day, including Tower of Power and Motown R & B, as well as highbrow jazz and funk. They played some original songs, but those leaned more towards jazz than the pop/rock material that Vallance liked to write.

Fairbairn, always a planner, scored a government grant to perform street concerts, and the group took on a parallel life as a clown band, playing parks and city streets.

Over the next few years, the members of Sunshyne became well-known, and were often employed as session players. Besides his work as a player, Vallance was also in demand as a writer and arranger for commercials and other ventures. Sunshyne faded away.

In 1976, Fairbairn, Vallance and the remnants of the band joined up with a new guitar player, Lindsay Mitchell, a veteran of local supergroup Seeds of Time. He, in turn, brought in his own cronies, including Jack and Tom Lavin. Mitchell had seen Ron Tabak fronting a forgettable band opening a rock concert and suggested him for the vocals.

Fairbairn made arrangements to take the project into the studio, and Vallance provided the songs he had demoed at home. With Vallance on drums, they played a couple of dates as Under Construction, complete with Men at Work signs and scaffolding on and around the stage. Then they named themselves Prism.

In the studio, Fairbairn took the controls as producer, his debut at the position (he would go on to become one of the top producers in the world, producing best-sellers for acts like Bon Jovi, Aerosmith and AC/DC), and Prism recorded seven songs from Vallance's demos. Vallance was writing under the name R. Higgs. Fairbairn negotiated a contract with an international record label and struck a deal with Bruce Allen to comanage the band. The new group was major news in the business.

To support their first album release, Prism took a trip down the West Coast of America, playing less than half a dozen dates. Vallance hated it. He hated the road. He preferred the studio, his cats and his own bed.

"You might say, Jim didn't travel well," remembered Mitchell with a smile. "Plus, he's a very reserved fellow, and being on the road with a rock band is not a reserved state of affairs. And he was also losing money out there. He could have been making a lot more at home writing charts. I don't think we had his complete attention."

"I couldn't relate to touring," confirmed Vallance with a grimace. "It was so inconvenient. It was this never-ending series of travel arrangements. I didn't mind performing, but I didn't like all the reservations, schedules, packing, unpacking, packing again...."

Vallance also had no love for life under a spotlight—and the band was already getting a lot of media attention. "Jim has always remained in the background," Adams was to tell his fan club in later years. "He doesn't really feel the need to speak out about what he does, and he doesn't really like the high profile. It's not that he's a shy person, it's just that I don't think he likes to talk with the press."

As the recording proceeded, musicians came and went.

Jack Lavin left to form the Powder Blues Band, later to be joined by brother Tom. New members coming in included keyboardist John Hall and bassist Al Harlow. Vallance left the drummer's chair as touring became a necessity. He was replaced by former Mitchell bandmate Rocket Norton.

This didn't leave Vallance much involvement. Fairbairn was firmly in control of the production, which itself was a point of contention. Vallance had always had a strong interest in producing, and had done some apprentice engineering. Mitchell later admitted that there was a little push and pull in the studio. "Those songs were [Vallance's] babies," he said. When all was said and done, acknowledges Mitchell, Vallance wrote seven of the nine songs, produced demos of the material that were closely emulated by Fairbairn, played drums, bass, keyboards and even a little guitar on the final sessions, and made a number of suggestions in the studio—but he did not receive a production credit on the record.

The eponymous album's first single, "Spaceship Superstar," written by Vallance, became a major hit in Canada, but by then he had divorced himself from the project. Prism later included two songs from his demo tapes on a second album, *See Forever Eyes*, but the band did not have his blessing. They would, however, reconcile in time for the third Prism album, *Armageddon*.

"It wasn't a war or anything," cautions Mitchell, "but there was tension. It was just business. There was publishing involved, and that's always touchy."

Meanwhile, Vallance wanted to promote his abilities as a writer and producer and perhaps find a new vehicle for his music. He decided to concentrate more heavily on that area by looking for a singer to record demos of his material.

Enter Bryan Adams.

Adams was a few months out of Sweeney Todd and looking to the jingle market to pay the rent, which was now his responsibility. His mother had met Bill Clark, a good-humoured, free-spirited European gentleman who was cut from the same cloth as Jane—denim. She was spending most of her time at his apartment, leaving Bryan and his brother,

Bruce, lodged with her furniture in a nice little house in Vancouver's Kitsilano district. Jane was still taking great pains to hide the family's whereabouts from Conrad.

Adams and Vallance embarked on a disciplined regimen of daily songwriting sessions, seven days a week, in Vallance's basement. Said Adams in a 1985 interview: "I'm not one of those guys that wakes up at five in the morning and goes, 'I have a great idea for a song,' and dashes down to the studio. Our songwriting is quite methodical; we really have to sit down and work at it."

"We are very disciplined," agreed Vallance. "Our songs don't just pop out of thin air."

Nor did they rely on drugs and alcohol. "I don't want to become a rock casualty," said Bryan. "Doing drugs for the sake of trying to become inspired would be really foolish."

"Hard work is what makes us successful," said Jim. "We work hard and put in long days."

Adams would check into the basement studio as if it were an office. He would arrive around noon, the two would chat for a bit, and then they would get to it, writing until early evening. After a break for a bite, they would be back at it until at least eleven or midnight. They would sit across from each other wearing quality headphones to make it seem more like a real studio. Vallance would play bass, preferring to "steer" the chords, while Adams played guitar. Vallance preferred the piano for ballads, and occasionally Adams did, too.

Bryan had taken the two thousand dollars Jane had in a fund for his university education and used it to buy a used Estey baby grand piano. "It drove my family out of their tree," he told *Kerrang!*, "but I taught myself the rudiments, the chords and their structure, within a year. And in that year I'd written 'Straight from the Heart' and a bunch of other songs, just toying with a piano. It was a good investment."

"I had two piano lessons and hated it," he told *Rock* magazine. "I had two guitar lessons and hated that. And I took one vocal lesson and really hated that. So, I decided to figure it out for myself."

Adams and Vallance would use a simple drum machine to keep them locked into their chosen tempo. There was no regular division of duties or talents. They both contributed to lyrics and music, though Adams was more in tune with melodies, whereas Vallance had a special feel for rhythms.

"Jim plays drums and bass, so it's logical he's more in sync with the rhythm section," explained Adams.

"It really helps sharing influences," said Vallance. "When we're recording demos, and he says to me, 'Try a John Bonham feel' for the drums, there's a reference point. We know what's being discussed.

"If we start writing a song, we can tell pretty early on if it's going to be a good one or not. If it doesn't feel good after writing the first minute, we'll go on to another one. We rarely argue or disagree. If Bryan puts forth an idea and I don't like it, or vice versa, there's no discussion, we just move on."

Vallance said that either each of them would come up with an idea on his own and bring it to the session, or they would start from scratch together by jamming until something felt right. A cassette was kept running the whole time to catch anything useful for future sessions. Hooks from old tapes occasionally made it to new songs.

Adams, who always admitted to being a poor judge of his own material, would run the new songs by his friends and family to get objective appraisals, sometimes staging informal "listening parties" at which he'd grill all in attendance for feedback.

"I bounced the songs off of everybody before they were finished," he said. "I thought it was important to bounce it off just people, because that's who I want to reach. I'd gauge their reactions." According to Adams, his mother would always say, "Yes, that's fine." If his brother, Bruce, liked it, he'd say, "Yeah, that's okay," and if he didn't like it, he'd ignore it. If a girlfriend of Bryan's liked it, he cracked, her sweater would stand out, and if she didn't, she'd leave the room.

When it came time to sell the songs, as well as his own

ability to perform them, he did his damnedest. As soon as he and Vallance had a couple on tape, he packaged the demos and sent them off to the record companies.

Adams said he spent time in Toronto to better pester the powers that be in the record industry. "I was very persistent," he said. "No one gave me a break. There were really hard times with my music. I lost lots of money and starved. But it would take a rock on the head to make me quit.

"I couldn't get their attention. I kept trying to get my foot in the door so they couldn't get rid of me. I knew I could work myself into a position where I could gain their respect."

He tells about waiting three hours for an appointment with a big national record rep, only to have the man brush by him on his way out the door.

"Got a manager?" he asked.

"No," said Adams.

"Got a band?"

"No."

"You'll never make it, kid."

And he was gone.

"More than that guy told me that," admitted Adams, "because I wasn't playing anywhere. They'd ask if they could come and see me, and I'd say no, and they'd say, 'Well, then, we can't help you.' It was really frustrating, because I thought the songs spoke for themselves.

"I'd be sitting in lobbies waiting for people to meet and just never meeting anybody. The only people who even talked to me were A & M and Capitol—that's it."

He brings up the topic of his rejection often, but in fact Adams had a major label deal with Sweeney Todd until the fall of 1977, and an international publishing deal and a record in the works by the fall of 1978. He spent less than one year unsigned from the age of sixteen on.

A & M Records had been founded by trumpeter Herb Alpert and partner Jerry Moss in Los Angeles in the late 1960s. It was the industry success story of the era—an aggressive independent that had worked its way up to the ranks of the "majors" in less than a decade. Bryan Adams wanted to be on A & M.

Michael Godin was the artist and repertoire (A & R) representative for A & M Records in Toronto, a position he held from 1975 to 1986. Irving-Almo Music of Canada Inc., the Canadian publishing arm of A & M, was housed in the same complex as the record company.

Godin recalled how Adams contacted him when he was still with Sweeney Todd. "He called me up. He introduced himself, said, 'I've got a tape I'd like to play for you. I'm from Vancouver, but I'm here in town. Can I make an appointment to see you?' I said, 'Yeah, sure.'

"He came to see me the next day and told me he was playing with Sweeney Todd at the Gasworks, but that wasn't something he was interested in—he wanted to talk to me about his career. He played a few songs and they were okay, but they weren't great. But he had a great attitude. He was very self-assured."

A great attitude wasn't enough. A record deal needed great songs. Godin told him to send more material when he had it.

"He sent me a letter the following March saying he'd met this guy named Jim Vallance, and shortly after, we got a couple of demos, which were pretty good." An immediate record deal was not forthcoming, much to Adams's chagrin, but he had gotten their attention.

"I remember talking to [Irving-Almo rep] Brian Chater about him in the summer," recalled Godin. "He was going to Vancouver on a business trip, so I gave him Bryan's number and said that he should get in touch with this guy."

Chater was one up on him. Adams had given him a tape, too, and he already knew all about Adams and Vallance from his discussions with Lynne Partridge at the Vancouver branch of the Performing Rights Organization of Canada, a licensing agency representing songwriters and publishers. He went to Vancouver in August 1978, met with them and brought back a tape with more songs, including "Let Me Take You Dancing." He wanted to sign them immediately to a writers' contract, but Adams was still holding out for a recording deal. To placate him, Chater also, in an unusual move, signed him to a production contract—making it Irving-Almo's obligation to record Adams and place him with a label.

Meanwhile, on the basis of the same demos, Godin decided he wanted to sign Adams as a recording artist. "He had developed quickly into a really good songwriter and into a really good singer," observed Godin.

The person in the middle was A & M President Gerry Lacoursiere. "He was being tag-teamed by the publishing company and the A & R department over [Adams and Vallance]," explained Godin, "so obviously he knew there was something happening."

Adams was contracted for the standard sum of one dollar; he and Vallance would record a minimum of four songs at Irving-Almo's expense. The company, in turn, would lease the rights to A & M's Toronto office for distribution and promotion in Canada and approach other companies for the rest of the world, starting with, but not restricted to, A & M's American arm.

"We were tired of having the artists that we signed in Canada ignored by the label in the States," said Godin. "If he was signed to the production deal, he could be shopped in the States to someone we knew really wanted him."

While A & M in Los Angeles was mulling over whether they really did want him internationally, Irving-Almo of Canada Inc. received word that RCA New York was interested in an international deal and was offering a big advance and even bigger royalty payments. Jerry Moss took another listen and made the decision to keep the kid in-house by signing him directly to A & M Canada and releasing his records on A & M internationally, with a separate writer's contract for Irving-Almo. Adams was ecstatic.

The writer's agreement effectively meant that Adams and Vallance, together or separately, handed over their demos to Irving-Almo to do whatever it wanted with the songs, as long as it paid the writers their royalties. That was fine, but Adams demanded control in the production deal. He got it. "They gave me all the responsibility that I wanted," he said. "I wanted to be the producer, I wanted to be the writer, I wanted to be the arranger and I wanted to be the musician, and they gave me that freedom. A & M just said we'll give you what you need."

He had learned his lessons with Sweeney Todd. This time he had a lawyer look at the contract.

The team prepared to record. Vallance would be producing, but while the deal was being completed, he had taken off to England to work on another project, BTO's *Rock n' Roll Nights* album, which proved a bonus for both Adams and Vallance as songwriters. Besides producing the project, Vallance wrote or cowrote four songs on the album with BTO, and Adams contributed a solo effort, "Wastin' Time."

When the duo finally started on their own material, the first record off the top was the reworking of "Let Me Take You Dancing." It was recorded at Pinewood in Vancouver and the remix was done in New York City.

When the subject of the remix comes up, Michael Godin winces. He had taken a little heat and a lot of ribbing when Adams complained that the tracks had been sped up, saying, "it made me sound like a chipmunk," a quote that went on to figure prominently in Adams's interviews and bios. Godin took pains to point out that dance mixes, then and now, always speed up the tracks slightly to an appropriate beats-per-minute and that the singer's vocal style at that time was much higher, à la Sweeney Todd. He added that Adams was well involved in the remix; he certainly would have heard the record before it was pressed, and nothing was said at the time about "chipmunks."

"Bryan was ecstatic to have a record deal. He was ecstatic to have a song, a dance song. It wasn't 'Let Me Take You Bluesing' or 'Let Me Take You Rock and Rolling.' It was 'Let Me Take You Dancing.' He was damn happy to have those sales out of New York City making it one of the top-ten dance records on the New York charts."

Adams himself made no apologies for the song: "What the hell is wrong with dancing? I don't care what anyone thinks of disco. Who cares? I had a good time with it, I loved it, I had a fabulous time, met some wonderful people, and it led on to doing an album."

"That song was written in August of 78, released February of 79, and it became a hit in the summer of 79," he recounted. "Disco was such a happening thing that year. Jim and I recorded it as a pop song, then disco started to take off—I didn't know anything about it before that—so we figured we'd make a twelve-inch of it, and it just took off in the clubs.

"Studio 54 was worth it alone, the ultimate human orgasm. I went through the ultimate disco experience, dancing and hearing your song at Studio 54. Absolutely stunning. It was really bizarre. Everybody from every kind of place, all doing something weird, wearing outrageous clothing, like girls with see-through dresses and guys with the crotch cut out of their jeans, and it's all hangin' out there.

"It was my first time in New York. I came in by plane, this big black guy picked me up in the limousine—it was this gala thing—and we chatted about it being my first time in town. He's got the disco station on and halfway through the trip 'Let Me Take You Dancing' comes on, and I say, 'Hey, that's my song,' and he says, 'You're kidding me, man. Shit, that's a big song here!' I said, 'What are you doing for the next little while?' We ended up driving all around New York from midnight till five in the morning. He took me all these crazy places, and we just had a great time. It was wonderful. New York is great."

"From the very beginning," recalled Michael Godin, "Bryan was involved absolutely and unequivocally in every element of his career. He watched everything, he wanted to know how his record was doing everywhere, more than any of the other artists, and he had his say."

On the campaign trail, Adams was racking up points. He made it his business to remember people's names; he had a natural ability to identify faces and voices and recall personal facts. He was polite and genuinely grateful; anytime a radio station added a record, he'd call up and say, 'Hey, man, thanks.' White disco suit aside, he was a regular guy.

It was 1979. Disco was at its peak. It had been on the rise

since the outbreak of *Saturday Night Fever* in late 1977, but
it was about to become inseparable from the word *sucks*. For
the time being, though, Bryan Guy Adams was a dance act.
"Let Me Take You Dancing" sold about 160,000 records in
the United States—80,000 of those in New York alone—
30,000 in Canada and 50,000 in the rest of the world, for a
total of 240,000 copies.

The first (and last) Canadian Disco Awards were staged at
a Vancouver hotel that year courtesy of PolyGram Records,
the home of such top disco acts as the Bee Gees and the
Village People. Both groups were in attendance, along with
other members of the music industry hierarchy. It was a big
night for Adams—he was both a nominee and a presenter.

Keith Sharp was covering the event for *Music Express*: "I
was walking through the hotel, and this kind of geeky guy
comes across the lobby and says, 'How you doing, Mr.
Sharp?' He had short hair, glasses and a suit. I had no idea
who he was. He says, 'Remember me? I'm Bryan Guy
Adams.' It was totally unbelievable, the different phase he
went through from our last meeting two years before."

The "disco king" phase itself would end with the summer
of '79. It had served its purpose, and Adams and Vallance
were ready to move into the trends of the eighties with a full-
length A & M album.

5

The Colonel and the General

Adams wanted and needed management, but not just any management. He wanted Bruce Allen.

"I ran into Adams in a clothing store just after he left Sweeney Todd," reported agent Brian Wadsworth. "I was with a guy who managed a fairly well-known local band that was doing pretty good. I asked Bryan what he was going to be doing, and he said he'd probably be going solo. I suggested he talk to the guy I was with, but he said, 'No, thanks, I'm going to be managed by Bruce Allen or nobody.' We laughed at him."

Bruce Allen was the top guy in the business. He was as big a celebrity to the music industry as his acts were to the general public. He had dug a foothold in the early seventies, establishing his booking agency, Bruce Allen Talent Promotion, as the largest of western Canada. He was managing a couple of local bar groups when Randy Bachman, a veteran of the Guess Who, a top Canadian recording act of the sixties, retained him to handle his new band, Brave Belt, which eventually evolved into Bachman Turner Overdrive.

BTO released a debut album early in 1973, the first of three increasingly successful LPs in two years. The third effort, *Not Fragile*, put the band on top—they sold millions of records and virtually owned the mid-seventies rock airwaves. They were listed in *Billboard* magazine's 1974 year-end poll as the #1 new group, the #1 new singles act and the #3 top albums act. The following year, the band topped itself by unequivocally winning the #1 spot in virtually all qualifying categories in all the major American music magazines, including *Billboard*, *Cashbox* and *Record World*. They also swept Canada's Juno Awards.

BTO was big news. So was Bruce Allen.

He was a colourful character, inflammatory, controversial and immensely quotable. He thrived on attention—as was subtly evidenced in the mid-eighties by the remote-controlled flashing applause sign hanging above his head in his downtown Vancouver office. Behind his desk, a sizable painting of a big, sweaty red eye watched his visitors. A regulation punching bag hung in a corner. A suction-cup pistol sat within easy reach on his desk. An oft-employed megaphone rested on the ledge by the window overlooking the building's parking lot; Allen gleefully took a keen (and vocal) interest in the comings and goings of his staff and the other tenants.

In later days, the decor changed, but Allen's well-honed public image as an intimidating rabble-rouser, an insult ace and a more than occasional loose cannon (with an ego the size of a small condominium) remained intact. He expanded his empire to include the management of a boxer and a couple of wrestlers (now the WWF's British Bulldogs); the co-ownership of a top-of-the-line NASCAR stock car racing team; and the near purchase of the city's major-league football club, the B.C. Lions (he noisily pulled out, blaming the stupidity of the league's head office). Allen was, as the personalized licence plate on his sleek black Corvette convertible attested, UNRULY.

He was also a tireless worker who required little sleep— an asset likely the result of too much caffeine and sugar. He gave an old meaning to the new phrase "coke addict" as he downed one can after another, plotting revenge on the cola company for phasing out bottles, changing the recipe and other offenses. Coca-Cola® should have been worried.

His reputation as a ferocious negotiator helped make him just that, and his oft-reported volatility provided motivation for those manning his machinery. "With a guy like Bruce looking over your shoulder, you make damn sure you're doin' your job," said one staffer.

"I'm not trying to be an intimidating asshole," said Allen. "What I'm trying to do is tell the truth, but nobody likes hearing it. Everybody wants you to say they're great."

At the same time, Allen admitted that his intimidating reputation had been a good thing. "It's worked tremendously for me. My reputation has been a plus business-wise.... I'd be a deterrent, though, at the radio level. Radio people have big egos. So do I. If we have a big clash, they're going to have the last word when I leave the station, so I'll motivate the record company to [deal with radio]. I deal with record companies, the groups, agents and promoters. And there isn't a manager in Canada who can motivate the record companies better than me.

"It's been a negative socially. But all I care about is that my acts like me. I can make mistakes—I've surrounded myself with enough good people that they can catch them. It's like 'Bruce Allen goes charging in headfirst with three or four people behind him to clean up the messes and put things in order.'"

Adams was aggressive, but Allen had a competitive streak that could span a galaxy. "I'm a great team player—providing I'm the captain," he said, straight-faced. "I can't play sports for fun—it drives me nuts. Everything's competitive to me. Pinball's competitive."

A former staffer remembered him at the New Orleans Mardi Gras one year: "He was standing with the crowd on the sidewalk watching the floats going by. They were tossing out candy and trinkets, and both Bruce and this little two-year-old reached for the same packet at the same time. The kid grabbed it, and Bruce yanked it out of his hand. The kid started to cry. Bruce felt bad and gave him the toy and a bunch of other stuff, but he just couldn't let the two-year-old beat him in the first place."

He took an equally confrontational stand in business. "People say to me, 'Bruce, it's good for the industry that [another Canadian band] did well!' What the fuck? Whaddaya mean it's good? With the stations only playing twenty or twenty-five records, they took [a chart position] away from me! They've got the one that I can't have now!"

As much as he liked being the aggressor, Bruce Allen confessed that he didn't have much respect for those he succeeded in intimidating. He maintained "you can't be scared in the business," because it signifies "a lack of conviction in your beliefs. If a guy with a band comes into my office and he's afraid of me, then sure as hell he's going to be afraid of the record companies. People like that are stupid. They haven't got any guts."

Adams certainly did not fit into that "no guts" category. He had more grit than all of Allen's other visitors put together. It didn't faze him that he was not the most welcome face around the office. The agency side of the operation had been left holding the contracts on a couple of dates—one of them New Year's Eve—when the young Adams walked out on Sweeney Todd. He had become bad news again when his song "Let Me Take You Dancing" hit the disco market. *Disco* was the dirtiest word there was to the live music industry. Nightclubs had been ditching the live format for taped dance music in droves. The entire industry had plummeted into one of its worst depressions of all time, and the agencies were hurting the worst of all.

Allen hated disco more than most. His strength had always been in the live music market, from the bar circuit on up. He had broken BTO through touring, and now he was well-established in the mainstream stadium rock niche. He had no idea what to do for the kid on his doorstep with a dance hit and no band, and he didn't much care. At the time, he had much more to worry about.

Allen was a great motivator with strong touring contacts, but his weakness had always been the business side of music. He had a university education—three years towards an arts degree with a major in labour economics—but (unlike Adams, said many) he had never been very interested in money.

"I have enough money," he said in an early interview, "so I pour it back into what I like doing. I put it all back into my groups. And I certainly won't manage their money. I tell the acts that I'll make them money, but what they do with it is their own business."

Crystal Harbidge worked for Allen from the early days until 1986 ("putting my messes in order," he said). "Bruce gets taken advantage of," she contended, "because he goes out and makes money but does not comprehend the making of money. He just makes it and hopes that everybody does what they're supposed to with it."

Allen needed a sounding board and a stabilizer to control the finances. For the past decade, that person had been Sam Feldman, his business partner since his doors opened. The name on the door was Bruce Allen Talent, but the mother company was A & F Music, owned equally by the two of them.

Feldman had been running the agency while Allen spent most of his time managing the artists, but Feldman also managed acts, including the progressively more successful Trooper. The band had had a string of Canadian hits, plus some luck on the international charts. Trooper and Feldman had become the competition.

"Once a month," said Harbidge, "he'd look at his Bruce-versus-Sam figures, and that's it. We get a monthly balance sheet that shows A & F Music, and it's got a page for Bruce Allen Talent and a page for S. L. Feldman. And every month he looks at the bottom figure that shows how much each person made. That's the only figure I've ever seen him look at."

It was that kind of competitive pressure that caused Feldman to jump ship early in 1979. The staff and agents were given the choice of going with Feldman or Allen. They all chose Feldman, down to the last secretary—including Allen's. He was devastated. To him, loyalty was sacred, and to break a deal was sacrilege.

"If I make a deal with a guy, that deal stays. I'll never

change it. It may be changed on me by somebody else, but I'll
never change a deal.... It would be foreign to me to leave an
act. That's why I don't have contracts. I do business on a
handshake. Just like it's hard for me to fire people on my
staff, which I've done very little of. It's a loyalty thing."

The finances were complicated. An agreement was made
calling for the partners to run separate operations from
separate headquarters but, for the sake of simplicity, to try to
maintain A & F Music. They would attempt it for one year,
then review the relationship.

Although Allen would be keeping the high-profile management end of the operation, Feldman was taking the steady
cash flow that had always provided development funds for
new management acts and served as a stabilizer for the
fluctuating careers of the established acts. The loss of this
cash flow would be disastrous.

BTO wasn't pulling them in the way it used to, especially
without Randy Bachman. Allen had signed an extremely
talented hopeful named Bim, but the project was taking on
water in a sea of record-industry politics. Prism was on its
way up, but then again, the band might be peaking; only the
next album would tell. Allen had two new acts in development: Powder Blues, so far riding one hit single, and a
project in the studio called Dogstar (produced by Sweeney
Todd's Marty Shaer, no less, until Allen fired him halfway
through the project). A bigger disco singer than Adams was
available in the form of Toronto teen Lisa Dalbello.

The last thing he needed was another act. Into this scenario
walked Bryan Adams. Three times a week.

"This was a driven guy," said Bruce Allen to *Rolling
Stone*. "He wore me down. He must have gone through most
of his life with blinders on, like a horse."

Allen recalled one time Adams was in his office, bugging
him, and they got into an argument. He made Allen so mad
that he kicked a wastepaper basket at the kid—hard.

"He just caught it and kept on talking," said Allen, shaking
his head in admiration. "He never skipped a beat."

"I remember Bruce booting a can at me," said Adams. "I

thought that was the 'hit the road' sign, so I said my piece and went to leave. But he called me back."

Adams also scored points by selling songs to Allen's clients, first BTO and then Prism. Prism was one of his biggest breaks to date. The band's previous album, *See Forever Eyes*, had done very well and all eyes were on their new release, *Armageddon*, which was about to be mastered and pressed. Adams and Vallance already had two songs on the album, the Adams solo "You Walked Away Again," and "Take It or Leave It," credited to Rodney Higgs and Bryan Adams.

"We had ten songs for the *Armageddon* record already shipped to Toronto," recalled Lindsay Mitchell. "They had the pressing plant booked for the next day—the album was going to be shipped platinum, we had that many pre-orders—and they phoned us late one day and said, 'We don't like this tune. We need another tune real fast. We've got the pressing plant booked for tomorrow evening. We have to have the tape of the song in Toronto by dinnertime tomorrow.'

"We were figuring out what to do, and I said to Bruce Fairbairn, "Well, jeez, I got this tune, 'Jealousy.' I hummed it to him over the phone. 'It's great,' he said, 'but it needs something.' I said, 'I'll phone Bryan.'

"I called him late, about ten or eleven o'clock at night, and I said, 'Bryan, I've got this song and it's about two-thirds written. I've got a chorus and a verse, but it needs something. But we have to have it finished by noon, because we've got to get it on a plane by dinner.'"

Adams was game for the challenge. Mitchell was up at 8:30 a.m. dropping off a cassette. "I need it finished in two hours," announced Mitchell. "I'm going for breakfast. I'll pick it up at ten-thirty."

"I came back about two hours later, and he had added a chord and he just sort of added this little twist in the verse, you know, turned it around a little bit, just made it two or three bars longer, and written an extra verse of lyric.

"We went into the studio at noon, we tracked it, set and recorded it, and by God, it was on a plane that evening and they went in the pressing plant the next day.... That was the only song Bryan and I ever wrote [together]. We tried to do it again, but we couldn't recapture that panic.

Armageddon was a hit. A songwriter's advance on his airplay royalties took the pressure off daily living for Adams. Times had been tight, with just some jingle money, as Adams waited for the cheques from his own dance single to trickle in through the paperwork.

Allen was even more impressed. The kid could support himself. He had gotten his own record deal (albeit a lousy one), he had coproduced, cowritten and performed a hit song (albeit disco), and now he was about to complete a full album deal with A & M. Adams was unstoppable in his drive to be a rock star; it was almost impossible for Allen *not* to manage him.

"Okay, Adams," barked Allen. "You got a deal. First thing, though, we have to live down Sweeney Todd and the disco hit." He sighed. "You have a real image problem, kid."

Allen was an Elvis Presley fanatic. He had always liked the idea of managing a single male artist, à la Colonel Parker. Given Allen's well-publicized overbearing antics and Adams's private nature, it is easy for the public to assume a Svengali-like relationship. Insiders find the notion that Allen controls Adams quite laughable, however. "Bruce Allen may fancy himself the colonel," cracked one observer, "but that makes Bryan Adams the general."

They were two peas in a pod. Their careers took priority over everything else, and they had seemingly unlimited energy. Both required little sleep, and thus one was usually up when the other called at all hours. Neither had much time or patience for the usual drugs, sex and other social functions of the industry.

Adams was cocky and pushy. Allen was arrogant and competitive. Both were aggressive and impetuous. Both loved to shock—they loved to get a reaction. Neither had any patience, but Adams was easily the less tolerant of the two. Neither cared much about material trappings. To Allen, success meant power. To Adams, it meant respect.

Allen was open and Adams was guarded, but both were mouthy. And both were loud. Said Adams: "Most people coming into a room during one of our phone discussions would go, 'Wow, man, what's going on?' But we're not yelling—well, we are yelling, but we're not fighting. We have a very loud way of talking to each other. Sometimes the best way to get things across is by yelling. And, actually, we do enjoy a good row."

Allen would take fifteen percent of Adams's earnings in all areas and take over all business dealings, with Adams approving all transactions and maintaining 100 percent creative control. In the Allen tradition, the deal was finalized with a handshake. ("Bruce did eventually send me a contract," confessed Adams, "but I didn't sign it.").

Allen also signed—figuratively speaking—a deal to manage Jim Vallance as a producer.

Adams and Vallance had entered the studio that November (Allen officially took them on in December) and went to work. Adams complained bitterly about the A & M recording contract.

"Bryan did not get a good record deal, generally speaking," A & M's Michael Godin freely admitted, "nor does any recording artist get a great record deal from the beginning. But when it comes time to renegotiate your deal, you make up for lost time, if you're in a strong position." Bruce Allen later renegotiated; it was the first of three such occurrences.

Adams and Vallance got together in the home studio and worked up detailed demos of the material chosen for the album. Adams wanted to work with his own group, but he said that Vallance nixed the idea. Adams never really forgave him.

"In those days Jim was really opposed to using a band," he explained. "He believed the way to do it was the old Todd Rundgren way, which was to just hire guys around you. With a band, you can work all the bugs out onstage, in rehearsal, but I didn't have one, so we did it all on demos."

The album was recorded at Manta Sound in Toronto, with some additional work done at Pinewood in Vancouver. A couple of songs were partially recorded in Los Angeles, during mixing sessions with ace engineer Bobby Schaper at the legendary Sunset Studios.

"It went quite fast at first," said Adams. "There was a track done a day. We finished most of the album within three weeks, but then we'd remix it and change guitar parts—we'd spend a lot of time fucking around with feels."

Vallance and technology provided most of the drum, bass and keyboard tracks; Adams supplied some guitars and piano, as well as his vocals. Hired guests included American studio aces Jeff "Skunk" Baxter (an exDoobie Brother) and David Hungate (Toto), and Canadians Fred Turner (BTO) and Jim Clench (exApril Wine).

"This album was done piece by piece," Adams related in 1980. "The sucker took three months. It wasn't spontaneous, although most of the vocals were done in one take. There was more feel lost because it wasn't with the band. I would have had a more spontaneous thing with a group, but I don't have a group, so I have to make the best of what I got. The next album there is going to be a band."

Bryan Adams was released February 12, 1980. Its nine songs included "Wait and See," cowritten with Allee Willis, an L.A.-based songwriter he'd met who had written for Earth, Wind and Fire; his own version of the song he wrote for BTO, "Wastin' Time"; and another solo effort, "Give Me Your Love."

Four songs on the record were by Adams and Vallance, and two others also had help from Eric Kagna, a folksinger turned lawyer who still kept his hand in music. He was a friend of Jim Vallance's who would occasionally shoot Adams some song ideas. Kagna contributed to "Hiding From Love," and "Win Some, Lose Some," which also had input from Loverboy guitarist Paul Dean.

"Win Some, Lose Some," like several other songs on the album, was written for Angela, who at the time was "on again, off again" with Adams, and living close by. He had grown out of his initial infatuation with her and into a more casual relationship. His career was the top priority, and besides, life on the road for a budding rock star was not an easy situation for either party.

"This girl lives six blocks from me, and I decided I have to write a song about her, because I've known her so long," Bryan told CFOX/Vancouver radio listeners when introducing the tune. "'You're six blocks over and I don't know what to say to you.' It's all very true. We wrote it when we needed a rock number. Jim had a hook, I had an idea. It's a great title. I don't know if she knows about the lyrics or not, but I'm sure she'll find out when she hears it. So—" he chuckled "—Win Some, Lose Some."

A & M Canada wanted to launch the album with more than the usual number of promotional copies, so they went to JVC in Japan to take advantage of the latest fad, half-speed mastering on virgin vinyl, which supposedly gave superior sound, and was usually only afforded top acts. The company also printed special foldout album covers. Just a thousand copies were manufactured for Canadian radio, key press people, record personnel, friends and family, while copies mastered at the regular speed were pressed for retail sales.

This decision caused Michael Godin's first major fight with Adams and Allen. "I remember going over to Bruce's house," related Godin. "I had some test pressings. I don't even remember whether Bryan was there or not, but the next thing I knew I was back at my hotel, four o'clock on Friday afternoon, and I get a call saying Bryan hated it—he didn't like the sound. They wanted me to call Toronto and stop it. They wanted the regular pressings sent instead.

"I said, 'Look, what can I do? It's the end of the day. They're all packaged, they're all prepared—I don't know if I can stop it in time.' And I couldn't. I call Toronto, but it's six-thirty, seven o'clock, Friday afternoon—who's there? Nobody."

Adams, meanwhile, paced half the night and finally phoned Allen at two in the morning. Allen told him to call the next day, but called back five minutes later, telling him to come over. The two spent the rest of the night verbally assaulting

A & M and planning revenge.

"Back in Toronto," continues Godin, "I get this telex—we didn't have faxes. It was from Bruce, ranting and raving with stuff like 'I told him he shouldn't have signed the record deal with A & M Canada,' 'It's amateur night at the Ritz,' 'If this is indicative of the future, we should stop it right here,' 'This is really amateurish,' 'This is not right and we told you that it shouldn't be coming out.' It was scathing."

Like the kid on the Sweeney Todd bus, Adams could drive his coworkers nuts with his energy and tenaciousness. Not all of them worked twenty-hour days like Bruce Allen.

"I think that there was an incredible amount of ongoing accommodation throughout the years," said Godin, quietly but firmly. "Adams," he recalled, "called me at one-thirty in the morning once, I think from an airport. He wanted to know why something was not happening or why something was happening, I can't recall, and it was the only time I ever got angry with Bryan. I said, 'Look, Bryan, if you want to call me at home, you can call me at home anytime, but if you want to call me at home on a Saturday night at one-thirty in the morning over something I can't do fuck-all about till Monday, call me on Monday.'"

It was a typically brazen move for Adams. Very early in his career with A & M, he had put in a call to A & M cofounder Jerry Moss to discuss the disco mix of "Let Me Take You Dancing." "I wanted to know what was going on," he explained. "I hadn't heard from anybody. And he did call me back."

Later on, he would regularly drop in on top L.A. executives like Moss, Chuck Kaye and Lance Freed (son of Alan Freed, who is credited with coining the term *rock and roll*). Adams had no fear.

Just before the record was released, he made a quick trip to England to shoot a video—referred to as "a film for the song" in those days—of "Hiding from Love" and "Coming Home," with a stop in France for a photo shoot and to capitalize on the success of "Let Me Take You Dancing." The trip reminded him of his youth and how much he loved to travel.

After the record came out, Adams went to work visiting radio music directors across Canada, attending giveaways and contests and making himself available for press interviews. "I didn't say no to anything. I met as many people as I could."

A & M, with the signing of acts like Joe Jackson and the Police, was doing well with the "new wave" of artists of the day, but had a hard time categorizing Adams. The album included fast, danceable pop songs like the first single, "Hiding From Love"; slower ones like the second single, "Give Me Your Love"; and fast pop rockers like the third single, "Remember." Called the purple album by the Adams family, the record didn't fit neatly in any one slot—pop, rock, new wave or disco. In an era when labelling music was so important, no one was quite sure what to do with it. The press was especially confused, and invariably brought up the subject. Adams quickly tired of it.

"It's eighties, but it's not new wave," Adams said lamely in answer to a query. "It's not really disco. It's just a good pop-rock record."

Adams would perk up, though, when asked how the album was doing. He could roll off the figures better than anyone: "It's been out a week, I've got twenty-seven stations in Canada on it, a few major markets in America—I got four stations in Cleveland today. The advance orders in B.C. are for five thousand records, they've shipped out twenty-five thousand already in Canada, and it's hitting the street in Toronto as we speak. I've got every station in Ottawa and Montreal. I've yet to pick up a couple of majors in Toronto, but I've got Q-107 and a couple of others. And I've got the eastern provinces, Edmonton, Calgary, Winnipeg and Regina, and CKLG in Vancouver."

And how did such early success feel, they asked? "It feels right. It's exactly what I want to do, and I'm just going to keep going. Bands can play forever in the clubs. If you can't write a good song, you're fucked."

A month down the road, the record was still doing well in

Canada, with only a few major stations in Toronto holding out; it was not doing much of anything in the States; and it was doing nothing at all in Britain. It wasn't a bad start, but it certainly wasn't good enough for either Adams or Allen.

"We've got to break that disco image," muttered Allen.

"We've gotta break Europe, you should be pushing me in Europe," insisted Adams.

As "Hiding From Love" faded from the charts, A & M prepared to release the ballad "Give Me Your Love." They needed a tour to focus attention on the record. Promotional tours, with the artist on a nonmusical road trip to do interviews and record-store autograph sessions, were no answer. Adams was severely tired of trying to explain to people what he was all about. "I wanted to show the people, not just tell them. People are one of the key things in music. They're the ones who look at your act and believe in it."

By early spring, the push was on to find a band.

It was about the worst time for Bruce Allen Talent Promotion. The battle with Feldman was at its height—his ex-partner had taken legal action in an effort to prevent Allen from smearing him all over the industry, something he was prone to do. BTO and Bim were gone from the roster, Susan Jacks had been added, and Lisa Dalbello was still being considered. Both Prism and Powder Blues were riding hits, and Dogstar was now Straight Lines and had a new album. Meanwhile, Capitol Records had asked Allen to manage its expensive new act, Tom Cochrane's Red Rider, and Loverboy was about to make its huge debut. BATP was on overload.

"I was in the office one day," remembered Lindsay Mitchell, "and Bruce is on the rampage. 'I've got too many acts!' he's yelling. 'I've got to clean house. That's it! Call Susan Jacks. And Straight Lines. They're gone! And Adams, he's gone!'

"I guess he didn't make the call," Mitchell chuckled in retrospect.

6

Bryan Adams Hasn't
Heard of You, Either

Bryan Adams may have been spared the purge, but he wasn't about to get Bruce Allen's undivided attention. He found himself on his own when it came to putting together a band. He had dreamed of going to England or L.A. and finding a group of hotshots, but he had to face the realities of budgets and logistics. Hotshots weren't interested in playing bars in Moose Jaw, Saskatchewan, for two hundred bucks a week. Instead, he approached a group that already existed, a local four-piece called Remote Control. It featured his old friend Steven Weakes on keyboards. Paul Iverson played bass, Daryl Kromm played guitar and sang backup, and Ross Hembling played the drums.

Early in May, Allen provided Adams and his new band with a warm-up spot on a Prism concert in Kelowna, British Columbia—the singer's first live appearance in three years. It was followed by a string of club and college dates, mostly in the west, and a summer jaunt through the east.

Remote Control wore paratrooper-style jumpsuits with plenty of zippers and incorporated just enough technology in their rock music to fit the "new wave" trends of 1980—futuristic fashions and high-tech sounds. For the club dates, the band first performed a set without Adams, covering material by Billy Joel, Gary Numan and Talking Heads.

They became the Bryan Adams Band when Adams, also in

a jumpsuit (although Allen soon put a stop to that by saying, "You're the star, you can't dress the same as the band"), came onstage and launched into "Hiding from Love." They continued with most of the songs from his debut album, as well as songs he and Vallance had given to other artists, including "Jealousy" by Prism. "Let Me Take You Dancing" was not on the set list.

"I know it's a great song," he told *West World* magazine. "But, I guess it would be the same as wearing the same underwear for two months—you just can't do it, you have to change. And if you don't change, well, God forbid!"

Paul Iverson remembered life on the road with Bryan Adams as nothing but phone calls and visits to radio stations. Adams talked nonstop to radio music programmers, disc jockeys, magazine writers and record company personnel. "He spent almost all his afternoons on the phone calling everyone in North America he could think of," reported Iverson. "He was actually pretty boring."

"If a radio station added his record, Adams would call and say, 'Thanks, man,'" confirmed Michael Godin, "and he'd never forget that station. Then he'd call the ones who weren't playing the record, and he'd say, 'Why didn't you add it?'"

"I was frustrated," Bryan told the Boston *Globe* a few years later. "'Why aren't you playing my music?' I'd ask radio people. And they'd say something like, 'Well, we researched it and found that the age group from six to seven wasn't responding.' I'd say, 'But what do you think of the songs?' I was a little confused about all of that. They never did it that way in the sixties."

According to Adams, he played every "pig hole" he could to reach people. "The band opened to a one-third-capacity crowd," a review in the Winnipeg *Free Press* said of his gig at the city's Plaza Motor Hotel, "but... this typically paltry Monday-night attendance didn't deter either band or head-liner from laying down some enthusiastic, sweaty sets.

"Although Adams made friends with his audience," the review continued, "his stage show needs to pack more punch if he wants to become a headliner. But it should be remembered that Canadian pubs are dismally poor settings in which to take the measure of any artist. If you're looking for an evening's worth of shiny pop/rock fun, you could do worse than check out Bryan Adams."

A *Music Express* review commented on the mixed signals given off at those early performances. "Perhaps feeling that the material was too pop oriented, Adams tried to beef up his live show by turning up his amplifiers and overpowering his way into our hearts. This didn't work either and the result was a confused public not knowing whether Adams was a pop or a rock artist."

"We were really loud," cracked one band member, "but we had to play over Bryan screaming at the drummer."

Steven Weakes's most vivid memory is from a show in Pointe-Claire, Quebec. They had just finished one of their better sets in front of a receptive audience. They unplugged their guitars and walked down a hall and through a door to wait out the applause before returning for an encore.

"The door slammed shut behind us," recalled Weakes, "and we were in a very dark alley and up past our ankles in mud and slush from the rain. The guys had their guitars, and we were just in sweaty T-shirts and stuff. We were all pounding on the door, but nobody could hear us. They were all calling for an encore. We were out there for quite a while."

A high point for Adams was in Montreal, when Lisa Dalbello, a young singer he had met in his disco days, came to the show. Dalbello's story was similar to his own. She was just sixteen and a rising star when she signed a lucrative recording contract with a major label, but she was dropped from the roster after just one album when the head office changed personnel. She bounced back with a hit record, and she was big news at the 1979 Canadian disco awards.

Dalbello and Adams got to know each other better in Montreal and really hit it off. She was living in California and writing for a new album. They talked about cowriting some material after he wrapped up his tour.

Back in the west, Adams played Lucifer's, the top club in

Calgary. He was not in the best of moods; he was tired and a little cranky. He was particularly incensed about a mildly negative review of a club date in Toronto. The contents of the story didn't bother him as much as the headline: Who Is Bryan Adams?

The Calgary club patrons took the brunt of it. Adams let loose at the audience for only dancing during the disco intermissions and "sitting there like logs" while he and the band "sweated their asses off" playing live music.

"Adams really railed into the crowd," remembered Iverson.

"They really did deserve it," said Weakes. "And it worked—they were up dancing after that. But the club manager wasn't very happy. He had a few choice things to say about it."

Iverson also remembered the panic on the face of road manager Mike Frelone. "It was like 'What's this stupid little kid doing?'" Frelone phoned Bruce Allen, and everyone ran for cover, expecting a blowup from the explosive manager. "That's my boy!" beamed Allen.

With new partner Lou Blair, Allen was experiencing major success with Loverboy. The band released its debut LP in the fall of 1980, and almost immediately it was an international hit. Adams's own album had been out for seven months, and apart from the marginal success of "Hiding from Love," it wasn't a happening record. Bryan accused A & M Records of trying to market it as disco, a charge the record company has vehemently denied. "They blew it," Adams told the Winnipeg *Sun.* "It just didn't happen."

He announced to the press that he was finished with the road, at least for the time being. He was determined to write and record a second album right away. He was going to call it *Bryan Adams Hasn't Heard of You, Either*. He promised the Calgary *Herald* that his new album would be "heavier" than the last, and that if it was not successful he planned to "move to California and start writing." He told another paper that he was "heading straight for the States" once the album came out, "because you can only play Regina so many times."

He told Remote Control, said Paul Iverson, that he would

not be requiring their services in the future, even if he did go back out on the road, because he didn't like their new drummer, Jim Wesley. He asked Weakes to stick with him, but Weakes chose to stay with Remote Control. (Later Kromm and Iverson, having caught the ear of producer Bruce Fairbairn, would go on to some success with their new band, Strange Advance.)

While Adams was on tour, Jim Vallance was in Toronto, producing Cano, an Ontario-based Francophone band whose membership included Rachel Paiement. She was destined to become Vallance's life partner. He remained in Toronto much longer than originally anticipated—"following his heart," said Adams. Adam's own love life was certainly no longer an issue. Bryan and Angela had split completely— with Angela eventually returning to Toronto—and with the exception of some very casual dating, he was concentrating one hundred percent on his music. He was anxious to begin writing for a new album, and he was impatient and annoyed that Vallance obviously had other interests.

Instead, he got together with Lisa Dalbello. He had earlier tried to collaborate with Peter Frampton, but the relationship hadn't progressed beyond a couple of phone calls. "It was done mostly via telephone," he told the *Toronto Star*. "And it was hard to do. It just doesn't work to say, 'Let's try an E minor seventh chord here' and have the other guy phone you back to say if it worked or not."

He had better luck in person with Dalbello, who, under pressure from her record company, was writing sequestered in a house in Santa Monica. Adams joined her, and the two of them were instructed to come up with some hits. The union produced three songs for her album *Drastic Measures*, released in the spring of 1981.

While in L.A., Adams made plans to record. Neither he nor the record company thought Vallance was the right coproducer for the next album.

"I think that one of the things that was really starting to establish itself was how good Bryan was live," said Michael Godin, "and they were looking for a producer—an engineer, basically—who could give Bryan that live kind of sound in the studio environment."

Adams met with A & M's David Kershenbaum—the two had established a great rapport—to discuss some names. "I need somebody who can get great sounds," said Adams. Kershenbaum, who himself ended up producing artists like Tracy Chapman and Joe Jackson, came up with a list that included Bob Clearmountain, who was recording Jim Carroll for the label. Adams liked what he heard, but he was a little put off by Clearmountain's disinterest.

"When I first talked to him," recalled Adams, "he was just finishing an album by [Hall and Oates guitarist] G. E. Smith, and next it was a toss-up between me and Blue Oyster Cult. I met with him, and he said, 'Bryan who? You're from where? Vancouver? That's somewhere on the West Coast, isn't it?' I played him some songs, and then I told him when he decided what he was going to do, he should call me. I never heard from him.

"It drove me crazy. I really wanted to work with him after I met him. I started listening to his stuff, and I found out some other things he'd done that I didn't know about.... I liked what he was up to. His records stood apart from everyone else's, even the early ones that he'd like to forget about like the Chic records.... The guy has a sixth sense. He can make things sound three-dimensional.

"I was skiing, and I called down to David Kershenbaum at A & M in Los Angeles and said, 'Let's get on with Clearmountain and find out what he's doing.' David called him and Bob said, 'Yeah.' And it turns out that day, if I hadn't called, he would have gone ahead and done Blue Oyster Cult. That's the way Bob works, really spontaneous."

Bruce Allen, in his usual role, was the bearer of the bad news when it came time to tell Vallance. Said Adams, "Bruce talked to Jim and said 'Look Jim, you can't produce the next album, Adams has to take a chance here.'" The decision caused tension between Vallance and Allen—Allen was also representing Vallance as a producer, and Vallance promptly fired him as his manager.

The tension did not affect the songwriting team. When Vallance returned from Toronto and met with Adams in the home studio, the results were more than pleasant. "As soon as we connected," Adams told Lenny Stoute of the *Sunshine News*, "we wrote six songs in two weeks, all of which ended up on *You Want It, You Got It*. That was around Christmas, and it was a very high time for us. The work was flowing; we knew this album would be even better than the first and we had a very good feeling about Clearmountain."

They continued writing in the New Year, and by March 1981 they were ready to record. The album took three days of rehearsals—Adams said that was all the musicians needed—and then just seventeen days of recording and mixing, mostly at the Power Station in New York, but also two days in Le Studio in Montreal.

"Most [of the musicians] were through Bob," said Adams in a 1981 interview with the *Georgia Straight*'s Ellie O'Day (also a CFOX radio broadcaster), "except for Jamie Glaser and the percussionist, Jimmy Maelen. Cindy Bullens was through him, and so was Tommy Mandel, Mickey Curry and Brian Stanley. We had a choice of a few bass players but we ended up with Brian just on the basis of his personality. For me, though, no matter what band I play with, the inspiration has to start from one place, and that's the drummer. [Mickey Curry]... was such a gas, so easy to work with and so happy to be doing a record."

"Besides being a powerhouse drummer," he told the *Sunshine News* later that year, "[Curry's] enthusiasm set up a momentum the whole project was built on. He's a tremendous guy and one day when I can afford to have him on the road I surely will."

Adams also alluded to "creative tension" from having to assemble a band from scratch. "Once we got to know each other it was a blast. And Bob, too, felt we had more fun doing that album. The band was so into it and so happy to be in the studio, and we all liked each other—which was the best thing about it...

"Clearmountain was perfect. His attitude was that he was

there to help you sound your best. I never really questioned
his work, or he mine. He never suggested 'maybe you should
add another line to the chorus' and I never said 'maybe you
should jack up the guitar part'. We each did our jobs and they
fit together fine."

"If it is that easy to make a record," he told O'Day, "I'll be
making them for a long time. [It was] fate, it seemed it was
meant to happen. It was meant for me to meet Clearmountain,
it was meant for me to be at the Power Station.... It was
spring, it was beautiful.... All these things seemed so right."

Adams, learned O'Day, had no fear of the big city. "I was
walking down the street, me, Bob, and his girlfriend Mary in
the middle. I see this guy coming right for me, I moved out
of his way—you could tell this guy was looking to run into
me, and sure enough, wham, he bashes my elbow and shoulder. Bob says 'don't look around, just keep walking, Don't
look around,' but I looked around and said 'Fuck you pal!"
We ended up having to run into the subway."

But, said Adams, it didn't dampen his enthusiasm. He
loved New York. "I look back on it very fondly," he told
Rolling Stone. "I had no girlfriend, I had no house, I had no
car, I owned nothing. There I was, a free man in New York
City. . ."

It was a typical Adams comment; he often worried that
success would slow his drive and dull his creativity. He told
Music Express's Davida Watson that he believed songwriters get trapped by success. "Money doesn't dull creativity,
but it dulls perception. If somebody has money in the bank,
they don't have to be perceptive any more. That's where the
true artist comes through. When money isn't the point, you
keep writing because you love to."

While Adams recorded in New York, Vallance stayed in
Vancouver. "I don't go to the studio unless I'm producing or
playing," said Jim. "You end up with too many chefs, for one
thing, but mostly I just don't like being a spectator. I like
being in the thick of it or not at all."

They still kept in constant touch, working on the songs
while they were being recorded. "Bryan would call me for

comments and sometimes ship the tapes overnight express, or he'd play them over the phone."

Adams still pushed to have his second album titled *Bryan Adams Hasn't Heard of You, Either*, but the end result was *You Want It, You Got It*. The album featured nine songs, including several "in your face" rockers like the title track, a version of "Jealousy," the song recorded by Prism, and the catchy first single, "Lonely Nights." Adams downshifted for a couple of well-placed ballads, "Coming Home" and "No One Makes It Right." There was nothing that could be construed as dance, and little that could even be called pop without the word *power* in the sentence. It was solid, straight-ahead rock and roll and, in contrast to the previous record, a bare-bones production.

"I like the sound of four guys playing together in the studio," said Adams, "and getting a real sense of oneness. No frills, no flashpot sounds. I've always liked that a lot. I didn't go for any gimmicks. The only one on the album is on 'One Good Reason' and it's a garbage can lid being slammed down. It was just fun."

Spirits remained high, although A & M Records was slow with the international release. The Canadian division shipped out "Lonely Nights," in June, but the head office in L.A. did not take similar action.

In an interview in August 1981, Adams applauded A & M Canada, but wasn't quite as enthusiastic about L.A. "A & M is amazing up here," he said, "but it's difficult for me to understand what happens in the States, because I don't really know everybody. But I think they're also really good. It's a matter of time, now, before they realize that I'm one of their artists."

The album's progress in Canada, meanwhile, was less than overwhelming. Although airplay in the West was strong from the start, the eastern response, especially in southern Ontario, was at first almost nonexistent. The record company blamed it on Adams's low visibility.

Adams was being heard a lot on the radio in 1981, but mostly as a songwriter. Lisa Dalbello had a strong Canadian hit with "She Wants to Know," and "Jealousy" by Prism had done well on the U.S. charts. It was immaterial. "Nobody pays attention to who writes those songs," said Adams. "They only care about who sings them."

The lack of recognition aside, Adams and Vallance were doing very well in the business of songwriting. The songs not used on *You Want It, You Got It* were being given to other artists, including Tim Bogert ("Try to See It My Way") and Prism ("Don't Let Him Know" and "Stay" for their *Small Change* LP). Ian Lloyd had put out versions of "Lonely Nights" and "I'm Ready" before Adams (Jim had flown to New York in the spring of '79 to work with Bruce Fairbairn on the recording.) and songs from the purple album were being covered by artists like former Fleetwood Mac guitarist Bob Welch ("Remember") and the band that rose from the ashes of the Bay City Rollers, Rosetta Stone ("Hiding from Love").

Adams had written "Straight From the Heart" in 1980 (from a title suggested by Eric Kagna) with Bonnie Tyler in mind after hearing Tyler's hit "It's a Heartache," and he was ecstatic when she decided to record it. He cowrote "Jump" with Paul Dean for the second Loverboy album. In 1981, he and Vallance were asked to cowrite a couple of songs with Kiss. By that point, the Vallance/Adams team had written nearly forty songs altogether, and almost all had made it to vinyl.

Among those credited to Adams was "Cover Girl," cowritten with Lindsay Mitchell and recorded as a single by Prism. The song was about Vancouverite Dorothy Stratten, who had been chosen the 1980 Playmate of the Year by *Playboy* magazine and then been murdered by her estranged husband later that year. Stratten had been close to the Bruce Allen camp—she had presented Prism with a gold record for *Armageddon* just months before her death—and her loss was mourned by the community.

Mitchell said he had the song written before he called Adams. "For some reason," said Mitchell, "I lacked confidence in the lyrics, so I took it to Bryan, and we did some rewrites. I liked the rewrites, but it turned out that our producer, John Carter, threw out all the new ideas and kept the originals. Adams had put in a couple days of work on it, so I still pieced him off with ten or fifteen percent."

Adams and Vallance ended up writing their own tribute to Stratten, the poignant "The Best Was Yet to Come," included on Adams's third album.

Singer Ron Tabak left Prism late in 1981, and Adams was asked to replace him. The idea was discussed at length, but they all eventually came to the obvious conclusion that it wouldn't work. He was an artist looking for a backup band, and Prism was a band looking for a singer.

"I didn't think Prism had the elements I wanted in a band," Adams told the Edmonton *Sun*. "I didn't feel right about it. They looked at a lot of people, not just me."

For Adams as a songwriter, 1981 was a high-profile year, but by the fall the public still didn't know who he was, and they weren't buying his record on spec. Adams, Allen and A & M agreed that touring was in order. He did a few quick promotional visits to some key American markets—Detroit, Dallas, Kansas City and Seattle—to promote *You Want It, You Got It* to music media and record retailers.

Back home, the search was on for a band. A tour with Marty Balin was under discussion, but it did not pan out. Meanwhile, A & M put the record on its October priority list and agreed to cosponsor a showcase tour of key club venues in major Canadian cities.

"I went on an all-night pub crawl in Vancouver, and the next day we had a band," said Adams. He had convinced three of Vancouver's top bar players, guitarist Keith Scott, keyboardist John Hannah and bassist Dave Reimer, to back him up on the dates. He and Scott had been first introduced back in 1976. Scott was one of Vancouver's top club guitarists even then, and Adams, just seventeen, was making his name with Sweeney Todd. They didn't hit it off right away, although they were destined to become the best of friends.

"I met Bryan in Toronto," recalled Keith. "We were both there visiting, and we were introduced by a mutual friend. I

heard from my friend later that Bryan was actually a fan of
mine and that he liked to watch me play. So I gather he was
a little nervous meeting me. What I understand about Bryan
now is that when he gets nervous he tends to mouth off
somewhat. He started to get downright insulting. I guess he
was bolstering up his confidence and overdid it. So I said to
my friend, 'Gee, this Bryan guy is kind of a twit. He's being
a jerk.' My friend said, 'Don't worry about it, he's really a
good guy.' I said, 'If you say so.' We ran into each other
again about six months later, and we broke the ice a bit and
started being good buddies after that."

John Hannah, too, had had a run-in with the teenage
Adams: "He was sixteen, I think. I was playing in a different
band and he sat in. He had real long hair, and he was
really...obnoxious. But he was a good singer, I recognized
that right off the bat.... He was just really making a bit of a
scene, that's all, just being Bryan, you know. That's Bryan—
he gets your attention." Hannah would go on to a long—
albeit rather bizarre—association with Adams.

It took longer to come up with a drummer, but Adams
grudgingly settled on Jim Wesley, the former Remote Control drummer he had earlier declined to play with.

In October, after a warm-up date at a club in North
Vancouver, the new group debuted at the Commodore Ballroom, a legendary thousand-seat licensed dancehall in downtown Vancouver. The gig attracted a Who's Who of the local
music industry, most of whom were impressed. Adams and
the band played a few more West Coast club dates, then hit
the road for a cross-Canada tour.

The tour started on a high note, with the shows in the West
attracting full houses and good reviews. Adams did get into
a minor tiff with an Edmonton club for overcharging the
audience. As he later described the meeting to MuchMusic
Vee Jay Monika Deol, at that time reporting for a small
Manitoba campus paper, he approached club manager John
Bell and told him, "'Look, I refuse to go on unless you bring
that ticket price down.' There's no way in the world that I'd
wanna pay $8.50 to see a band. So why should they have to

wanna pay $8.50 to see a band? It's only rock 'n' roll! Eight-fifty, man! You can go out and buy the record! I just hope the people that night thought it was worth $8.50."

It turns out that the money was for a worthy cause.

"I had to charge $8.50," said Bell, "because I had to pay Adams almost $3,000 a night—he charged me four times what he had charged me the first time he played. The liquor board only allowed the club two hundred and seventy-five seats, and no one was allowed to stand. What was I supposed to do?"

In the weaker markets, the exposure was working. When Adams and the band hit Winnipeg, the local stations were not playing the record. After well-received live performances and in-person visits to all the radio programmers, Adams was on the charts.

Things slowed considerably farther east. The band played smaller centres like Thunder Bay and Hamilton, as well as a sleepy, half-filled room in Ottawa and several indifferent dates in Toronto, including a major media showcase at the El Mocambo. He also played Toronto's Massey Hall, opening for the Canadian band Saga. The audience was hostile—it was Saga's big homecoming concert, and the fans had little interest in an opening act. Adams knew it would be tough, and he was unfazed. "Up until a month ago I didn't know who Saga was," he told Lenny Stoute, "but hey, I'll take on anybody's crowd and I'll move them too."

A review in *Sunshine News* told the story: "Bryan took the stage to the typically prejudiced reaction. Chants for Saga, whistles, and scattered boos lasted for the first three numbers, then the tide slowly turned. The singer's energy and commitment welded to his hook-laden, body twitching tunes could not be denied. He got them. By the end of the set they were cheering. They know who Bryan Adams is now, but you know how it is, openers don't get to do encores."

A & M Records in Toronto threw a sizable party for the El Mocambo showcase, and so the majority of patrons filling the room were invited guests—music industry personnel and media—not paying customers. A mobile studio was brought in to record the set. The show went well, but it wasn't the best night for the players, so a hastily arranged second recorded performance took place the next night at a private birthday party for a friend of an A & M staffer. The bash was at Toronto's Casa Loma, a castlelike tourist attraction. The guests got more entertainment than they bargained for.

The party was quite the rave-up, and Adams and the band got well caught up in the merrymaking. "Bryan made [guitarist Keith Scott] drink a whole bottle of wine between songs," recalled Michael Godin. "I remember they were running back and forth to the truck where the recording gear was. It was like 'That's shit, man,' 'That's dogmeat,' and 'Hey, Keith, how could you play like that?' Bryan had this big silly grin on his face—he was pissed drunk—and he'd be pointing at Keith, going, 'Hey man, you're shitfaced!'"

The tapes went back to Vancouver for patching up by Adams and Jim Vallance. That seems to have taken some work. According to Dave Reimer, when the end result was released—a three-song EP (extended play) called *You Want It, You Got It—Live*, with "Fits Ya Good," "Don't Look Now" and "Lonely Nights"—his own tracks had been "patched up" right off the record, apparently replaced completely by Vallance's overdubs.

The showcase didn't seem to change much in the Toronto market. "They made the big deal about him playing at the El Mocambo," recalled Keith Sharp of *Music Express*. "It was the big media event, then three days later he's playing down the street at this little dive, the Jarvis House, and there must have been no more than thirty or forty people there, mostly really disinterested.

"He finished his set and we went over and he says 'C'mon, come upstairs with me and have a beer.' So we went up to the dressing room and cracked a case of beer. He said, 'Cheers to me,' and I said, 'Why?' He said, 'It's my twenty-first birthday today.'"

As Adams, band and crew celebrated in the dingy dressing room, somebody called out a toast.

"Here's to promises."

"Here's to delivery," answered Adams.

"I thought it was very sad," said Sharp.

With *You Want It, You Got It* still on the "to be ignored" list in the States, the Toronto showcase was particularly important because some major American radio personnel were expected to attend, including Ed Levine, a music director from Rochester, New York, an important market. If Levine added the record to his playlist, others would follow suit.

The man walked out shortly after the set began. Bryan was livid. After the show, the Adams family members plotted revenge on the errant consultant, drank themselves fearless—which didn't take too much—and proceeded to wreck the man's hotel room while he was out. The radio exec wrote up the incident in a music-industry tip sheet. Luckily, he had a sense of humour.

"All the station programmers were impressed," Adams smugly told Graham Hicks of the Edmonton *Sun*. "Anybody who'd trash Levine's room, they said, was all right with them."

Sure enough, radio stations in New York started playing Bryan Adams. Shortly after, he was offered one live American date, a last-minute concert in Buffalo, New York, in early December. He said the show convinced the A & M people in the States that he was worth the effort, and they finally began to promote the record.

The ballad "Coming Home" was released as the next single. Bryan and the band opened ten days of western Canadian dates for Loverboy, and headlined a few clubs. It was at this time that Adams made a change in bass players, trading Dave Reimer for Dave Taylor, another one of his local bar band heroes.

Late in 1981, Keith Scott, who knew Taylor fairly well, suggested him to Bryan. "Before that," recalled Taylor, "I had only heard Bryan's 'Let Me Take You Dancing,' which was okay, but then he played me 'You Want It, You Got It' and I was really sold! I *really* wanted to play in his band."

By January 1982, "Lonely Nights" was finally taking off

in the States, and Adams and Allen were determined to put the act on the road south. They succeeded in scoring the opening slot for the Kinks on a U.S. tour. Adams was elated—the Kinks were among his childhood heroes, the band had been key players in the British invasion of the mid-sixties, and they were in the midst of a substantial comeback.

"It was an incredible opportunity for us," Adams said, "and we didn't know about the tour until two days before. We were [waiting] for two weeks. Bruce was going out of his brain—me being there going, 'Are we going to get it? Why are they waiting till the last minute?' and Bruce going, 'Adams, leave me alone!' Finally we get a call Monday, and we flew out [to Toronto] Tuesday morning."

The next day, they drove to Cleveland to do a live noon-hour radio broadcast. He was still on Vancouver time, as he pointed out to Ellie O'Day: "I went onstage at eight o'clock in the morning... I never sing that hard at eight o'clock in the morning. I blew my voice out completely. For a week and a half I was rasping, my voice was cracking and all kinds of stuff. And that never happens.... Iron lungs here. I can sing forever."

Adams joined the Kinks the following night in Buffalo. If he was expecting an easy time of it, he was sadly mistaken. He recalled the details in a posttour interview with O'Day: "The lights went down," said Adams, "the crowd roared, the band was introduced and [the crowd] went, 'Oh, come on, we want the Kinks, we paid ten bucks to see the Kinks.' We ran into that in a lot of places. The Kinks's fans are not just fans, they're fanatic. We'd get up there and they'd go, "Piss off! We don't care who you are! We wanna see the Kinks!'

"The biggest place we played was the Meadowlands, twenty thousand, in New Jersey. It was kind of impersonal, and they're not really there to see you anyway. 'Oh, like there's a band there? Hey, Bob, pass the popcorn!' And you only get half the power, you only get half the lights and that's just the way it is."

Adams said he didn't mind so much not getting a sound check ("With me, it's just 'The mike works. Right. The guitar's on. Okay, I'm ready to go'"), but he hated being ignored by the audience.

"You have to impress them, and I hate trying to impress people," said Adams. "You either like my music or you don't. I'm not saying that I don't want to work at it, but we'll have a bum night and I'll walk back and scream at the drummer, 'Come on, Jim, what the fuck is wrong with you, man? Everything is two beats too slow!' But I was ten times [more] adrenalized than anybody else. I was going too fast. He was going, 'Just leave me alone.'"

"One night," said Adams to the *Sunday Express*, 'the lights went down, the [emcee] was just about to announce me, so I grabbed the microphone and said, 'Listen, we've got forty-five minutes to be on stage no matter what. Why don't you sit down and have a listen?" And they listened. And we won 'em over.

Tour highlights, he recalled, included Memphis, New Haven, Syracuse, and especially Springfield, Massachusetts. "We walked out onstage and it's like eight thousand people holding up their Bic lighters. It was like Christmas or something. It's amazing to know that some people are there to actually see you, and they've only been playing the record for a couple of weeks."

He also learned a disturbing lesson about his audiences: "People are animals," he stated flatly. "It's not funny. I broke a string in the first song [in Plattsburgh, New York] and I was so pissed off, I grabbed my strings, yanked them all off and hurled my guitar over my head and said, 'Hey, look at this!' And the crowd went crazy, they loved it, and that's when I realized the more violent you are, and the more things you destroy..."

"People love that shit," he lamented. "And it makes me think, you know, here I am, Mr. Mild-Mannered Guy, and I have to give something I don't have, you know. It's scary."

Adams dropped the ballads from his set and added "Jump," the song he'd written for Loverboy. "We've got to come out stomping," he said.

By reputation, the Kinks were a hard-living bunch with a

road show described as a travelling brawl, but Adams had no experience judging degrees of disorder backstage at coliseum-size concerts, and no access to the Kinks to observe the band's lifestyle. He ran into guitarist Dave Davies in the hall backstage the first night and introduced himself, but Davies thought he was meeting his new guitar roadie, not his opening act. Adams didn't meet Kinks leader Ray Davies until the last night of the tour. He asked for and received an autograph—a rare event—but not much else. The singer wasn't up for a chat.

"He just didn't wanna know about anything," said a disappointed Adams.

He was getting his first taste of touring in the big leagues, travelling in a rented bus all night and visiting radio stations all day. Unlike his previous stints, this tour took him to a different city almost every day—no three-nighters at a single club on this circuit. Bryan and his band lived backstage and in the bus and rarely had the luxury of hotel rooms. Over the next few years, they would spend more nights on the road than they would at home.

The tour paid off that same month. "Lonely Nights" entered the *Billboard* American singles chart at #180 and jumped to #161. Prism's "Don't Let Him Know," written by Adams and Vallance, was a fast-rising bonus at #76 on that same chart.

"We've broken into the U.S. market," enthused Adams to Ellie O'Day. "There's no longer a boundary; there's no longer a border."

You Want It, You Got It spawned just a minor American hit, but Adams saw it as a major breakthrough. "I look at this as digging the highway," said Adams. "Not paving the highway, not driving the highway, but digging it."

7

First Cuts

February 1982. Bryan Adams had made inroads in the States on the Kinks tour, and he and Bruce Allen wanted to keep the momentum going with more roadwork. They wanted all the exposure possible for *You Want It, You Got It,* and Adams was also thinking about his next album. In the six-month period between the recording of *You Want It, You Got It* and the first tour, he and Jim Vallance had written a half dozen or so new songs, and Adams was testing different arrangements on the road, using the audience as a gauge.

Allen had used his old BTO connections to keep Loverboy on the road for 251 days in 1981, opening for acts like Kansas, ZZ Top and Journey; the band's 1982 calendar included headline engagements and some stadium shows with Foreigner and Aerosmith. The managers and tour promoters of all these acts were Bruce's buddies—they had all come up in the ranks together. He had no problem booking Adams onto that same circuit, initially on a two-month tour with Foreigner, starting in the southern states. There were also more dates with Loverboy.

Adams and crew were home from the Kinks tour for not much more than a week, and his stay did not qualify as time off. "I've had so much to do," he told Ellie O'Day. "I've had one night off and went and had a curry and drunk a bunch of booze, and that's all I've done to really relax. And I went to a hockey game the other night, which was cool. But I haven't had time to sleep or go, 'Oh yeah, nothing to do today, great.' I can't wait until next week to see how Foreigner's audiences are. I feel great and I know I'm going to walk on that stage and eat the front row. I can't help but think that their audience is going to be more receptive to us than the Kinks'."

They were. Bryan and the band were well-received throughout the South as they toured with Foreigner, who were on the heels of their album *Foreigner 4* and selling out coliseum-size venues nightly. In spite of Foreigner's box-office success, though, their press had been mostly bad. Critics labelled them faceless corporate rock. Adams was bewildered by the media response, especially the negative connotations so many scribes gave the words *commercial* and *mainstream*.

"Doesn't 'commercial' mean people like you and buy your records?" asked Adams. "And what's wrong with mainstream? My music is very mainstream—straight-ahead, acceptable. It's not wimpy." He was quick to dismiss the electro-pop dance music labelled "alternative" by those same critics. "The new music they're flogging is just rehashed disco—the same stuff everybody was crying about four years ago."

The Foreigner tour was an otherwise pleasant experience for Adams. "They were the nicest bunch of guys, and they had the most helpful crew," he told Kingston, Ontario, reporter Greg Burliuk. "From them I learned that you have to get a certain kind of persona both on stage and off stage. It's something you have to experience, but it's a diplomatic, polite, professional approach you use in dealing with a mass audience."

Adams played for his largest audiences ever at all-day festivals for upwards of forty-five thousand people at both the Tangerine Bowl in Orlando and the Orange Bowl in Miami. Adams and his band had received a last-minute call to replace Ozzy Osbourne on the shows when Osbourne guitarist Randy Rhoads was killed in a plane crash while buzzing his band's tour bus.

With the touring and showcasing in the American northeast, the single "Lonely Nights" had climbed the regional charts—it went to #1 in upstate New York—and by early March, now nine months old, it was given status in *Billboard* magazine as a national breakout. It was a good step, but the song stalled without support from radio broadcasters in Toronto and Los Angeles—his weakest markets.

Adams's longstanding enthusiasm for New York City was equal in intensity to his distaste for L.A. He hated that city. "It's big, cold and impersonal—I can't call anybody up and say, 'Hey, let's go out and have a good time," said Adams. Worse, he couldn't get the radio stations to play his record, however much he tried. A staffer at one major station in particular incurred his wrath by telling Adams to his face that the station had no intention of playing his music.

"I was just stunned," related Adams. "What do you mean you can't play the record? You don't like it? The guy insulted me. Fuck you, you don't like my record, you know it's a fine record. It's better than half the shit you're playing on your stupid radio station. I really took it personally. When I found out he added my record [after it was a hit elsewhere], I thought, 'You dink.'"

The Foreigner tour swung north in early April to include back-to-back shows in Montreal and Ottawa. Adams had come through the area six months earlier with Remote Control, and Ottawa audiences were scheduled to see him three more times in the next three weeks—the Foreigner concert, a club appearance at Faces the following night, and a return to the Civic Centre opening for Loverboy May 1. He was saturating the market.

His Ottawa roots guaranteed that he was well covered by that city's media. On one trip through town, he was interviewed by Margaret Trudeau. The former prime minister's ex-wife, herself well-known in rock and roll circles after a well-publicized rendezvous with the Rolling Stones, was cohosting a morning TV show in the Canadian capital.

"So what's it like travelling around with rock stars?" asked Trudeau.

"Gee, Margaret, you should know," Adams fired back.

The Foreigner concert was wildly successful. "Foreigner had the fanfare but it was the up-and-coming challenger, Bryan Adams, who impressed the most Tuesday night at the Civic Centre," wrote Bill Provick of the Ottawa *Citizen*. "The only things that kept Adams from stealing the show were the intrinsic advantages of being the headline act: better, bigger sound, more elaborate lighting and stage effects and, of course, a longer lists of hit songs from which to draw. Otherwise, Adams and his equally hard-working band put on the better performance.... They packed so much energy and music into their tight and taut 45-minute set that it was hard to believe that so much had been accomplished in so little time."

The review and word of mouth drew a large crowd with high expectations to Faces the following night, but Adams was a no-show. According to Faces owner Rick Saikaley, a crew member came to the club in the afternoon and told him his sound system was inadequate. Saikaley said Adams himself did not come to the club, no equipment was set up, and no sound checks took place.

"I get a lotta acts in here bigger than Bryan Adams," complained Saikaley, "and none of them ever had this problem." He took his case to the musicians' union, the Toronto booking agency responsible for the gig, and the media. The *Citizen* printed a feature news story that included interviews with clubgoers just after the cancellation announcement was made.

"Who does he [Adams] think he is? Mick Jagger?" said one angry kid. Another promised to attend the Loverboy concert: "I want to get within range of the stage because I have a few things to say to him."

Adams sneaked out of town without commenting on the affair. Back home in Vancouver for a couple of weeks, he and Jim Vallance did a little writing, and then they flew to L.A. to do additional work with Kiss. At the end of April, the Adams entourage hit the road with Loverboy. When he returned to the Civic Centre, he was served with court papers from Faces demanding a $5,000 settlement for advertising costs and lost concert revenues.

"It took two years," said Saikaley, "but I got it."

The Loverboy tour moved west across Canada through mid-May. There was still an underlying rivalry between the two acts. Adams was given the respect due a fellow member of the Bruce Allen stable, but the opening-act syndrome did incite the occasional flare-up; on one occasion Keith Scott infringed on the Loverboy colour scheme (red, yellow and black) by wearing a red shirt.

Adams didn't help matters any. "Don't compare me to Loverboy," he would growl at the press. His mouth didn't stop there. "We're happy with our sound, but we're willing to stretch—unlike Loverboy," he told *Faces* magazine.

He may have been stretching, but it was Loverboy who were headlining and thus paying the office bills. Headliners on major tours pulled in major revenue—moneys from ticket receipts and merchandising usually far exceed that generated by record sales and songwriting royalties—but opening acts were rarely paid enough even to cover their expenses. By this point, Bruce Allen had sunk close to $100,000 into keeping Adams on the road, money that Bryan would have to pay back eventually. It was obvious that his tour support was being made possible by the success of Loverboy.

Both bands returned home later that spring for a giant homecoming concert at the Pacific Coliseum. Adams was well received, but again the spotlight was on Loverboy.

For the next two months, Adams and Vallance mostly concentrated on amassing material for a new album. They had a half-dozen songs already in place, the ones that Bryan and the band had fine-tuned before live audiences.

"My goal is to make the songs that sound great in concert sound great on record," Adams told the press. "This whole record is designed for AOR [album-oriented rock] radio."

Road-tested rockers included "This Time," "The Only One," "What's It Gonna Be?" and "Let Him Know" (the rebuttal to "Don't Let Him Know" recorded by Prism). Two of the most popular songs passing the test were the 1979 Adams/Vallance rocker "I'm Ready" (recorded by Ian Lloyd) and an in-concert highlight, "Take Me Back," with its monologue about the woes of love. Not everyone liked the latter. "'Take Me Back,'" offered critic Tom Harrison in *Music Express*, "has a spoken part in the middle where the protagonist gets to tell the love of his life to fuck off. [It's] a cheap shot. A sell-out. Especially if the writer in question is capable of so much better."

"Yeah, but you know what?" Bryan answered. "That song has saved my ass [during slow concerts] so many times. It's a low blow—I'm not denying that—but it works."

Jim and Bryan's liaison with Kiss had generated two songs on the Kiss album *Creatures of the Night*. It also spawned a song cowritten with Kiss drummer Eric Carr, "Don't Leave Me Lonely," earmarked for the new Bryan Adams album. Also on tap for the new album were a couple of Adams/Vallance ballads—"The Best Was Yet to Come" and "Cuts Like a Knife," which would become the title track. It was written, said Adams, from a mumble.

"I think that I'm one of the world's best mumblers," he told his fan club. "I can mumble some of the best lyrics! Putting them together is another story. That's where Jim is really good. He can piece a story together for me.... 'Cuts Like a Knife' was literally a mumble. We looked at each other, rolled the tape back and it sounded like 'Cuts Like a Knife,' so we started singing that."

"My songs are love fantasies all the way," he told *Hit Parader*. "I haven't had that many intense love affairs. I have had my share of flings that have made me able to talk about it. I've also watched a lot of people and how they approach love. It's good to talk about it. I'm a romantic and I like singing about romance."

In August 1982, he began recording at Vancouver's Little Mountain Sound. Bob Clearmountain was again brought in to coproduce, a move that Adams said was questioned by Vallance because of the previous album's overall lack of sales and airplay.

"I like that sound, though," he said in Clearmountain's defence. "I go into the studio knowing exactly what arrangement of what is gonna happen, and then he just takes it from there. And I know Bob hates me saying this but he does take care of the sound and I take care of the arrangements. I knew exactly how I wanted those tunes to come off. Nobody could tell me any different, because I road-tested them."

Keith Scott, of course, would play guitar, Dave Taylor would be playing bass, and Mickey Curry and Tommy Mandel were again recruited for drums and keyboards respectively. Adams desperately wanted Curry and Mandel as permanent band members, and he put the pressure on, with some success—they agreed in principle. He considered *Cuts Like a Knife* the inaugural point of his new group.

"I really wanted to make sure the guys [in the band] were on this album," Bryan told Tom Harrison. "The last album the players were mainly pick-up musicians who didn't go out on the road with me, so the band I had on the road didn't really feel as involved with the songs."

"In the studio I wanted it to feel like it felt live," said Adams, "and that's very difficult to do because basically you're dealing with [the problem] of not having an audience. The adrenaline is a lot higher when you're playing in a concert, so I had to get the band in that feeling. I've always thought I was pretty good at motivating people." His biggest asset in this regard, he said, was his own ability to rev up instantly. "I can be on in two seconds."

Foreigner's Lou Gramm recorded backup vocals for most of the tracks at the Power Station in New York. Adams likened their duets to "two trains going at 100 miles per hour, trying to beat each other but still staying even." Background vocals were also provided by Keith Scott and Chic's Alfa Anderson. A gathering of friends and family contributed the "na na nas" (à la "Hey Jude") for "Cuts Like a Knife."

As an afterthought—the album needed another ballad— "Straight From the Heart," which had now been recorded by several different artists, including Bonnie Tyler, was brought to the table and quickly put on tape. Adams and Clearmountain mixed the record in Montreal and New York in September.

As with all his records, Adams would say it was his

favourite album. "Lyrically, I'm saying something," he told
Hit Parader. "Musically, I feel very strong. The production
is better and the band is playing better. This record is better
than anything I've ever done. In my life I haven't done many
things, so this album is even better than any girlfriend I've
ever had."

In October of 1982, with all recording complete, Adams
and Vallance learned that "Let Him Know" had been nominated for Pop Song of the Year at the prestigious Yamaha
Music Festival in Japan. The competition was at the end of
the month, and Adams made arrangements to perform there.
Since Mickey Curry was tied up on another project, Jim
Vallance agreed to play drums.

A year or two previously, Bryan, unbeknownst to Jane,
had tracked down his father through the consular service.
Conrad Adams had remarried and been posted to Tokyo with
his new wife, Hiroma. Father and son spoke, but Conrad
really had no idea what Bryan was up to until just a few days
before the concert. During a business reception, someone
pointed out a story on a budding Canadian rock star, Bryan
Adams. Conrad was embarrassed to admit that, yes, it was
his son, but he knew nothing about the boy or his career.

After Bryan got to Japan, he gave Conrad a call at his
office at the Canadian embassy, and they made arrangements
to get together. The two met that evening, alone, and caught
up on the previous nine years. The tête-à-tête did much to
clear the air between them, and Adams invited his father to
the next evening's performance. Adams played the concert
on a real high, but his mood deflated when Conrad, appalled
by the volume, left halfway through.

"He said it wasn't his cup of tea," Adams ruefully recalled.
Back home in November, he had no time to dwell on the snub
as he prepared for the release of *Cuts Like a Knife*. If
anything, he became more determined.

He assumed the first single would be the title track, and
was both surprised and dismayed when the powers that be at
A & M chose "Straight From the Heart." He strongly opposed the move. "The first single should be a rock song," he

said. "I don't think "Straight From the Heart" is Top 40 material." He did not get his own way. The song was shipped to radio December 2, with an announcement that the album would follow in January.

Adams spent Christmas at home, then opened for Loverboy again, first in Las Vegas and then on New Year's Eve at the Forum in Los Angeles. At this point, he still expected to be joined by Curry and Mandel. A press release issued by A & M in January 1983 listed the two as band members for the pending Canadian tour, but it was becoming painfully clear that they would not be available. Curry had recorded *Private Eyes* with Hall and Oates in 1981, just before he first worked with Adams; the hits were still pouring off the album, and he was going on the road with that very successful duo. Mandel was also making good money in New York doing jingles and session work for acts ranging from Dire Straits to the Clash. Adams couldn't pay him enough to make him leave his happy home.

"The hardest thing in the world is to find guys who will stick with you," lamented Adams to Tom Harrison, "especially when it's almost entirely your trip." John Hannah returned to play keyboards, and Jim Wesley was hurriedly called in to again play drums.

That month, Adams also shot a video in L.A. for "Cuts Like a Knife" at the Berwin Entertainment Complex. It featured scenes of a woman in a bathing suit diving into an empty pool, a shot of a hand holding a knife, and one of Adams peeling an apple. It was destined to get him into a spot of trouble with a few feminists. At the first hint of criticism, Adams launched a massive counterattack. Many thought he overreacted.

"Some girl is taking her clothes off, and in the meantime I'm peeling an apple and throwing the knife around," Bryan indignantly snorted to *Rock*'s Daina Darzin. "You can see more suggestive stuff watching "Kojak." No one saw the humour in it. Fuck 'em."

"They're just full of shit," he raged to *Smash Hits*'s Sandy Robertson. "Look," he added. "I'm just a regular guy with

regular adult feelings and y'know, if women didn't want to
dress in bikinis they wouldn't dress in bikinis, right?"

"Anyone who thinks [the video] is violent or pornographic
is a prude," he told *Maclean's* magazine.

"Bryan didn't mind being known as a bit of a chauvinist,"
observed one insider. "He probably liked the idea of a little
controversy, maybe even manipulated it. It was a macho
thing to do. He and Bruce had always been targeting the
young male market."

Another source disagreed: "I doubt that Bruce or Bryan
manipulated that kind of press. I don't think they were that
sophisticated."

During the first few months of 1983, it became apparent
Adams had two hit songs—"Straight From the Heart" through
Top 40 radio, and "Cuts Like a Knife" through MTV and FM
album rock stations. Meanwhile, Adams was about to go on
tour, but he wanted another drummer. "Jim Wesley was a bit
depressing," commented a backstage observer. "Adams would
be pumping everybody up to go onstage, and Wesley would
be looking like his mother just died."

He called up Frankie LaRoca, a New Yorker he had met
first at his publisher's office and again at the Tangerine and
Orange Bowl festivals. He had been in John Waite's band at
the time, but told Bryan to give him a call if he ever needed
a drummer. Laroca arrived in Vancouver for a few days of
rehearsals, then hit the road with the band.

The tour started at the end of January on the Canadian East
Coast, and moved into chilly central Canada in February.
The band was headlining small concerts, mostly at the local
colleges. Attendance generally wasn't that great, but the
immediate future held bigger and better things to cheer them
up. Allen had already scored a massive U.S. tour with
Journey, and these sleepy Canadian dates were essentially a
rehearsal for the Adams assault on the States.

Laroca was not a happy camper. He had assumed he would
be paid in American funds and was receiving his money in
substantially devalued Canadian dollars instead. He found
himself trapped on a small-town Canada "Motel 6 tour" in

the middle of a very rough winter, travelling on black ice through blizzards in a creaky bus.

"He was calling the Bruce Allen office almost everyday to complain, until "Crystal [Harbidge] stopped accepting his collect calls," chuckled one source.

It didn't help matters when a bomb scare cancelled the last half of a show in Halifax, one of the first stops on the tour. That was the tour lowlight. The highlight was Montreal, where he accepted an award from *Music Express* for winning the top male vocalist category in a year-end readers' poll, played a hot show at McGill University and squeezed in an opening spot with Aerosmith at the Forum.

Several dates on the tour were cobilled with either the Headpins or Harlequin—both acts with stronger sales and profiles—and it alternated as to who opened and who closed. The only disagreement was prior to yet another gig in Ottawa. Adams was scheduled to go on first, but, claiming hometown status, asked for the headliner's slot. He lost the battle, but he had the last laugh when the review came out.

"All the best moments happened before the night was half over," wrote the Ottawa *Citizen*. "It might have been a mistake for Harlequin—who have been playing the same way for seven years—to tie onto a fresh phenomenon like Bryan Adams. They ended up looking fairly crass by comparison."

The schedule included several major shows with Hall and Oates, but Adams and Allen blew gaskets and pulled out of the dates when they were cut back to just a thirty-minute set and given a start time that was ten minutes before the advertised time of the show. The industry rumour mill claimed that Hall and Oates felt that Adams was too strong an act and used these measures to drive him off the bill.

"It was a real dog of a tour," recalled crew member Mike Harling. "The Hall and Oates dates had been the main carrot, so everyone was really bummed out. The only good thing that happened was that Sudbury was cancelled. We didn't have to go to Sudbury." The town, hundreds of miles off the beaten track, was considered the hellhole of Canadian touring due to its remote and unappealing geography and traditionally ugly audiences.

"It's still a battle," Adams told Tom Harrison in a phone interview from Cornwall, Ontario. "Every step of the way you think it's going to get easier, but it doesn't. It's still the same.... I want to be home, man! Everybody wants to get back so bad. It's too cold out here!"

Adams did make it home, but not for long. He and the band played a couple of hometown dates as warm-ups, and on March 26 in Seattle they embarked on a five-month, eighty-seven-show tour with Journey. "By fall I'm going to be totally bagged," declared Adams to the press, "but everybody in the States is going to know who I am."

Within a few weeks of its release in late January, *Cuts Like a Knife* was the most-added record to radio station playlists in the States and Canada. "Straight From the Heart" was on a brisk and steady rise up the *Billboard* Hot 100—it would peak at #10—and the title song was high on charts listing the most-played album tracks. By April, "Cuts Like a Knife" had been released as an official second single, and it, too, quickly climbed the Hot 100 (it eventually peaked at #15). Bryan Adams was one of the fastest-rising acts in America.

In Canada, he finally won a Juno award—Male Vocalist of the Year for 1982. The small size of the Canadian music industry made Juno nominations commonplace for marginally successful artists. Adams had been up for Most Promising Male Vocalist in 1979 and again in 1980, but had lost out to Walter Rossi the first year and Graham Shaw the next. He hadn't been nominated for any award in 1981.

A breather in the schedule in April was used to shoot a video for "This Time" (without the band, much to their chagrin) at Edwards Air Force Base in California. The Journey tour was again interrupted in May as Adams and the band spent a few days at home, then flew to New York for two shows at the Bottomline, historically the most important music club in the city. The audience was jammed with rock stars, including Mick Jagger, Rick Nielsen (Cheap Trick), Nils Lofgren, John Waite and Rick Derringer, and friends like Paul Dean from Loverboy and Gene Simmons and Paul Stanley from Kiss.

Adams was hot, but the stars were really out for Stevie Ray Vaughan, Jimmy Vaughan's guitar-whiz little brother, a musician's musician who was also making his big debut at the club that night. Bryan's presence was incidental, but he made the most of it by circulating among the rockers and the moguls.

In the crowd was the ever-surly John McEnroe, and the tennis star was his moody self that night. In the course of the evening, Adams came over to meet him. "I bought your tape", McEnroe muttered sourly. "Hey, man," replied Adams, "don't let it get you down. It was only eight bucks!"

Once onstage, Adams and the band never quite got their illustrious audience's attention. They were being upstaged by a rookie who didn't even have a record on the charts. Adams did his best to manufacture some energy, and at the end of his set, he rounded up Waite, Derringer and Dean for a rendition of "Hound Dog."

Backstage after the show, he was greeted by Mick Jagger.

"You Bryan Adams?" asked Jagger.

"Yeah," said Adams.

"Well, I'm your dad," cracked Jagger.

"Hey, Dad, have a seat."

For the rest of the conversation, Jagger was "Dad" and Adams was "the lad."

From New York, it was onto L.A. and the taping of Adams's first appearance on Dick Clark's "American Bandstand." If that didn't drive home the artist's success, the fact that his album went gold in the States that same week certainly did. Adams had sold 500,000 copies of *Cuts Like a Knife* south of the border, and another 100,000 in Canada— platinum there.

In late June, with a show scheduled in Detroit with Journey, Adams zipped up to nearby Toronto for a not overly well-attended appearance at Canada's Wonderland, a theme park.

"The security at Wonderland are a bunch of seventeen-year-old assholes who think they're cops," recalled one member of the audience, Louise Allen, "They were pulling their usual tricks, like telling the audience to sit down—we couldn't stand up and dance. Adams put his foot on one guy's head, a guard in front of the stage facing the crowd, and said, 'This is a Bryan Adams concert. I'm Bryan Adams, and I say they can get up and dance.' So we got up and danced."

By late July, the new album had raced to platinum status in the States—one million records—and as the tour hit the West Coast, the feat was celebrated at a "pool party" at the Berwin Entertainment Complex, the scene of the "Cuts Like a Knife" video. The press thought that it was particularly endearing that Adams gave the mounted platinum record to his mom, Jane.

According to those in attendance, the party was a real "smoker." "A & M found out the hard way never to barbecue in an empty indoor pool," recalled Crystal Harbidge. "The smoke and the fumes just hung there. All the guests were asphyxiated. It was great fun, but you don't score a lot of points when you kill off the people who were playing your record."

Adams had retained "Take Me Back" and its midsong monologue as the high point in the live set. He'd talk about waking up in the morning with his girlfriend gone, and how he had come down to the breakfast table, poured himself a bowl of cornflakes and ate them while she approached him in a slinky negligee, begging to come back. All of this led to his notorious onstage response, "Fuck You!"

The Journey band and crew, hearing the spiel for the eighty-seventh time in less than five months, sought revenge. As Adams launched into the monologue at one of the last shows of the tour, a huge sack bearing the contents of sixty econo-size boxes of cornflakes was unceremoniously dumped on his head, much of it becoming immediate mush as the flakes hit his sweaty body. "Good humour!" laughed Adams.

The extended road trip had its moments, admitted Adams, but it really wasn't much fun. "By the end of the Journey tour," he later told the Pittsburgh *Press*, "I was fed up with being a support act.... We were living on the bus and sleeping in the hall. We never had a hotel. It was really horrible. I'm glad it's over. I don't think I could have done much more like that."

Adams and Allen were targeting young male fans when they toured with Journey and Foreigner, but "Straight From the Heart" and "Cuts Like a Knife" were appealing to teenage girls in a major way. He was a natural: He was young, handsome and blond, and he was a rocker who sang love ballads.

His face was splashed across glossy fan-magazine covers, and inside they poured out all the crucial details of his life. His favourite colour was red (sometimes platinum), and he liked Indian food, fresh cocoa and plums in Paris, Italian food, marmalade made by his buddy Steve Weakes, sci-fi films (especially *The Blob)* and Johnny Carson. His favourite breakfast was a fresh cup of coffee or a hot cup of tea, a croissant, marmalade and unsalted butter. He liked dogs—he'd grown up with a wirehaired fox terrier named Gypsy, and now had one called Puddles. ("You can guess why," said Adams.)

He liked foreign-language films, and he hated soap operas. "I like real things. I like real people in real situations... I don't like phoney interpretations of day-to-day life..." He read a book a month (at the time he was reading a Kurt Vonnegut novel and a book about the Beatles), and he went to the gym twice a week for weight training.

As for "Bryan's Ideal Girl," she had to be intelligent above all else, he told *Bop*, and "she's also got to have something real striking about her. I like women who are kind of exotic! Not in a sexual sense, but just the way someone carries herself."

"I like girls who almost seem untouchable," he told his newly formed fan club. "Mystique is very important. I find mystique attractive in people. Even relating it to myself, I think it's important for fans to know what I'm like... But sometimes I think I'd like to leave a little to the imagination—that mystique thing again."

Bryan told his fan club quite a bit. He was nocturnal and liked to party. He didn't drink much or do any drugs but sometimes got "too excited," and consequently earned nicknames like "the brat" and "the menace". "That's when my mouth starts to work," he said. "My own greatest fault is probably my mouth. I'm not a brat, okay? That's a bad word for me to use 'cause I don't think that I am. I get a little over the top, you know, more of a menace, the kind of guy you wouldn't want in your neighbourhood."

He admitted to a short temper. "Patience isn't my middle name," he told the interviewer. "I can't tolerate incompetence in any respect. My temperament varies only in that when I have to deal with people who aren't doing their job properly I get moody, you know.... I think that I'm reasonably personable but I'm not that easy to get to know, just because I like to keep to myself. The other day on the TV news I heard the guy say, 'Bryan Adams, known as the Canadian Prince of Pop and also as an arrogant little brat.' Anyone that says that about me doesn't know me at all. They interpret 'excitable boy' for arrogance, which is a misunderstanding I think."

Adams turned to someone in the room: "Dave, would you say I'm arrogant?"

Pause. "Yeah."

"Oh." Adams continued, unruffled. "He said I was. But being arrogant and knowing what you want and trying to get it, there's a fine line there. Confidence is often mistaken for arrogance."

To his closest acquaintances, he's "Adams."

"What kind of people do you like?" asked the fan-club interviewer.

"I like my friends," was the answer.

"Adams doesn't have a lot of friends to begin with," commented one observer. "And even they won't say they really know him. He's got these rooms in his life, and he lets some people into some, but not others. Different people get to know different rooms, but nobody really knows the whole layout."

"The first thing that attracts me to another person is intelligence," said Adams. "I go for people who are basically straightforward and don't try to pull anything on me. [I don't like] people who try to pretend they are something they're not. I can see through that kind of shit right away."

"Bryan is exactly as you see him—he doesn't modify his behaviour for anyone," confirmed Crystal Harbidge. "He was the only artist I was allowed to speak my mind to. And he never treated me like a girl, a bimbo secretary. He was consistent—you always knew where you stood with him. There was no pussyfooting around, and none of this backstabbing stuff."

On the downside, said another insider, he could be very thoughtless when it came to other people. And, they added, he had the worst table manners on the planet: "Rachel, Jim's wife, got to the point where she she couldn't eat with him, he was so disgusting—grabbing food with his hands, talking with his mouth full, laughing, telling rude jokes...."

"Adams got away with a lot with that cute little 'aw, shucks' naughty-boy smile," observed Harbidge. "He was like a big kid. Sometimes he was just—inappropriate."

The more popular he became, the less privacy Adams got. He had moved into a large but modest two-storey rented house in a nice part of North Vancouver, sharing it with his brother, Bruce. Bryan hated the place; he thought it was 'tacky' and called it his "dumping ground." So-called friends and wannabe friends would drop around to say hi. The special-delivery man would wake him up early in the morning for a chat.

Never one for subtlety, Bryan put a sign on his front door that read Attention! Do Not Disturb this House under Any Circumstances. Please Go Away. Thank You." The doorbell was labelled Death Ray.

He occasionally allowed reporters to come by for interviews, but he was furious when they described his home or lifestyle.

"Aside from the BMW in the driveway, the baby grand in

the basement, and the six gold and platinum albums hanging on his wall," noted the Vancouver *Sun*, "Adams's place looks like that of any other 23-year-old bachelor. It's sparsely decorated, somewhat unkempt, and the sink full of yesterday's dirty dishes."

"In the garage is a three-year-old, metallic green BMW car," Les Wiseman wrote in *Vancouver Magazine*. "In the kitchen is a three-day-old, green plastic garbage bag. In the house is a female platonic housemate who shares the rent and looks after the place when Adams is on the road."

Adams declared his home life, friends and family off-limits to the press. He wasn't hiding any dark secrets. Wiseman was describing Anna Skokan, who had met Adams when she was working in the office of a local jingle company. Late in the summer of 1983, she was watching Adams record a Labatts commercial for the company when it came up in conversation that she was looking for a place to live. Adams told her that with his brother moving out to his own pad, he had an empty, fully furnished five-bedroom house on his hands, and that he was looking for a roommate who could take care of the place while he was on the road. A deal was struck.

A few weeks later, Skokan was lodged comfortably in the "dumping ground" while Adams was on his way to Europe. Over the next year and some, people would variously refer to her as Adams's girlfriend, friend, platonic friend, housekeeper and housemate. Yet, as Skokan emphasized, "We were just roommates, like any other roommates sharing a place, except he paid more of the rent."

"It was a big house," she said, "and we each had our own space. I liked cooking, and he didn't, so I cooked. He made sandwiches. I liked my living space cleaner than Bryan liked his, so I cleaned more. When he was in town, in the morning we'd have our tea, and late at night we'd watch [the British comedy] "Fawlty Towers" on TV. The time between, he'd be working."

He worked all the time, said Skokan. If he wasn't on the road or in the studio with Vallance, he was on the phone doing business. "Every night, he'd write up this big list of things he'd have to get done, and the next day he'd whip right through it. He had more energy, drive and determination than anyone I know."

He was never one to go out on the town, but Adams and Skokan would occasionally have small dinner parties at home, always with the same select group of friends—Jim and his wife, Rachel, Chris "Beanbag" Ainscough, Keith Scott, and Dave Taylor and his wife Donna.

Adams made sure reporters knew he rented his house, that he didn't spend money on partying and that he gave to charity, but any real questions regarding his financial status were off-limits. He felt most uncomfortable when others eyed his few trappings of success. His "Let Me Take You Dancing" money had bought a Volkswagen convertible, and then the songwriting boom of 1981 paid for a brand-new BMW—it was before the car became *the* yuppie symbol, but he was still a little embarrassed by it. He didn't own up to taking a Caribbean vacation, and barely admitted to buying a motorcycle.

"There's something very impersonal about success," said Adams. "It's not so much that you change, but people's attitudes towards you change. I've never taken advantage of my popularity, and I've never flaunted it. People respect that."

He certainly didn't flaunt his riches. By now, *Cuts Like a Knife* was bringing in big money. He and his mother, Jane, a director of his company, Adams Communications, were reportedly investing it in safe ventures like term deposits ("He's not buying shopping malls," Bruce Allen told one reporter), but there was no outward sign of wealth. He certainly wasn't spending more than he had to. According to most sources, he paid notoriously low wages and offered little in the way of bonuses.

His penny-pinching ways were also legendary in the service industry. One gardening professional recalled Adams's decrepit old lawnmower and marvelled at how he defied all attempts to get him to buy a new machine. "It works, doesn't it?" Adams would say audaciously.

A repair shop recalled that same lawnmower—it had stopped working. Adams still wouldn't buy a new one. While they fixed it, the shop staff chuckled that such an affluent rock star would own such a wreck, then laughed out loud when Adams complained about the bill and refused to pay the full amount.

"I don't think Adams ever paid the amount listed on an invoice, at least not without an argument," recalled one insider. "I think that came from growing up in Portugal and Israel. He learned to barter."

"He was tight," added a former coworker, "but he was also very suspicious about people taking advantage of him—gougers, bootleggers, freeloaders.... Both he and Bruce hated the thought of other people making money from their success—unless they had a piece of it."

Adams was also growing more distrustful and intolerant when it came to the media, and it was showing during interviews. And it was duly noted by the press. "Don't send out a limousine for Bryan Adams," advised journalist Liz Braun in one article. "Don't try to categorize his brand of rock music, don't compare him to Bruce Springsteen, don't query the lack of social issues in his songs. And please don't ask him what it's like to be a rock star."

"I'm getting really bored looking at my face," Adams told Sandy Robertson in 1983. "My picture seems to be everywhere right now, in all the magazines. And the interviewers are so dumb. You get all these guys with their list of questions who know nothing about me, going, 'Do you have a girlfriend?' or 'Do you have sex with six?' or 'Do you pick your toenails?', y'know?"

"I believe that there should be some respect," he told the *Toronto Star*. "I think people forget that these artists are individuals; living, breathing, human, thinking people with feelings. I'm not just a piece of vinyl. Behind all this music I do is a human being. But I don't necessarily want people to know about it."

8

Heaven and Hell: Reckless to the End

For the second half of 1983, Bryan Adams was off the road for only one week in August and ten days in September, but he still managed to release another hit record. He just didn't know it at the time, and he certainly didn't expect it.

Coming into the eighties, songs from movie soundtrack albums evoked the same response in radio programmers as elevator music. But record companies and recording artists found that movie tie-ins paid well, and a fee from Hollywood could more than make up for a lack of sales and airplay income when the record stiffed. Adams and Jim Vallance had been exploring this lucrative area—"Hiding From Love" and "Lonely Nights" had just been sold to the movie *Class*, starring Jacqueline Bisset. The two whipped up the song "Heaven" on spec after hearing that a production-in-progress titled *A Night in Heaven* was in need of material. Their timing was impeccable. They were on top of a trend that would quickly breed the era of hit soundtracks like those of *Footloose, Top Gun* and "Miami Vice."

Their taste in cinema left something to be desired. The flick starred Christopher Atkins, the teenage blond sex-symbol from *The Blue Lagoon*, and it promised good things at the box office. It lied. It was a dud. *A Night in Heaven*, the story of a promiscuous high school student—a male stripper by night—who seduces his teacher to get a better grade was bloody awful. Fortunately, the tune fared much better.

"Heaven" took just two days to write, and was recorded that summer at the Power Station in New York, with Bob Clearmountain coproducing. Tommy Mandel was brought in to play keyboards; Mickey Curry was asked to play drums.

A 10 a.m. session was scheduled to record the song. Curry had a Hall and Oates rehearsal at noon a few blocks away, and he left just as the recording was about to get under way. Adams was not a very happy man, and he reportedly made a phone call.

"Bryan knew I had to go," said Curry in fan club interview, "so I said, 'Look, I'll be back around five o'clock. I've got it down, and when I come back, I'll nail it!'"

By the time Curry returned, the drum track had already been nailed. He walked in to find Adams, the band and Clearmountain in the control room with Journey drummer Steve Smith, listening to completed bed tracks.

"Bryan pulled me aside," related Curry, "and said, 'Hey, Steve was in town and stopped by, and we just started playing.' I said, 'Great—it sounds great!' They had five or six takes and they pieced it all together, like Bryan likes to do. I guess he was feeling kind of bad, so he offered to pay me for the day. I said, 'Bryan, it's okay, man—don't worry about it!'"

At the time, added Curry, it was just another session, and a mere soundtrack session at that. When the soundtrack album *A Night in Heaven* was released that fall, no one gave it a second thought. The news that Canada's biggest star, Anne Murray, was going to cover "Straight From the Heart" was much more exciting.

In mid-September, Adams and the band—Scott, Taylor, Hannah and LaRoca—embarked on Adams's first tour of Europe. He had fought for the trip—Bruce Allen was not a fan of the European market.

"Bruce hated the idea," confirmed Adams. "He hated Europe. We went head-to-head on it, but I told him we can only play Canada so many times. Things get boring if you do. People get too familiar with you, you lose the excitement."

Adams had no worries about that in England—there was no excitement to lose. The European tour lasted six weeks and hit eleven countries. Some markets were better than others, but for the most part, the experience was the opposite of North America; the band was thrilled to be travelling and the audiences weren't thrilled with the band.

A "Rockpalast" TV show out of Germany, watched by two and a half million viewers, helped break the ice in much of Europe, but the British were still wary of mainstream North American rockers. The "Cuts Like a Knife" video had aired on "Top of the Pops," his album was getting smatterings of airplay, and Adams had made the cover of *Sounds*, one of the more important U.K. music weeklies. Still, his concert at the half-filled 2,500-seat Dominion Theatre in London drew a thoroughly indifferent crowd. The reviews were mixed. Tom Harrison, writing for Canada's *Music Express*, was particularly hard on the performance. "What should have been a blockbuster night for Bryan Adams and London, in the end was a loud odourless fart... Ultimately Bryan won his two encores, as I imagine he has done in every city where he was unknown through sheer force of will and positivism, but this was neither the ideal introduction to Bryan Adams nor the show to make his name here."

Harrison went on to accuse Adams of using "arena rock jive" and presenting an "act" with little real character.

"They respond to energy," said Adams of his European audiences. "They don't know me or my songs, but they do know energy and that's what we give them."

A notable exception to the lukewarm initial response was at a university in Sheffield—a concert Adams will never forget. "England was a very tough, tough market for us to break," he said in a radio interview, "but we packed them in at Sheffield. It was strange—people had come from everywhere to see this concert. I don't know why. We went onstage that night and it was kinetic. There was something so wild about that show. The audience was really listening. After we walked off, we thought we'd get the same reaction that we'd been getting in Europe.... Suddenly the crowd went berserk. They all started singing, 'You'll Never Walk Alone' by Gerry and the Pacemakers, a huge football song, which is probably the biggest compliment any musician can be paid, never mind a football team. If they start singing that song at a football game they think you are the best. A security guard came over to me and he said, 'I've worked here for five years and no one has ever got this reaction.' That was a moment that I'll never forget ever, and anybody who was there will know that it was special, too."

Living in different countries as a diplomat's son had been the perfect preparation for life on the road in Europe. He was comfortable with new customs, different languages and foreign people. ("I'm not afraid of anything," said Adams.) Adams was also a happy traveller. He didn't mind living in hotels, he had a passion for exotic food and he loved sightseeing. While in Europe, he spent as much time as he could visiting places he remembered from his childhood.

He also visited relatives. "My cousin James is currently at Sandhurst," Adams told *Record* magazine, "and my grandfather still doesn't understand why I'm not there. I'm an Adams, aren't I? It really came out during the Falklands war. Fiery blood flowed through the Adams family once again."

He arrived back in Vancouver, only to leave a few days later for a handful of key concerts in Japan starting the first of November. Frankie LaRoca had passport problems and arrived a day late, missing a TV taping at which crew member Michael "Bilko" Bilkoski was recruited to sit at the drum stool during the lip-synced shoot.

Adams was becoming increasingly frustrated with LaRoca, and he would wish out loud in front of him and Hannah that he had the budget to hire Curry and Mandel. Road manager Graeme Lagden was also on their case, riding Hannah for his constant preoccupation with billiards, and LaRoca for anything that came to mind at the time. LaRoca, in turn, stewed about not being on a retainer.

By mid-November, the band was back on its home turf and busy with a western Canadian tour. Meanwhile, *A Night in Heaven* and its soundtrack were released with little fanfare.

By year's end, music industry accolades were starting to pile up. They included three major American awards—Best Selling New Artist (presented by the National Association of Record Merchandisers), #2 Male AOR Artist (the U.S. music-trade publication *Album Network*) and #3 Most Played AOR Album (*Radio and Records*, another American trade). Over the previous year, Adams and crew had spent 283 days on the road.

Adams was home for Christmas, and early in the New Year he and Vallance went song-crazy writing for a new album. "We can't write without each other," he told James Muretich of the Calgary *Herald*. "When I'm on the road I can't really write without Jim. I've been back in Vancouver now for four days and already we've written a song. It is like a marriage. If you hadn't seen your wife for two months, what's the first thing you'd do when you got home? You're not going to go out for dinner, that's for sure! And the first thing we do is get together and write songs."

Late in February 1984, the opportunity to tour down under with the Police came up. Adams jumped on it, but he wanted to continue writing with Vallance and he was short a drummer—Curry, as usual, was tied up, and Frankie LaRoca was on a job in Europe, flaunting his independence. (This was the last of LaRoca, as far as Adams was concerned.) Both problems were solved when Vallance agreed to play drums on the tour.

"I wasn't adverse to the more exotic tour stops or vacation spots," said Vallance.

The first stop was Hawaii. "I've seen some frightening things at large outdoor festivals," Adams told *Record Mirror*. "The worse for me was in Hawaii. A fight broke out at the front of the stage between the natives and the U.S. Navy. One guy has another in a headlock. He just stood there grinning at me while pounding this guy's head in time with the music. It was so sickening I stopped the band. Luckily that's not my audience. I once saw another band go on stage with crash helmets and literally say 'come and get us.'"

New Zealand, too, proved to be a hot spot. Adams played

a major outdoor event as the third act of a six-band bill headlined by the Police. He was "pretty jacked up" according to the New Zealand media, and he did his best to get the crowd equally jacked up. And his best was pretty good. The end result was a riot.

"It's your show, and you can do anything you want!" screamed Adams. "Have a wild time!"

His invitation was the cue for thousands of kids outside the gates to break down the fences and flood the stadium, which was already packed with thirty-five thousand Police fans. The press roasted him for inciting the melee.

Things were a little quieter in Australia, largely because the public didn't know Adams from Adam: "It was, 'G'day, mate.' They didn't know who the hell I was!" Once they were back in Vancouver, the push to come up with more material for the fourth album continued, with an emphasis on variety and humour. The Adams/Vallance team wrote steadily until the end of March. One of the first songs chosen for the new album was "Run to You," written for submission to Blue Oyster Cult. When that band took a pass, Keith Scott convinced Bryan to record it himself.

"Summer of '69" was the hardest song on the album to write, according to Adams. "'Summer of '69' is Jim, but it's a song about our youth, both Jim and I, growing up as musicians. The year is immaterial, although it was a great year—I was only ten, of course, but I remember the moon landing, the Beatles breaking up, Woodstock.... That song took more rewrites than any of the others, and I only let it go on [the record] because I didn't know what else I could do with it."

"Kids Wanna Rock" evolved much more quickly. "It was kind of a natural song for us to write," Adams told the press. "Vallance and I have been saying that phrase for years. 'Hey, Vallance, kids wanna rock!' Or 'Hey, Vallance, what kinda songs are we gonna write?' 'Hmmm, I don't know, Adams. Kids wanna rock!'"

In a British radio interview, Adams revealed that the original lyrics of the song were quite different: "It was so difficult getting a break here in England on our first couple of tours," revealed Adams. "We had a [line in 'Kids Wanna Rock'] that used to go 'What's Sir Lew Grade got against me, I can't get my songs on the BBC.' Ha ha. But we didn't think it was very good for the record, so we changed it." Adams actually meant Stephen Grade from the British radio network, not publishing magnate Lew Grade.

"I Need Somebody" was influenced by the Police in a roundabout way. "Jim had come up with a bass line," explained Adams, "and I started singing a melody, and the words 'I need somebody,' and I said, 'No, that's too corny.'" Vallance responded by singing "De do do do, de da da da," the title and chorus of the hit record by the Police. "After that, it didn't seem so corny."

"Ain't Gonna Cry" was an exercise in humour that many said didn't work. Critics accused him of making light of family violence with lyrics about rearranging an unfaithful loved one's face.

Mark Mehler brought the subject up in an interview in *Record* magazine. "I'm writing in the third person there," Adams explained, adding with a touch of annoyance, "Why must everything be tied directly to my personal life?"

Reviewer Tom Harrison also took a shot at Adams in *Graffiti* magazine, saying this attempt at humour—and recklessness—backfired horribly. Adams was phlegmatically defensive "I've never hit a woman in my life," he told Harrison. "It's just a joke. We have a funny thing that goes on between the band, myself and Jim. It's not meant to be a violent thing—it's a humorous thing.... It got a reaction, anyway."

"Emotions are a funny thing," he said to Harrison. "If you want to dig here, I didn't exactly have the best childhood—it wasn't exactly rosy. Everyone wasn't always nice to each other. I've heard everything from 'I love you' to 'I hate you,' and that's just the way humans are. Don't tell me you've never threatened anybody."

A few songs didn't make the cut. Adams and Vallance originally wrote "Edge of a Dream" with a movie in mind, but then they decided to record it for the new album. They cut a good demo in the basement, but didn't like the studio version and dropped it.

Bruce Allen hit the roof when Adams gave the song "Boys Night Out" to Krokus—it was one of Allen's favourite "attitude" songs. Another reject was a tough little rocker called "Reckless." The decision to drop it was not taken lightly, considering it was planned as the title track. *Reckless* remained the album title, but the song was turned into "Dangerous" and recorded by Loverboy.

The band started recording early in April in Vancouver at Little Mountain Sound, with Mickey Curry and Tommy Mandel flying in for the sessions. It was an Adams/ Clearmountain coproduction, with Vallance credited as associate producer. The sessions initially went well. "Run to You," one of the first songs recorded, was cut in one take.

It went downhill from there. "I never rehearsed for the album," said Adams. "I thought we'd try to capture some spontaneity."

In this case, however, "spontaneity" took endless hours of rehearsing, recording, rerecording, editing, splicing and mixing. When we went into the studio, it wasn't a matter of how many hours I could go without taking a break—it was how many days. I think for the first part of the record, I ended up spending seven days a week and probably sixteen hours a day. Finally I realized I was losing my objectivity. Not only was I overworking myself, I was overworking everyone else around me, and that attitude doesn't make for being very spontaneous or very creative."

"I'll never do it again," he told Wilder Penfield III of the Toronto *Sun*. "It wasn't worth the anguish it took to make this record. There was too much pressure, so many loose ends to tie up. I found myself at odds with everybody in the room, and totally unobjective... Bob Clearmountain is a brilliant engineer, but it gets wearing on him, and the others can't stand me as a producer because I'm so demanding. I'll do it in a nice way, but there's a point when everyone will go, 'What! Is! Wrong! With! That!,' and I'll go, 'It isn't right yet, and when it's right, I'll let you know.'"

It was mid-May, and *Reckless* still wasn't right. It had been almost two months of hell, and each new week brought a new set of scheduling problems. Both Clearmountain and the studio had other bookings. So, naturally, did Mandel and Curry. Curry was due to start recording *Big Bam Boom* with Hall and Oates, and he wasn't about to forsake that duo, just as Mandel wasn't about to leave his other session work, especially for the money Adams was willing to pay. The sessions collapsed.

By that point, Adams had a new woman in his life—Elizabeth Dawson. Liz was another dark blonde; she was petite, older than he by two or three years, and she was in advertising—an executive with one of the major agencies. She visited the studio often, but she had never seen him perform live.

When he finally did take a necessary break from recording, he worked on his new house in West Vancouver, a small but charming two-bedroom Tudor-style home with a spectacular view. It would be several months before he could move in—it needed a lot of work in terms of general renovations and landscaping, plus more fundamental items like plumbing and wiring. The house was his hobby that summer; he said he found the work relaxing, especially the gardening.

Some inspiration was forthcoming at the end of June. Adams and the band had recorded "It's Only Love," and Adams went after Tina Turner to make the song a duet. Adams had long been an enthusiastic fan. He had attended a Tina Turner Revue concert at the Commodore Ballroom in the late Seventies, and the event was indelibly stamped in his memory. "Within two songs she had me on top of the table, you know, standing up and screaming and shouting like everybody else. I remember going backstage and trying to meet her. I wanted to play her a song that I had, but, you know, that was three years ago and I was just another fan."

He did smuggle himself backstage, only to be forcibly ejected, apparently at the request of Turner. "She didn't feel too good, and I guess she didn't have time so that didn't work out," he told *Look In* magazine. He provided more details to the *Daily Star*: "I had just enough time to say, 'Hello' when this burly bouncer grabbed me by the collar and threw me out into the street. I tried a safer approach the second time. I posted her some tapes of my songs and she sent a car round to collect me."

Adams and Vallance had submitted a song for Turner's *Private Dancer* album, with no luck. Adams knew her producer, Carter, and approached him regarding the possibility of a duet. Carter said yes, maybe, and told him to send a tape of the song. Adams promptly sent off a copy of "It's Only Love." A prompt reply was not forthcoming, but he persisted.

Turner was scheduled for several concerts in Vancouver the last two days of June, opening for Lionel Ritchie. On Adams's instructions, another demo tape of the song was sent to Turner's hotel and a meeting was arranged for backstage at the Coliseum after her set. Adams smiled as he was respectfully ushered past the guards and into her sizable dressing room.

"I just sat backstage waiting to see what would happen," recalled Adams. Turner made a beeline for him through a crowd of press and promoters. "I want to do this song," she enthused. "It rocks! Can we do it Saturday?"

"She came into the studio and it was just like, 'All right! Let's do it,'" said Adams. "We had to work out where she was going to fit, because at first the song was a bit low for her voice.... With a lady like that you want to give her a lot of room, so that's what we did."

Adams's sagging spirits had been revitalized but there were other tracks on the album that he was still not happy with. Mickey Curry had already been flying in and out on a delicately balanced schedule. Hall and Oates were putting the finishing touches on *Big Bam Boom*, and they were preparing to go on a massive world tour in October.

From Curry's perspective, there seemed no end to the *Reckless* recording. When Adams wanted him to redo more tracks again, Curry refused. Adams was choked.

Clearmountain also wanted to go with the tracks as they were, but it was Adams's turn to refuse. The record company, originally expecting a late summer release, had an anxiety attack. Adams was expected to be the top A & M release of the season, if not the year.

"Why is Mickey Curry out and Pat Steward in?" queried a writer for *Sounds*. "Because there was a serious lack of fire," answered Adams. "I need spontaneity. I wanted the guy to come in and kick my ass, and he didn't."

Just before leaving for Australia with the Police the previous February, Adams and Keith Scott had gone on a bar cruise looking for a drummer for the touring band. Scott led the way to a small, run-down club in an unsavoury neighbourhood. There they had found Pat Steward playing with some longtime mates in a respected but struggling local band called Rubber Biscuit.

Said Adams: "I remember seeing this guy play and thinking 'Wow, good energy!' We went up and talked to him, bought him a beer and chatted with him for a while.... We dropped a hint heavily that we were looking for somebody and we needed some energy in the tracks, and he said he'd be into trying a couple of jams out."

"I didn't know who he was," recalled Steward, "but we sat down and talked for a couple of minutes. I asked him his name and when he said 'Bryan' I put it together. The fact that we were talking about me doing some playing for him was all hush-hush because of [Rubber Biscuit]. We were all living in the same house. It was like sneaking out to drink beer before you're old enough."

With Curry out of the picture, Adams returned to the studio in late July with Steward, rehearsing and recording the new drummer as the clock ticked on. Steward recorded new tracks for "Summer of '69," "Kids Wanna Rock" and "One Night Love Affair." Things clicked, and Adams asked him to join the band.

"I didn't decide right away." said Pat. "I was freaking out for about five months because I was in a band that I started, a band I really liked that was doing really well." It was a once-in-a-lifetime offer, though. By September, Steward was a full-fledged member of the Adams family.

A last-minute decision was made to include "Heaven" on *Reckless* after the marginal success of the *A Night in Heaven* soundtrack and following an excellent response from Adams's friends and cronies. Bruce Adams had paid attention. Anna Skokan's sweater had stood out. Others had given it the thumbs-up. Not everybody was a fan of the song, however.

"I remember playing the record for this producer," said Adams in a British radio interview, "and him saying to me,'You know, it's a good record, but there's two songs you should take off.' 'Oh, yeah? What songs are those?' 'You should take 'Heaven' and 'Summer of '69' off the record, they're not right for this album.' I said, 'Oh, man,' and by that time I'd already given the record away to the record company." The producer was the ultrasuccessful Jimmy Iovine.

For the cover of *Reckless*, A & M forked out in excess of $20,000 for a stark black-and-white photo of Adams by Hiro, a prominent Japanese portrait photographer. The processing of the shot and the ensuing artwork to match the theme took some time. The theme was again matched by the video treatment of "Run to You."

Adams flew to England to shoot that video, and it was there he met Vicki Russell. She was the daughter of movie director Ken Russell *(Altered States, Lisztomania)* and the sister of *Kerrang!* writer Xavier. Vicki had played the young Sally Simpson in the movie version of *Tommy*, directed by her father. She was hired by the Adams video producers as a stylist—a costume/image designer and consultant. It would lead to a six-year affair—and eventually the end of Bryan's relationship with Elizabeth Dawson.

"Run to You" was released as a single and video in early October, and the great things A & M was expecting from *Reckless* were already in evidence. The song was chart-bound in North America and, to Adams' considerable pleasure, England, as well. He desperately wanted success in the U.K., but the English press made no secret of their distaste

▲ **1** Yearbook photo 1975

▲ **2** Yearbook photo 1976

▼ **3** Sweeney Todd 1977

◀ **4** Bryan and Martin Shaer 19

▼ **5** Bryan with Keith Scott, 198

▲ 6

▲ **8** Dave Taylor, Bryan, Keith Scott

◄ **7**

▲ **9** Bryan with his mom Jane and her husband Bill Clark

▲ **10** Conrad Adams

▲ **11** Bruce Adams

▼ 12 Bryan and Keith, 1985

▲ 13 Duet with
Tina Turner,
1985

▲ 14 Bryan and Jim Vallance accepting
Juno, 1985

▶ 15

▲ 16　Amnesty International, 1986. Bryan seen here with Bono, Sting and Peter Gabriel.

▲ 17　Bryan, girlfriend Vicky Russell and Jim Vallance at 1986 Junos

▲ **18** From l to r: Pat Steward, Dave Taylor, John Hannah, Bryan, Keith Scott, 1985.

▲ 19

▲ **20** Bryan and Keith, 1987

▲ **21** From l to r: Keith Scott, John Hannah, Mickey Curry, Bryan, Dave Taylor

▲ **22** The "Into the Fire" tour, 1987

▲ **24** Bryan and Bruce Allen in New York

◀ **23**

▲ **25** Bryan with MuchMusic vj Natalie Richard,
1993

for the overtly "American" rocker, who many said was too similar to Bruce Springsteen for their tastes.

As the inevitable Springsteen comparisons grew with the success of "Run to You," Adams was having dinner with the Boss himself in a Vancouver restaurant. They had met in passing a couple of times before through Bob Clearmountain, who had done some album mixes for Springsteen. This time they went out for seafood the night before Springsteen's mid-October concert.

Adams said that after seeing Springsteen live, he had a better understanding of the comparisons: "It's the live performances, and I think more than anything, it's the common man thing. But really, you can't compare yourself to anyone else."

It had been decided that Adams would be the first artist ever to release a single, album, CD, chrome cassette and thirty-minute video package simultaneously. The date was set for November 5.

It was a race against time for the video package, which was unique and unprecedented. It contained a series of five songs—"Run to You," "Somebody," "Kids Wanna Rock," "Summer of '69" and "Heaven"—that told a continuous story of lost love featuring a young character, Natalie, who drifts in and out of the storyline. She was played by Lysette Anthony, a twenty-one-year-old actress whose main claim to fame to date was a starring role in the movie *Krull*.

Also included in the package was an edited version of "This Time," the third single from *Cuts Like a Knife*. Besides that song and "Run to You," shot earlier in England and incorporating some footage from the Beverly Theater in Beverly Hills, California, the other four video clips had to be completed in eight days flat. Crews would be working from 8 a.m. to 2:00 a.m. at various locations in and around Vancouver.

The concert footage required a theatre full of fans. On Friday, October 19, word spread of a free Adams show at the city's Orpheum Theatre. Within hours, hundreds of fans were camped on the sidewalk outside the sponsoring radio station in anticipation of a ticket giveaway at 6:00 a.m. Monday for the Wednesday concert.

Bruce Allen showed up, surveyed the situation, and bought the happy campers pizza and coffee. The scene turned ugly, however, as the giveaway began. Line-crashing and general chaos resulted in several minor injuries, and a number of people who had waited in line overnight or longer did not get tickets. News reporters wrote up the incident in a bad light, escalating a media battle that had been brewing for some time. The Allen office put a news blackout in effect for the event; journalists were barred from attending, even though the concert was free. Of course, the Vancouver press wrote up that story, too.

The Orpheum shoot was an all-day affair that began with the filming of Lysette/Natalie amid the empty seats. For his part, Adams paced the stage, nervously playing his harmonica and worrying audibly that his new drummer hadn't had enough rehearsal time and that his sound system and monitors were untested.

He was reassured by Bruce Allen: "It'll be great, Adams!" Later the tables were turned, with Allen himself taping a scene in the dressing room.

That evening, the audience took their seats at a dead run. The venue's capacity was 2,600 people, but seats were at a premium because a counterfeiter had printed up some six hundred phony tickets. The overcrowding handily added to the air of excitement and anticipation. An emcee prepped the audience, and then the band launched into "Heaven," playing to a tape of the song blaring in the background. The scene was completed in three takes. Next up was "Kids Wanna Rock," which would require six takes, and then five more takes for another scene from "Heaven."

Adams kept the audience pumped during the breaks. "Some guy from a high school printed up about six hundred tickets for tonight," he said. "For those of you who bought them, I want you to find the guy and do a number on him." He thanked the fans for coming out, especially the ones who waited all night for tickets. He talked about his new album and introduced Pat "The Axe" Steward. "He's only twenty-two and he's an animal!" said Adams. Video director Steve Barron also took a bow.

Adams revved them up as the cameras rolled. He asked for fists in the air and shouts during "Kids Wanna Rock," and encouraged swaying and waving from the crowd for "Heaven." Several young girls climbed onstage to hug him. "Don't throw them out!", he shouted. "Just put them back!" The stage was cleared and a good-natured Bryan made a "You can touch, but don't grab!" deal with his admirers.

After completing the video shoot, Adams and the band launched into a full concert, opening with "Remember" and playing eight more songs in rapid succession: "Teacher, Teacher," "Cuts Like a Knife," "Lonely Nights," "Long Gone," "This Time," "Straight From the Heart," "Run to You" and "Take Me Back."

"I was really worried about tonight," he confessed to the audience. "We haven't played live since March in Australia. And a lot of these songs we've never played for an audience before tonight. We didn't have as many rehearsals as we wanted, and we wanted to give you a great show—but I'm not worried now! I don't know about you, but I'm having one hell of a good time!"

The band closed with "I'm Ready," then returned to deafening applause for an encore, "One Night Love Affair."

Backstage, record execs, management staff, and friends and family—including Jane and Bill, Bruce Adams, Liz Dawson, Jim Vallance, David Foster, Loverboy's Paul Dean, and others—milled around the dressing room before being called upstairs for a special presentation of a platinum award for the as-yet-unreleased album. The initial airplay from "Run to You" and Bryan's solid reputation had encouraged Canadian retailers to place advance orders in excess of a hundred thousand copies. *Reckless* was still two weeks away from being available to the public.

Exhausted, but still smiling, Adams thanked the crew, the staff and the band, said his goodbyes, signed some autographs outside the theatre and then headed home alone. It was a wrap.

The video production was rumoured to have cost the record company half a million dollars. The new album was a relative bargain at $325,000.

The *Reckless* package was released on schedule November 5, 1984, Bryan's twenty-fifth birthday. The next three months would see a constant barrage of interviews, photo sessions, tour planning and band rehearsals as he embarked on one of the of the most gruelling schedules of his career. On top of his new album release, he was moving into his new home.

His first stop was a quick press tour of Europe, and then it was back to Toronto for the 1984 Juno Awards. Traditionally held in the spring, the event had been moved to late fall. (The change meant that the awards covered music released in 1983 and most of 1984.) Adams had seven nominations. He attended the December 5 event with Liz, Bruce Allen and Jim, and took four awards—Album and Producer of the Year for *Cuts Like a Knife*, Best Male Vocalist, and the composer award,with Jim Vallance, for the title song.

Interview requests grew rapidly with the strong Juno showing. One of Adams' more memorable media appearances was on MuchMusic, Canada's national music-video channel. Through some technical mix-up or other, the station aired five minutes of hardcore pornography over top of the audio portion of an interview conducted by J. D. Roberts. As Roberts calmly discussed *Reckless* and the Junos with Adams, pictures of group sex, oral sex and other endeavours were being flashed across the country.

Although his other interviews weren't quite that exciting, he was flippantly revealing in several. "I've been going out with a girl called Liz for a few months," he told the London *Sun*. "But she's not in the music business. She's in lingerie."

"I love being on the road," he said later to the *Record Mirror*. "But I get short periods when I feel like cooking my own breakfast or going home just to hang around the flat and see my girlfriend. It's difficult trying to keep a relationship together. Ours is as shaky as a guy on a tightrope—but I'm a young guy."

Two days after the Junos, Adams was in New York for an MTV Christmas special with Pee Wee Herman. The show's premise had Pee Wee alone at MTV on Christmas Eve, deserted by his hosts. Bryan comes to his rescue (out of a TV screen) and throws a party. He performed "Reggae Christmas," a song that had been pressed and sent out to the Adams fan club. (Among the dancers on the floor were Liz Dawson and Crystal Harbidge.)

From there, he and Liz flew off to spend a week in the Caribbean. It was his first real vacation, and he hated it. He had never been one to comfortably do nothing, and within three days he was chomping at the bit to come home—and on the fourth day, he did just that.

Adams spent Christmas Eve with brother Bruce, Jane and Bill after making an unscheduled visit to a Vancouver children's hospital to sign autographs and hand out gifts. But for Adams and crew, the holiday season was anything but a holiday. The band was booked for a yearlong world tour starting on December 27, and they were heavily involved in the advance planning such a mammoth task required.

There were also heated discussions over the second single off *Reckless*. The record company had selected "Heaven," but Adams and Allen were violently opposed. Earlier in the summer, Adams had gotten enough positive feedback on the song to put it on the album, but releasing it as the all-important second single was another matter. A & M was insisting. Adams and Allen conducted another of their informal opinion polls.

"He asked me to name my favourite song," recalled Keith Sharp of *Music Express*, "and I named 'Heaven.' Adams said, 'Are you stupid? That was in that film about the male stripper; it came out on the soundtrack and nothing happened.' I said, "Well, you asked me!' Bruce was scribbling something in the background. Two weeks later, Bruce told me 'Heaven' was the next single."

9

Reckless on the Road:
Tears, Tours, and
Oh, Chute, Why Me?

December 27, 1984. Bryan Adams and his band—Keith Scott, Dave Taylor, Pat Steward, and John Hannah—embarked on the Reckless tour, dubbed "World Wide in '85." It would be true to its title.

The tour began in Chicago, Illinois, encompassed a handful of dates in the American Northeast, then moved into Canada for a nationwide trek kicking off in Halifax. Opening acts included Honeymoon Suite and Platinum Blonde. Adams was hot stuff. He had sold more than a quarter of a million copies of *Reckless* in Canada, and a million more in the U.S., all in six short weeks. The concerts were sellouts, including three dates at Toronto's Massey Hall, which were also taped for a live video.

Naturally, he was ecstatic. He was on the road, he was headlining, and his music was racing up the charts.

Those early tour dates were not without problems. He cancelled a Quebec City concert because of laryngitis, and he played what he called the worst concert of his career (next to a showcase for music industry executives at the Roxy in L.A. during the Journey tour) in Sudbury, Ontario, where he was faced with a rowdy crowd that insisted on throwing things. He warned them once, to no avail, then became totally enraged and walked off the stage when he was hit between the eyes with a coin. Adams told the audience not to expect him back "to take this abuse from those in the front row."

"We are human beings just like you!" he shouted.

The tour skipped Vancouver and swung south down the West Coast. In Seattle, Liz saw him perform live for the first time. It was a nail in the coffin for their relationship. "Adams was a different person when he was on the road," commented one observer. "He could be a real asshole—he was so focused. Plus he'd get even rowdier and more obnoxious."

That tour culminated with two sold-out shows at the Palladium in L.A. The city's Mayor, Tom Bradley, proclaimed February 1 Bryan Adams Day. Adams stopped by a local radio station to receive an official copy of the proclamation from a Bradley representative. "Bryan Adams is 'Somebody,'" reported the press.

Adams was on a high, but his bubble burst the next day, when the Los Angeles *Times* slammed his Palladium performances. "The people who write about me don't really know me," Adams later told *Record* magazine. "No critic knows me; none is close enough to me to judge what I do. I have only a couple of close friends who do know. Last week we played Los Angeles—and everybody, the band and the audience, had a wonderful time. But the *Times* panned the show. It makes no difference to me whatsoever. That's where I leave off, because it can't touch me. I know how great that show was. I always give my audience 110 percent. They paid for it and they deserve it."

Late in 1984, Irish musician Bob Geldof, a one-time Vancouverite, had selflessly invented a project called Band-Aid, an African famine relief fund fed by the profits of an all-star hit record, Geldof's "Do They Know It's Christmas." The recording session had featured the cream of the British music scene, including Sting, Phil Collins, George Michael and U2's Bono. The English benefit single was followed by an American song, "We Are the World," produced by Quincy Jones at the request of Geldof and featuring the top Americans—Michael Jackson, Bruce Springsteen, Diana Ross and Bob Dylan among them. Jones proposed a whole album of fundraising songs, and contacted Victoria, British Columbia, native David Foster about a contribution from Canada. Foster was one of the hottest names in music at that time, as both a producer and musician. Although mostly based in L.A., he had bought a house in Vancouver, and he was recording Adams's rostermates the Payola$ when he received the call from Jones. He had all of two weeks to complete his assignment.

Foster naturally called Bruce Allen to spearhead the gathering of the talent; Allen, Lou Blair and the rest of the office threw themselves into the task of contacting and coordinating a Who's Who of Canadian performers.

The typical scenario at the Allen office had an underling at Allen's elbow listing the names of practically every act in the country as Allen barked back their status. ("In!" shouted Allen. "Still pending! Fuck 'em, they're nowhere! Nobody cares!")

Foster had come up with a basic melody. He ran into Jim Vallance at Little Mountain that day, and the two moved the project to Jim's studio to finish and record a demo of the song. A title, "Tears Are Not Enough," was suggested by Paul Hyde of the Payola$.

Adams returned home the day after his last gig in L.A. and called Vallance soon after his plane landed. Foster's description of the event in the "Tears Are Not Enough" documentary made it fairly obvious Adams had jostled his way into the writing session: "He rang up and said, 'What's going on?'" recalled Foster. "'Oh, well, we're demoing this song.' 'Oh, I'm coming over. Can I come over?'"

Adams may have been uninvited, but his input was not unwelcome. He arrived late enough to find Foster and Vallance about to call it a night—they had the melody and some rhythm patterns down and planned to pick up where they had left off the next day. Foster still packed it in, but Adams and Vallance worked on the lyrics in the basement studio until morning as Jim's wife, Rachel, translated them into French upstairs. Foster got a 9:00 a.m. wake-up call from Adams. The song was finished.

They demoed it, with Adams providing the vocals, and recorded the bed tracks a couple of days later in Vancouver, with Vallance on drums, Foster on keyboards and Loverboy's Paul Dean and Doug Johnson on guitars and keyboards respectively. The massive recording session was just a week later, Sunday, February 10. The scheduling for Adams was no easy task. He had to fly to Toronto just hours after a prestigious appearance on "Saturday Night Live" in New York City.

Allen and his team had done their work: The biggest names in Canadian music, working collectively as Northern Lights, were on hand for the historic "Tears Are Not Enough" sessions. The roll call included Anne Murray, Neil Young, Gordon Lightfoot, actor John Candy, Tom Cochrane, Burton Cummings, Lisa Dalbello, Corey Hart, Ronnie Hawkins, Geddy Lee of Rush, Murray McLauchlan, Joni Mitchell, Kim Mitchell, Loverboy's Mike Reno, and David Letterman sidekick Paul Shafer.

At the studio, Adams was at his best as a performer and as a schmoozer. He also put in his two bucks' worth of production advice—much of it from over Foster's shoulder. He coached a number of the singers, mostly the women, over the course of the day. He was obviously in total awe of Joni Mitchell—at one point the documentary camera caught him staring at her with incredible intensity and emotion—but that didn't prevent him from respectfully offering her advice, too, when she sang her line.

"Tears Are Not Enough" was a #1 Canadian hit, eventually grossing $4.5 million, but domestic success wasn't enough for the Adams camp. They pushed to have the song released internationally as a second single from the *U.S.A. for Africa* album. It was not to be.

Adams told the American radio show "Rockline," "It wasn't released as a single in this country primarily because I think the public might have gotten to the saturation point. It got to the point where if you heard "We Are the World' one more time you were ready to throw your car stereo out the window."

Naturally, Adams would have liked to have "Tears Are Not Enough" played all over the world, but his main concern was that it wouldn't be generating international sales for the benefit of the fund.

Within a week of the "Tears" session in Toronto, Adams went overseas to tour Europe with Tina Turner—twenty-eight shows in nine weeks, starting February 17 in Helsinki and ending April 16 in Brussels. Everything was right for this one: Adams loved touring Europe; "Run to You" was establishing itself as his first hit record on the English charts; Turner was on the comeback trail with *Private Dancer,* a monstrous hit album; and all eyes were watching this tour.

And Bryan was happy for the opportunity to get to know Vicki Russell a lot better. She was shorter and not quite as attractive as Princess Diana, but there were similarities. She was also much like Angela—blonde and spunky—but she was cool and sophisticated, too. Adams was fascinated by the woman—she was intelligent, artistic, rambunctious, and even a little mysterious. She turned him down when he first asked her out. That made him all the more persistent, and Russell eventually accepted. Their time together was what Adams called "a mad-on" full of rowdy behaviour, spending sprees and food fights in fancy restaurants.

Neither Adams nor Russell was the least bit inhibited by the other's status. Russell was well acquainted with the trappings of celebrity life. That included life on the road—she had grown up with "life on location," travelling from movie set to movie set, and didn't see much difference in touring. She really had little or no interest in the music business, anyway; what she knew of it, she didn't like. She was able to ignore it: she was almost as heavily preoccupied with the movies as Adams was with music.

The tour lived up to expectations. Tina Turner obviously drew a different audience from the young males Adams usually targeted, but Adams and Allen realized that careerwise, this was a bonus, not a problem—there were more people in the world over thirty than under twenty-five. Still, it wasn't easy.

"Opening for Tina was tough," Adams told *Music Express*. "We got a good reaction, but it wasn't our audience. I'd be looking at a woman in the front row, wearing a mink coat dripping in diamonds, and I'd say to myself, 'Who are these people?' "Kids Wanna Rock"? I don't think they want to know.'"

Bryan would open the show with a forty-five-minute set, then Tina would bring him out towards the end of her own set to sing "It's Only Love." He'd come on stage clutching his black Charvell guitar and sing nose-to-nose with Turner.

"When we sang, you could feel her sexuality," said Adams. "She was the most exciting performer I'd ever worked with onstage."

"I remember the first night in Helsinki," recalled drum technician Michael (Bilko) Bilkoski, "with Tina and Adams on stage together. It was magic, it was just incredible. It was a long night—we had to sit and wait every night for two hours for Bryan to do that last song—but I never got tired of that performance."

One night in Belgium, Adams literally stopped the show. As usual, he made his appearance when summoned by Turner—but on this occasion he had secretly blacked out his front teeth. "I sang the first verse with my mouth sort of closed so she couldn't see my teeth," recalled Adams, "and then as soon as she started singing her line I smiled at her." Turner laughed so hard she had to stop the song. The last night of the tour, though, her band got even. Adams was nailed with a pie in the face.

They had a few days off in March and took advantage of the break to shoot a second video for "Heaven" in London. By the end of the Tina Turner tour, Adams had garnered enough attention to headline three shows of his own at the Hammersmith Odeon. The standing-room-only crowds cheered on a great concert, and Adams suitably impressed his many relatives in attendance.

At least one critic in the audience was not as enamoured: David Quantick of *New Musical Express*. He hated Adams. "[Someone] could show him something mildly peculiar, say a newspaper held upside-down," wrote Quantick, "and Bryan's eyes would widen in horror, his head would burst and his brains would be scattered to the four winds.... I will never question people who say that rock is meaningless.... Bryan Adams has taken the fight out of me, defused all my arguments by his mere crass existence." He finished the review with a reference that Adams had "vomited over pop music."

Adams may not have scored with the press, but he was garnering the attention of his peers. Celebrity encounters were occurring with increasing frequency. Adams's European schedule had included two concerts for a Tina Turner Home Box Office special with guest David Bowie. Four shows at Wembley Arena had drawn a star-studded backstage crowd that included Roger Daltrey and John Entwistle of the Who—major heroes—and Elton John. Adams had always likened the Adam/Vallance partnership to that of Elton John and his cowriter Bernie Taupin, and often commented that one of the most pleasant memories of his youth was seeing Elton perform live in 1974. Bryan, as usual, was the kid in the front, standing on his chair, pumping the air with his fist. Now they were shaking hands.

Although several papers, like *New Musical Express*, targeted Adams as the stock, formulaic American rocker they loved to hate, many others in the British press corps found Adams an interesting subject who tended to blurt out the truth in a straightforward manner.

"Will Bryan Adams be getting a Grammy one day?" asked a writer for *Sounds* magazine. Replied Adams: "They don't nominate Canadians, they think we're all lumberjacks."

To what would he attribute his sudden U.K. ascent, then?

"Perseverance. And 'Run to You' was a good song for England. There was also a change of the head guy at the record company. Things are much better now."

It was the song "Diana" that put him on the front pages of the tabloids. It was obviously written for the princess of Wales; the lyrics asked what she was doing "with a guy like him," and Adams offered to bring the ladder if she brings the limousine. "Diana" was originally scheduled as the flip side of "Heaven," but Adams had decided against it.

"Further accounts on Mr. Adams suggest that the bounder was about to release a love tribute to our very own Princess Diana," reported the *Record Mirror*.

"It was supposed to be tongue-in-cheek," Adams told the London *Sun*, "but I know how much the British love the royal family, and I thought they may get the wrong impression about the song."

With "Run to You" peaking at #11 on the English charts, Adams was a hot topic—a simple trip to a soccer game was covered by a half-dozen papers. The "Bryan and Di" gossip ran hot and heavy. Of course, due to popular demand, the song was released with "Heaven" in Europe that May. In North America, the song became a huge import hit before being made available domestically as part of an *Adamix* EP.

The "Diana" chitchat was both amusing and advantageous, but coverage of another fantasy romance ignited the rocker's short fuse early the following year, when an American syndicated gossip columnist reported that Adams and Tina Turner were having an affair. Adams lashed out with overly vehement denials and condemnations.

"It's rubbish," snapped Adams, "and my family—my grandparents—are reading that junk. They asked me if it was true.... My relationship [with Tina] is great, but it's never more than professional. I've never worked with anyone as professional as her. And for God's sake, she has a son my age!"

When Adams returned from Europe later in April—he stayed a few extra days to visit relatives—he was home for only a matter of days before launching the American leg of World Wide in '85.

The American tour was a tightly scheduled, with little time and a lot of distance between shows, but by now the Adams band and crew were a well-oiled machine.

They were travelling through the States in four buses—including one labelled You Guest It, and another whose sign read Nobody You Know—with video and cassette decks, a microwave, fridge, and other amenities. The band gear, sound, lights and merchandise (mostly T-shirts, sweatshirts and jackets) followed in four tractor-trailers.

Showing a loyalty unusual for the music industry, Adams and Allen had stayed with a local Vancouver sound company, Jason Sound, run by old friend Jeff Lilly. The same loyalty (and business acumen) was evident when they retained what in effect was an in-house merchandising company, Rock Merchandise, owned by another associate and friend, Craig McDowall. Other managers and artists almost invariably hooked up with one of a handful of large American sound outfits and merchandisers.

Gone were the days when a promoter would hire the band, the sound and the lights, pay the fees and take care of the production. The business focus of any concert and tour now centred around the band and the road show, not the promoter or the venue. The promoters would basically take a production fee of ten to twenty percent of the gate receipts, less show costs like advertising, hall rental and the opening act. Adams would be offered a guarantee in the neighbourhood of $50,000 to $65,000 by the promoter, but most of the money—usually eighty percent—would be handed over to the tour accountant to pay the road crew and to cover bills for sound, lights and stage rentals, hotel accommodations and travel costs stemming from buses, trucks and airplanes.

Altogether, World Wide in '85 employed thirty-five travelling crew members. The list included riggers, carpenters, sound, lighting and stage technicians, bus and truck drivers, merchandisers, an accountant, and a wardrobe person.

Obviously, the Adams tour was big business. In 1987, *Canadian Business* magazine estimated that one concert at Toronto's Maple Leaf Gardens brought in $310,000 in gate receipts and that Adams netted $75,000 after expenses. They also guessed that he garnered thirty percent of $125,000 generated that night from the sale of official Bryan Adams merchandise. The magazine estimated that over the course of a year, one hundred and fifty Adams concerts would gross $45 million from ticket sales and yield $15 million in profits.

They also tallied up his career revenues and concluded that he had earned no less than $35 million.

Typically, as soon as one show was completed, the band and crew would hit the highway and drive through the night to the tour's next destination. Band members would check into a hotel upon arrival, but most of the crew would carry on to the venue. Some would be on call immediately to catch a 7 a.m. load-in and rigging call. The others would catch some shut-eye on their respective buses. For the crew, hotels were a luxury reserved for days off only.

The fifty-six giant speakers, the lighting trusses and the other gear were usually unloaded in just ninety minutes or so, courtesy of twenty or thirty local stagehands.

One of the first things set up was the production office. Operating as a sort of command central, it was equipped with temporary phone lines and filing cabinets, a typewriter, a photocopier, a stereo, and the ever-present Polaroid camera and laminating machine. One function of the production office was to issue backstage passes, including photo ID for all regular crew and certain special visitors. (In backstage social circles, those with a "laminate" were big deals. "All Access" crew stickers placed the bearer next in the pecking order, but provided no dressing room access. "After Show" stickers weren't cool at all.)

The continuous presence of the Polaroid camera made for an interesting chronicle of backstage life. A large photo display board hauled carefully from city to city recalled some of the tour's more irreverent moments. Candid shots of band and crew in various stages of inebriation, undress, elation and exhaustion were marked with rudely humorous captions.

The key crew members were technicians Bilkoski, Gerry Berg (an old bandmate of Keith's), and Bob Loney, responsible for looking after the guitars, drums and keyboards respectively; sound mixers Jody Perpick and Glen Collett from Jason Sound; lighting director Brian Hall (later Robbie Morrow); and stage manager Don Finch. Kathy Baker, in charge of wardrobe, was the only working female on the tour.

They were all based in Vancouver. The top dogs on the road were at first Bryan's long-suffering road manager, Graeme Lagden, and then longtime Loverboy production chief Doug Grover. The two switched off as dictated by the Bruce Allen office to accommodate other acts on the roster. Inside sources say the full job was eventually given to Grover permanently when Adams grew tired of harassing Lagden—apparently a favourite pastime.

A few years before, while on tour with Adams, a member of the Journey entourage entertained himself by making up his own set of backstage passes for his tourmates. Adams's read Dennis the Menace—a moniker that stuck through the years. Lagden's nickname was Mr. Wilson. It was indicative of their early relationship.

"Adams caused Lagden no end of grief," confirmed Bilkoski. "If Lagden told Adams to turn right, he'd turn left. If Graeme told Adams not to go somewhere, you'd know he'd be there. I remember Lagden telling him not to climb some piece of scaffolding one night, there was something wrong with it. Sure enough, just into the set, Adams sticks the mike in his pants and shimmies up the thing."

"Adams used to wind Graeme up, get him all fired up about something or someone, and then turn him loose and laugh at the results," recalled one insider. "Bruce used to do the same with Crystal. She could be a real fire-breather, and Bruce liked that—he called her Pistol. He'd light the fuse and send her off, then he'd sit back and go, 'Atta girl!'"

The Adams crew were known as among the most professional in the business, although they certainly weren't among the best paid for their efforts. They were much closer to the worst. Other bands in the industry paid up to five times as much as Adams—including Loverboy.

"He had a good crew," speculates a crew chief who toured with one of the opening acts. "They complained about the money, but they still worked hard. They knew what they were doing. It ran like a military base, military precision. They were pretty easy to work with.... If shit came down, it was always Bruce Allen, Grover or Lagden.... You never heard from Adams, but you still got the feeling he had a pretty good hand in it all."

Adams and the band would check into hotels under assumed names—Keith Scott's favourite was "Travis Bickle," the character from the movie *Taxi Driver*. Adams used "Mike Hunt," mainly, said one source, because "he liked to hear the women at the office say it really fast." Another choice was "Dick Gozinya."

The long hauls on the bus weren't good for much rest—the band would play cribbage, watch movies and make up silly songs rather than hit the hay. Once checked into the hotel, however, the band would most often sleep till noon. So would Adams, providing he didn't have to appear on a TV or radio morning show. He'd start his day with his customary breakfast, along with the first of his interviews and phone calls. Radio-station in-person visits were the norm en route to the afternoon sound check. Check-in time at the venue was 4:00 p.m. with Bryan and the band arriving together via either a mini-bus or on later tours, a Lincoln Town Car— never a limousine.

Most of the shows were in coliseums, arenas or small stadiums, so the backstage layout was usually pretty much the same from one concert to the next. Specific requirements at every show were covered by the "rider" sent to the promoter with the original artist contract. It dealt with the fine details of meals, refreshments, furniture, decor and other creature comforts. The dressing room had to be large and roomy, with plants and comfortable couches. The actual changing area was, ideally, a smaller room off the main backstage area.

Kathy Baker did a good job of turning it into a home away from home. Snackers could munch on vegetables, fruit and hot hors d'oeuvres, while drinking a beer or Perrier. A blender was close at hand so that Baker could whip up jugs full of daiquiris. A dartboard graced the side of a large wardrobe.

The sound check would begin by 4:30. The band would amble through four or five songs—some on the night's set list, some just for fun. By 5:30 or 6:00, the caterers would have laid out a hot meal—the rider called for a variety of food, including the usual fish, meat, pastas, vegetables, salads and desserts, and specifically two plain baked chickens. Adams had given up red meat. He was very conscious of the need to keep his body healthy enough to keep up with the physical and mental demands placed on him. Occasionally he'd race off for a quick dinner with a record rep, friend or interviewer, but usually they'd all eat backstage together.

Adams would invariably be scheduled for TV and other interviews once back from dinner, and there was always a certain number of contest winners to entertain. As was the case with many concert dates, record companies, promoters and sponsoring radio stations would offer the public a chance to schmooze backstage with the headlining artist. In Adams's case, he would meet winners in a separate area, and chat and sign autographs for ten to twenty minutes while the opening band performed out front. (He would rarely get to watch his support acts himself).

While Adams took care of his various responsibilities, the band relaxed in the dressing room, watched a movie or read on the bus parked behind the venue, or warmed up in a separate practice room. They would gather in the dressing room a half hour before the curtain call. With twenty minutes to go, the room was cleared of everyone except the band and key working staff. The performers changed into their stage clothes and psyched up with shouts and jibes. As they neared the stage, they'd stop for a traditional band cheer. Graeme or Grover would lead them to the darkened stage with a flashlight—the crowd invariably erupted into a frenzy at the sight of the penlight, well before the spotlights were turned on the band.

Adams would wear his customary white T-shirt and blue jeans, the type of garb that won him a place in *Creem* magazine's Rock Slobs Hall of Shame. His wardrobe, or lack thereof, was an ongoing point of contention with management.

"Bruce Allen and I have enormous arguments over that,"

said Adams. "To me, what you project musically and visually has got to be sincere. I've always worn old jeans. I happen to like them.... Flash isn't important. What is important to me is being able to feel normal. I don't make excuses for the way I look. I never have and I never will."

The staging was as simple as his wardrobe—the show offered few effects other than lighting, Adams didn't like gimmicks, and he was also health-conscious. "I won't have any smoke or dry ice on stage," Adams told *Q* magazine, "and I have the air-conditioning turned off in buildings. They just blow enormous fans of cold air onto the stage. It's a hockey arena, they're meant to refrigerate ice, it's too cold. If you get really hot and sweaty and then they blow cold air down your back, you can get a chill, and next thing you know you can be on your back.

"I have to really take care of my voice. It's just a muscle that I've trained. I get it checked all the time.... Sometimes I think that I work it a bit too hard."

A typical night would see Adams rip through a long set before returning for two long encores, playing for over two hours in total. He'd open with "Remember," the fast-paced rocker from his second album, and fans would respond by waving Canadian flags and tossing stuffed animals, flowers, notes, hats, jewellery and sunglasses on the stage. "We'd like to play some songs for you from our last four LPs," he would announce early on. "Some of the songs you're going to know. Some of the songs you're going to get used to."

Early in the set, "Kids Wanna Rock" would raise the energy level to a raucous high as the crowd belted out the chorus. If the fans looked like they were getting out of hand over the course of the evening, or pressing too hard in front of the stage, Adams would make sure they were brought in check.

"Turn around and tell the a-hole behind you to step back!" he commanded one audience. "You've got some people up here in the front row that look like ham sandwiches."

"Let's act like human beings, not pigs," he snapped at another crowd. "I'm going to stand here until you get it together."

On an occasion when a scuffle broke out, he asked, "Are we all through back there? Can we carry on now? Are you guys through playing in the sandbox?"

The early part of the evening would feature such older songs as "Cuts Like a Knife," "This Time," "The Best Was Yet to Come" and "Lonely Nights." Later in the set, the first notes of "Heaven," now released as a single, evoked a frenzy that intensified with the opening chords of "Run to You." "Somebody" featured an audience-participation game in which Adams would call for the crowd to sing louder than Keith Scott's riffs. From that feel-good high point, the show would climax with "I'm Ready." Called back for encores, the band would launch into "Straight From the Heart," "She's Only Happy When She's Dancing" and "Summer of '69."

Postconcert, the dressing room was again off-limits for at least fifteen minutes to allow Adams and the band to shower and wind down. Occasionally, old friends and ranking musicians would be ushered in for private meetings. After thirty or forty minutes, Adams and the band would make their way out of the building, stopping for a few minutes more to mingle with the "After Shows"—record retailers, radio reps and other casual "meet-and-greets." Within ninety minutes of playing the last chord, Adams and the band were most often on a bus heading for the next town a few hundred miles away.

An average week on the road would have three, sometimes four, shows back-to-back followed by one day off and at least two more consecutive shows. In spite of the work load, it was a pleasant and very special time. The road show was artistically and commercially successful. The touring unit developed a strong camaraderie on the road.

Adams was the boss; he was not really one of the boys.

"He knows what he wants," said Pat Steward at the time. "Other people have been in the same seat I'm in, but attitude-wise, couldn't handle the 'Hey, it's gotta be like this.' He wants to be perfect. So I strive to be like him."

"He's a workaholic," said keyboard player John Hannah,

"an overachiever. He knows what he wants and he goes out and gets it. And he's not afraid to do what is necessary to get it. I don't think there's anybody who's successful in any line of business who doesn't do the same things. I'm sure that his ingredients for success are universal: perseverance, hard work, dedication...believing in yourself, believing in your product. He has all those things. And I'm sure that if he didn't he wouldn't be where he is today."

Hannah was well aware of the extent of Adams's perseverance. The predominant activity for Adams on World Wide in '85 was harassing John Hannah.

On previous tours, the various drummers had taken most of the heat, although Hannah had never fared well in the Adams abuse department. He was not officially in the band—Tommy Mandel was still the keyboard player of record. But with Pat Steward official (complete with his photo on the album sleeve), Hannah became the sole remaining target, and he got it full-blast. Adams was merciless. He'd jump all over him for minor infractions and take pains not to give him any credit. Every snide remark and pie-in-the-face prank Adams could muster was directed at Hannah.

If the prank of the day was spitballs, Adams first shot would be a wet one aimed at Hannah's face. If a fan was taking a photo, Adams would be holding two fingers up over Hannah's head. The band and crew would pounce on Hannah as he slept, sometimes landing some serious blows. Adams nicknamed him "Johnny Blitz," ostensibly an endearing gesture, but really just a ploy to prevent him from getting any kudos under his real name.

Outwardly, Hannah remained unfazed—it was water off a duck's back. At the height of the Reckless tour, a reporter asked him if he thought success had changed Bryan Adams. "No," Hannah cheerfully volunteered. "He's still an asshole."

John Hannah and the quiet Dave Taylor were "the two old married guys" on the tour, and their all-engrossing form of entertainment was a never-ending cribbage tournament. Occasionally they'd put down their cards for a bit of sight-seeing, and once in a while Taylor would play social coordinator and organize a band dinner.

Keith Scott was the tour's most eligible bachelor. "It wasn't so much that Keith was out hustling women all the time, it's just that he drew them like this huge magnet," observed one insider. "Girls who worked at the venue, girls from the radio station, girls who snuck in past the guards— every girl that came within twenty feet would be offering to take him out somewhere. They'd hang out with him all day, and he'd be peeling them off to get on the bus every night."

Scott rarely checked out clubs. "I spent ten years in nightclubs," he said with a grimace. "The novelty has kind of worn off." He was more inclined to play tourist during the day. "I'll bring out my camera and see the sights. We'll go to a museum that somebody told us about or go to a movie. Or if it's somebody's birthday or something, we'll drag him out to dinner and get him soaked."

Pat Steward was a young, energetic and wide-eyed kid on his first major tour, and he wanted to rock—he wanted to hang out at the beach and look at girls by day, and make the club scene by night. But even when he did get the time, he couldn't always find some company.

"I'll go out for dinner, go to some clubs or take in a movie and come back for a late-night swim in the hotel pool—as long as I have someone to go with," said Steward. "Bryan might be interested, but he's so busy I never even ask him. He probably has to get up and go do something in the morning. Dave's usually into it—that is, when he's not playing crib with John, which actually isn't that often—and I try to talk Keith into going. A lot of the crew guys like that stuff, but they're always working."

Thus, more often than not, sighed Steward, he found himself in a hotel room or bus with a couple of movies and a beer.

The main off-time activity on the road for Adams and Scott (and later Steward) was riding the mountain bikes that were carried along with the gear. A bike was the perfect toy, providing transportation to see the sights and serving as a getaway vehicle for Adams when he wanted to dodge unwanted attention. Impromptu bike races also provided a competitive form of exercise.

Another favourite Adams activity, of course, was food. He frequently lamented the fact that he rarely had time to sample the local cuisine; whenever possible, he scheduled interviews and meetings at exotic restaurants.

The road show arrived in Tulsa, Oklahoma, May 1, 1985, for a couple days of rehearsals before performing May 3 to what would be the first of many standing-room-only crowds. The first show was a big hit—Adams bashed himself in the mouth with a microphone.

On the fourth date, the entourage, most of whom had been away from home since Christmas, suffered a strong attack of homesickness as they found themselves in Texas in the middle of the Stanley Cup hockey final. Austin was anything but a hockey town. But where there's a will, there's a way. A satellite dish was rented and set up in the parking lot, with a feed going into the bus. The band had to play as the game went into the third and final period, but Grover ran back and forth from the bus to the stage with the latest game reports, which Adams passed on to the audience. By the end of the night, Austin had an arenaful of hockey fans.

In Houston, they played the grand opening of the outdoor Southern Star Amphitheater to a packed house of eighteen thousand. The plan was for the band to charge on stage amid a fireworks display and jump right into some high-energy rock and roll. Even with all that potential excitement, the air was literally charged with electricity—a storm was brewing.

Adams hit the stage on cue, simultaneously with the fireworks, a flash of real lightning, a roll of thunder and a deafening ovation from the audience. That spectacular intro was followed immediately by a torrential downpour. The rain blew sideways across the stage as the players hurriedly unplugged themselves from their instruments, their first chords gone with the wind. The show dissolved into mass confusion.

Still in Houston, Adams met Steve Marriott, the anchor of top English bands Small Faces and Humble Pie. Both groups had influenced Adams strongly as a boy.

"I picked up a paper and it said, 'Steve Marriott, tonight' at this club. So, boom, me and the boys get in the car, and head down to see this band. Sure enough, Steve Marriott comes on. He had a broken leg, he hobbles on stage and says, 'All right boys, let's play.' The guy sang great, he scared me.

"This is the kind of stuff I have more respect for, because after all is said and done, after all the gold records, after all the money, after everything else, the reason they are in the business, the reason they love it, is because they still want to sing.

"I went to up to Steve afterward and I said, 'Steve, man, why don't you put out a record? You kill me, you're amazing.' He says, 'I've done it. I've seen everything I want to see, all I want is to just play my music. Everyone should just leave me alone. I just want to sing. Why can't I have that privilege?' I said, 'Hey, no one is taking it away from you, it's always yours, you know, you keep going as long as you wanna go.'"

It was an intense experience for Adams. Marriott would die in a fire a few years later.

Towards the end of May, a series of concerts in Florida were followed by a five-day break that provided a chance for some sun-and-surf at the beach. Adams, never one for relaxation, flew back to Vancouver to briefly tend the home fires.

The tour resumed June 1 in Birmingham, and a few days later, the Adams family took a rare day off in Memphis. Bryan's first inclination was to hang around the hotel, the famed and elegant Peabody. "The Peabody," recalled Adams, "was kind of neat. It has this 'duck walk.' Every morning at eleven, these ducks come down the elevator from the top floor, walk across the lobby on this red carpet and get into this little swimming pool—this little fountain in the middle of the lobby—and eat and swim around all day and march back up in the evening."

The Peabody ducks weren't the only thrill to be found on the Memphis stopover. Road manager Doug Grover had organized a skydiving outing for a half dozen or so members of the crew at a nearby airstrip. Keith Scott caught wind of it and asked to come along; Grover called Bruce Allen for permission, but it was not forthcoming. Keith was to be grounded. "And whatever you do," added Allen, "make sure Adams doesn't go."

Said Bilko, "As soon as Adams heard about it and was told he couldn't jump, that was it, he was heading for the plane."

Grover was nervous. "If you die, I die," he reminded Adams.

The novices were given instructions in "tandem free-fall," a relatively new method whereby an experienced jumper straps on to the harness of the newcomer and both jump on the same parachute.

The plane climbed to 6,500 feet and circled the target area. Several people jumped before Bryan with no problem—they enjoyed ten seconds of exhilarating free-fall, pulled their chutes and drifted to the ground for perfect landings.

Adams's plunge wasn't so easy. "Just before I jumped," he told *Q* magazine, "one of the guys in the plane looked over as he pulled open the De Havilland door, and yelled 'Blue sky! Black death!' and then we all jumped out of the plane. And [the instructor] got quite excited, I guess, about having me tied to him, and did these intentional back flips—like, to give me the ride of my life?—so instead of soaring through the air looking at the ground coming towards me, it was like, earth-sky-earth-sky-earth-sky-earth-sky. To get control, he pulled the parachute, and it came up between our legs and tangled up with us."

"I was just enjoying the ride," recalled Adams in another interview. "I thought it was just great. I had no idea. But once I realized the parachute had wrapped around our legs, I thought, 'Wait a minute! This isn't right!'"

Doug Grover watched in disbelief ("My life is shit! My life is shit!" he muttered), as Adams and his cojumper fell without a workable chute for twenty-four seconds. Four thousand feet they plunged, much of the time still spinning crazily out of control.

"I guess we're going home early," sighed Scott.

"Everybody turned and looked at Keith when he said that," remembered Bilko. "It was crazy. Keith laughed, because it was just so bizarre."

As Adams plummeted towards earth, the instructor attempted to cut loose the main chute, then pulled the emergency back up, which also came precariously close to tangling. Finally, in the last few seconds, it filled with air and they dropped into a farmer's field, a mile or so from the original target.

A jumper with a video camera attached to his helmet had left the plane right after Bryan and had captured the entire incident. He hit the ground a few seconds later and ran towards them, the camera still rolling.

The footage showed Bryan and his instructor sitting up slowly after lying still on the ground for a minute or so. As the others ran towards him, Bryan managed a shaky smile, and then a grin. "Big-time malfunction," said an equally shaky instructor. "You know what?" said Bryan. "I'm alive. Let's get back and get me a beer!"

Bruce Allen exploded when he heard of the misadventure. "There's ten guys jumping out of an airplane!" roared Allen. "Nine of 'em are roadies, who fuckin' cares, but whose chute doesn't open? It's unbelievable!"

"It was something I wanted to do because I like to try everything once," said Adams shortly after the incident. "If I was going to jump out of a plane again, it would be on a static line, not the tandem way. But I think it might be easier going parasailing off a boat. I'm going to try that."

Adams told the *Record Mirror* that he had never thought he was about to die. "I knew that wasn't it. There was no way. But I did think it was terrible. It happened in seconds, and you don't think a lot in that short time."

There was a silver lining to this particular cloud, however. The video footage landed Adams a long-sought invitation to the David Letterman Show. "I was about six seconds away from being pizza," he said, grinning at Letterman, later that month.

His grin widened when Letterman held up the latest issue of *Billboard*. "Heaven" was #1.

10

Live Aid, Amnesty,
Royalty and Victory

June 13, 1985. Adams had just flown into Chicago from an MTV appearance in New York when he got the call from Bruce Allen. "Heaven" had hit the top.

"I never in a million years thought 'Heaven' would be a #1 record," said Adams. "It's strange, too, because that song was written and recorded over two years ago. It should be old news, but it's #1."

The call had come just before showtime. The concert at Poplar Creek that night was an onstage celebration—Adams and the band were revved. After the show they cracked some champagne, but there was little time for a party. They had to be in Cuyahoga Falls, Ohio, the next day—Friday—for the Blossom Music Festival, Cincinnati on Saturday, and Louisville, Kentucky, on Sunday. They partied along the way.

They were particularly frisky over the next few days. Backstage in Cincinnati, Adams and the crew tossed fire-crackers at each other, launched Roman candles above the crowd, and threatened to throw rocks at a flotilla of pleasure boats anchored nearby on the Ohio River.

In Washington, D.C., Adams offered the visiting Bruce Allen Talent Promotion accountant, Chu Chu Shekh, a ride to New York, their next stop. "It was great," related Shekh, "because I hated flying—I hadn't travelled much at that

point, it was all new to me. I didn't mind being on the bus.
I had gotten in late—I was sleepy and I dozed off. The next
thing I know, Adams is waking me up, saying, 'We're here,
we're at your hotel.' I was still pretty sleepy. He helped me
off the bus, got my suitcase out and put it on the sidewalk. He
said goodbye, and got back on the bus and it pulled away. I
looked around, and the first thing I thought was 'This city is
all black people.' Then I looked closer, and the little shit had
let me out in the worst section of Harlem he could find. I
wasn't anywhere near my hotel!"

For the whole week, most of the shows were in the New
York area, and Bryan was joined by Vicki Russell. In between concerts, interviews and doing business, they grabbed
what time they could to play tourist—the agenda included
trips to the Guggenheim Museum and a Broadway production of the hit musical *Cats*, and an excursion to the Philadelphia Museum of Art to view an exhibit of Chagall paintings.

They were inseparable—she even came with him to interviews. He'd introduce her as "the bag" or "Miss Bag," but
he'd refuse to give her name or any details of their relationship. If the reporter questioned her, she was coolly but
playfully evasive, clearly enjoying her role as the "mystery
lady."

Two shows in the Boston area the following week had
more than the usual exciting moments. The keyboard player
for Fiona, the opening act, was arrested as he came off the
stage—the warrant cited adjudication of paternity, false
representation to the department of public welfare to secure
support, and nonsupport of an illegitimate child.

During his own set, Adams dashed to the side of the stage,
jumped on top of a speaker cabinet and reached out to touch
the outstretched hands of the screaming fans. The speaker
tilted under his weight, and down he went into a sea of
flailing arms. The members of Aerosmith, just hanging out
backstage, stood ten feet away, watching in disbelief.

"I'm all right, leave me alone!" Adams shouted at the
security and crew who reached out to help him. He clambered
back onto the stage under his own steam and nonchalantly

took up where he left off. "One small step for man, huh?" he laughed.

That same show saw ex–J.Geils Band frontman Peter Wolf, a Boston native, join Adams for a medley of "Hound Dog," "Blue Suede Shoes" and "Whole Lotta Shakin' Goin' On."

The initial opening act on this tour had been Survivor, but their stint was cut short by a week when they scored a series of Top 10 singles and moved to their own headline tour. Fiona, led by Fiona Flanagan, took over.

"Fiona was great," said Adams. "We've also had Shooting Star, Autograph and Kim Mitchell open shows for us. Kim's another Canadian. He's a real good dude. We really liked him. Actually, I rather enjoyed Autograph, too. I think of all our opening acts so far, they've been my favourite." Adams and the crew, by all accounts, treated his openers well.

The tension mounted as the band toured into July. Back at the office, frantic phone calls were being exchanged with the promoters of what promised to be the largest concert in history. Band Aid organizer Bob Geldof was ready to move on to the next phase of his ambitious plan to Feed the World (the campaign's slogan), and in June he had announced details of Live Aid, two giant outdoor shows to be held in mid-July—one at London's Wembley Stadium, the other across the Atlantic at Philadelphia's John F. Kennedy Stadium. The shows would be broadcast to more than a billion people worldwide, and donations would be solicited during the telecast via a toll-free telephone line.

Fifty top names announced plans to perform. The ten-hour Wembley show would feature Elvis Costello, U2, Bryan Ferry, Elton John, George Michael, Paul McCartney, the Who, Queen and David Bowie, among others.

In Philadelphia, the biggest buzz was to be generated by three unique all-star groupings: the reunited Jimmy Page and Robert Plant of Led Zeppelin fame, playing together for the first time in five years; the trio of Bob Dylan and Rolling Stone members Ron Wood and Keith Richards; and the hot pairing of Tina Turner and Mick Jagger. Also on the American bill were Madonna, Eric Clapton, Paul Simon, Stevie Wonder and Dire Straits. Phil Collins and Duran Duran made plans to perform at both shows.

Adams was determined to be a part of it, but first the logistics had to be worked out. The Live Aid show in Philadelphia was scheduled for Saturday, July 13, the same day Adams was booked for a late-afternoon headline performance at Legend Valley, near Columbus, Ohio. Adams was important, but not important enough to warrant a late slot amid that sea of stars. He settled for a noon appearance on the Live Aid schedule and booked a Lear Jet to enable him to wing it from one gig to the other.

He played before a sellout crowd Thursday, July 11, in Fort Wayne, Indiana, then left immediately after the concert for Columbus, 160 miles away. After a short rest at the Columbus Hyatt, he caught an early-evening flight on Friday to Philadelphia, while the crew and band drove out to the Legend Valley concert site, fifty miles from Columbus, for a sound check. They joined him in Philadelphia later that evening.

Adams was at the Live Aid site by midmorning on Saturday. The Hard Rock Café had set up shop backstage and was doling out first-rate food, but he didn't have time to eat. It wasn't a great time to meet his peers, either—the heavyweights were all scheduled later in the day, although Adams happily chatted with Carl Wilson and Mike Love from the Beach Boys, and Rob Halford from Judas Priest.

The Live Aid performance went off without a hitch, although the TV viewing audience saw commercials instead of "Tears Are Not Enough," which was performed with fellow Canadian Paul Shafer, the musical director of the David Letterman show. The four-song, seventeen-minute set also featured "Kids Wanna Rock," "Summer of '69" and "Cuts Like a Knife."

The Adams segment ended at 12:15 p.m. Eastern Time, and it took thirty minutes just to run the gamut of backstage media and well-wishers.

"The press kept asking me if I was nervous playing in front

of a billion TV viewers," he told his fan club, "but I never look at live TV that way. I look at my performances as a very intimate thing. I always try to single out three or five people—or at least the people in front of me—and try to play to them."

Within the hour, he and his band and crew were en route to the Columbus, Ohio, airport in two private Lear Jets. By 4:45, they were onstage at Newark, Ohio's Legend Valley Park.

After that concert, Adams and the band treated themselves to a substantial Japanese dinner at a restaurant in Columbus, then drove to Detroit for the next day's show at Pine Knob. A few days later, Adams received word of yet another career landmark. As he was driving into Duluth, a call to the office yielded the information that *Reckless*, spurred on by the success of the album's third single, "Summer of '69," would be in the #1 position on the album chart in the next issue of *Billboard*.

It had taken *Reckless* thirty-seven weeks to climb all the way to the pinnacle of American success. It replaced the Tears For Fears album *Songs from the Big Chair*, which had clung to the top for a month. The last time a Canadian album had made it to #1 was 1974, when both Gordon Lightfoot's *Sundown* and BTO's *Not Fragile* accomplished the feat. The only other Canadian who had racked up a #1 album before then was Neil Young, with *Harvest* in 1972.

Again, there was no time to celebrate, although two days later they did take an afternoon off in Rapid City, South Dakota, as the band and crew—all except Keith, who went bike riding—went to see Mount Rushmore. The day after that, Adams was on a plane home. He could have taken a few days off, but instead he raced back into the studio to record "Christmas Time," an Adams/Vallance contribution to the movie *Santa Claus*. While he was in the studio, it turned out Donna Summer was just down the hall with producer David Foster. Foster put down a piano track on "Christmas Time" while Keith Scott played a guitar solo on a Donna Summer song.

Adams had no rest on the break, and he paid for it. Two dates after resuming the tour, he lost his voice, and a July 28 Kansas City concert was cancelled. Meanwhile, back in Vancouver, pandemonium broke out with the announcement of Adams's September 2 homecoming show. Frantic ticket buyers jammed phone lines at the rate of fifty thousand calls an hour as they attempted to get through to the city's ticket outlets. The overload knocked out the major phone exchange in the downtown core. A second show was added September 1, and it sold out in twenty-four hours.

In Montreal, fights broke out at the Forum and other ticket outlets as thousands of screaming, shoving fans snapped up fifteen thousand tickets in two hours flat. Six police cars were needed to control the crowd. In New York, both mid-September shows at Madison Square Garden were also advance sellouts.

The two Vancouver concerts immediately followed back-to-back shows in the Pacific Northwest—he played five days in a row. "The best part about coming home," he told the press, "is sleeping in my own bed, not having to dial eight to get [an outside line] and no more room service."

After his hometown shows, Adams moved on to Michigan to resume the American tour. He performed eleven of the next thirteen nights, using one of his off days to attend the MTV Awards in New York—the *Reckless* video package had eight nominations, although no wins were forthcoming.

The following night was the first of two shows at Madison Square Garden. The show went well, with the lone downer being a subsequent review in the New York *Times*. Critic Stephen Holden described Adams's stage appearance as "emotionally lifeless...imitation rock." Holden said the material was diluted, secondhand and cookie-cutter derivative.

Adams was staying at the swanky, old-fashioned Pierre Hotel on Fifth Avenue, and after a full day of interviews, he decided that the fastest route from the hotel to the Garden for the second show was the subway. (He also had at least one member of the press in tow, which may have influenced his decision.) Only a few people recognized him on the train, and no one approached him. Once on the street again near the Garden, a fan talked to him.

"Hey, man, what are you doing?" asked a fifteen-year old.

"Just going to the gig," answered Adams.

"Man, you're walking down the street!"

"Gotta go to the show."

"Well, I'm in section E."

"Great."

After the concert, there was a triple-platinum award presentation and a party at a cajun restaurant, How's Bayou, in lower Manhattan. It was a low-key but star-studded affair with Eddie Van Halen and bride Valerie Bertinelli commanding most of the attention. The rest of the Van Halen band were on hand as were Simple Minds' Jim Kerr (Adams's copresenter at the MTV Awards), Superman Christopher Reeve, Julian Lennon and hometown pals Mike Reno and Paul Dean of Loverboy. A number of reporters were also in attendance.

Bryan—who was overtly more interested in eating than mingling—had shown up with Vicki, but as usual he would only introduce her as Miss Bag. Also front and centre were Jane, wearing denim, and husband Bill Clark, in leather. They stood beaming in the middle of a crowd, accepting congratulations and fielding queries from the press.

"His brother Bruce is mostly into sailing," Jane said to one scribe, fearlessly breaking the "no discussing family" rule.

"Really, Bryan is a simple, straightforward kind of person," she told another reporter. "You know what they say—there is no such thing as an extraordinary person, just an ordinary person with extraordinary determination."

"At home, we just get in the van and follow him," Jane told writer Tom Harrison. "We try not to make any trouble."

There was little Bryan could do to control his mother. Jane loved to chat, as did the sociable, heavily accented Bill Clark.

"Jane Clark may look like a typical sweet little old lady—except for the flame-red-hair—but she's very eccentric," said one insider. "She's sharp—she's a schemer—and she's very strong-willed," said another. "I don't imagine she likes sharing him with too many people. And she's just as tight with money as Adams."

"Jane's like a lion protecting her cub with Bryan," added a third. "She is involved in pretty well every aspect of his career. She picks up his mail, she does his banking, she takes care of all the house stuff, seeing as he's never there. She's up in the Bruce Allen office at least two or three times a week, always with Bill in tow."

The North American arm of the tour drew to a close on October 5 in Philadelphia. Over the course of that week, Adams made several trips to Toronto. He attended the premiere of the movie *Tears Are Not Enough*. He joined Vallance in accepting the William Harold Moon Award for international achievement from the copyright society PROCAN (he wore jeans and a white shirt, buttoned to the collar, at the black-tie affair). And he recorded with Glass Tiger, a rock band from Ontario whose debut album Vallance was producing.

While Adams saw "Heaven" and *Reckless* at #1, Jim Vallance had his own Top 10 hit. He had cowritten three songs for the band Toronto in the early Eighties, two of which had made it onto record. The third had been rejected by the band's producer. "What About Love?", cowritten by Vallance with Toronto members Sheron Alton and Brian Allen, sat on the shelf for two years before a publishing company representative sent it to Heart's Ann and Nancy Wilson. They loved the song, and it launched the Seattle-based group's renaissance in 1985, eventually reaching #10 in Billboard and #7 on the Canadian charts.

Glass Tiger would prove to be an even bigger success that year. Vallance had been playing the tapes for Adams as the production progressed over a four-month period. When Adams and Keith Scott were in Toronto, they offered their services, with the former singing a distinctive backup line on "Don't Forget Me (When I'm Gone)." That was the album's lead single, and in February 1986 it rocketed straight to #1 in Canada. Six months later, it would go all the way to #2 in America.

"I wanted to give [Glass Tiger] a break," said Adams. "I wish someone would have given me a break in the beginning. And I wanted Jim to have a hit record."

World Wide in '85 was winding down. Adams had two weeks off, then spent the last few days of October in Japan, performing in Osaka and Tokyo. Then he was officially off the road.

Immediately upon his return to Canada, he attended the Juno Awards in Toronto on November 4 and accepted three more trophies—Best Album (*Reckless*), Best Male Vocalist and, with Jim Vallance, Composer of the Year. He also turned in a sizzling performance with Tina Turner on the Juno broadcast, and took part in a choral rendition of "Tears Are Not Enough" for the show's finale.

Adams dedicated his Male Vocalist award to his mom "and, of course, the people of Canada. Remember, I'm a Canadian, and I'm out there for ya."

At the end of the month, he was back in England to appear in a video with Roger Daltrey. Bryan had met him through Vicki, who had worked with him on the movie *Tommy*. Adams got Russell to invite Daltrey over for dinner, and they hit it off.

Adams and Vallance ended up writing two songs for Daltrey, "I'm a Rebel," and "Let Me Down Easy." The video was for the latter.

Said Adams: "There wasn't any pretensions, or any big star things. He was just into the songs. He wanted something that had a real good lyric and something he could really sink his teeth into. I was inspired by that, because here is a guy who is pretty well at the top of the rock and roll business and he's managed to keep his sanity, his edge and his voice."

Adams told the press: "Roger wants to be an actor now, which is kind of disappointing. It's funny how guys after a while get so good at what they do to a certain point in their career and they decide they don't want to do that anymore. I wouldn't want to go into acting. I've sat on a couple of film sets, and believe me, it's not what it's cut out to be. Unless you are a really brilliant actor and you can make the situation work for you, I can't imagine why you'd want to do it."

Later Daltrey said that Adams had so much energy, and such a positive outlook on life, that it inspired him to go back into the studio.

In December, Bryan received the prestigious Diamond Award at a ceremony in Vancouver commemorating the sale of one million copies of *Reckless* across Canada—he was the only Canadian artist ever to achieve that goal. The event was celebrated with a private buffet dinner in a small Vancouver restaurant for Adams, his band, his road crew, family and record company officials. A & M Records president Gerry Lacoursiere presented Adams with the Diamond Award plaque. Adams credited his success to "hard work and team-work."

At the end of the year, Billboard named Bryan Adams their 1985 #1 Top Male Pop Singles Artist, #3 Top Male Pop Album Artist, and #5 Top Pop Artist. Those ratings were based on chart success, and it had indeed been a remarkable year for a man who had scored six Top 20 hits in twelve months.

Early in 1986, Adams was nominated for two Grammy Awards: Best Male Rock Performance for *Reckless* and Best Rock Performance by a Duo or Group for "It's Only Love," with Tina Turner.

"I mean, I'm up against Mick Jagger!" he told Liz Braun in the Toronto *Sun*. "John Fogerty, John Cougar and Don Henley—and these guys have been around for donkey's years! And what am I? Just some Canuck." (Adams eventually lost the solo honour to Henley and the group award to Dire Straits.)

Adams told Braun he found awards ceremonies completely nerve-wracking. "I can't bear it. I may look like a cool cucumber up there, but believe me, inside I'm freaking," he laughed. "Do I seem nervous?" he asked her earnestly. "It's ironic that I can go out and play a concert for people and be totally comfortable, and never really feel that nervous. I feel excited and enthusiastic, you know, but never nervous. I guess the biggest thing about those ceremonies is that it's all industry people, and it's all eyeballs on you."

Now that *Reckless* had run its course and been duly celebrated as one of the biggest rock records of all time, Adams the workaholic was ready to plunge right back into a new cycle of writing, recording and touring. Over the next few months, he and Vallance spent every possible hour together, writing songs for a new album.

They were in England for most of March, writing and cutting demos. Much to their surprise, "Cuts Like a Knife" was again climbing the British charts—three and a half years after its release. While in London, they were invited to a formal charity function at London's Royal Albert Hall where Supertramp played for Charles and Diana. The predominant media story on Adams at that time was how he took a bus to the event.

"Ten minutes before I arrived," Adams told the press, "I realized we didn't have a taxi, so I took the Kensington night bus straight to Albert Hall. It was a strange feeling to get off the bus in front, then go in to meet the prince and princess."

The real news was inside. Jim Vallance was on hand, and he told the story to writer William Deverell: "There were about twenty-five people, including Supertramp, backstage in this reception area. A fellow from the palace came in and said the royal couple will be arriving soon, but we shouldn't speak to them unless they spoke to us first. And if they do speak to us, we should address them as sir and ma'am, which is as informal as the royals get. So a few minutes go by, the door opens, and there they are. As soon as Bryan sees the prince, he hollers, 'Charles!' I wanted to disappear into the collar of my shirt. But he actually came over and talked to us for a bit." Apparently, he wanted to know who they were.

At the end of the month, Bryan flew from London to New York to work on Tina Turner's forthcoming album. Adams was trying on a new hat—he was producing two songs, one of them written by Adams and Vallance. He used his own band—Mickey Curry, Tommy Mandel, Dave Taylor and Keith Scott—on the Turner sessions, and played piano and guitar and sang backup vocal.

The bed tracks were recorded without Turner's participation. "A week later we recorded her in Europe," said Adams. "She was brilliant. The first song we produced is called 'Back Where You Started,' and we also produced the flip side of the new single ['Typical Male'] which is called 'Don't Turn Around.' She thought I was a nitpicker—until she heard the final product, and then she couldn't believe it."

Turner apparently concurred. "I told him he was nitpicking, trying to get every syllable perfect," she told *Rolling Stone*. "But when I listened back in the control room it sounded fantastic."

Back in Vancouver, the city was hosting the world's fair, Expo 86, that summer. The Bruce Allen office had been put in charge of lining up entertainers for the opening gala. The guests of honour would be the prince and princess of Wales. The song "Diana" was still big news, as was anything connected with the princess. The show was a natural for Adams, a second opportunity to rub shoulders with royalty.

May 2, 1986, the opening of Expo 86. The world turned its attention on Vancouver. The British tabloids had reporters following Adams's every move. Would he or would he not play "Diana" with the prince and princess in attendance? He had a glint in his eye when he took the stage at Expo Theatre for the afternoon sound check. After running through a couple of other tunes, he and the band launched into "Diana." As the chords drifted out of the open-air theatre, the press ran for the phones. But it was only a tease. They had to refile their stories after waiting in vain to hear the tune that evening.

"Star's love song to Di is banned," the London *Daily Mirror* screamed in a front-page headline. "But Charles can't stop her flirting."

The so-called "ban" was pure Fleet Street fancy, however. "We never intended to play that song live," said Adams, "but at no time did anyone tell us or suggest to us that we couldn't."

At $86 per ticket, the Expo 86 gala drew a mixed crowd outfitted in everything from tuxes to jeans. The fashion press, well represented, noted that Diana was dressed in a conservative black tuxedo-style jacket and pants with a white ruffled blouse. Charles was in a dark suit and yellow tie. The crowd was seated when the royal entourage swept into the theatre to take their box seats in the middle of the 4,100-seat room.

A synthesized version of Loverboy's "Turn Me Loose" began an overture that featured snatches of music from each of the evening's artists—Idle Eyes, Sheena Easton, Bryan Adams, Loverboy, Véronique Béliveau and Kenny Rogers. Comedian Howie Mandel was the emcee, regaling the audience with gems like "You want to know what a gala is? A gala is $80 more than a show."

Adams came out unannounced as the last act of the first half, dressed in a white shirt and black pants. He and the band launched into "Summer of '69," then "Straight From the Heart." A woman shrieked at the opening chords of the latter, but shrank back in her seat, embarrassed, when she realized she was a lone voice in the staid crowd. He followed with "Run to You" and finished with "Tears Are Not Enough." Former Canadian prime minister John Turner led the standing ovation.

"I didn't enjoy it that much," said Adams later. "It was awful. It was too rushed, and there were a lot of mums and dads there. It was boring."

Two of the "mums and dads" were Jane, with husband Bill Clark, and ex-husband Conrad Adams, the latter seeing his son onstage for only the second time. It was a tense evening. Neither Jane nor Conrad had any desire to be in the same room, even one that held 4,100 people. Juggling seating arrangements, backstage reception invitations and the like had been a nightmare for Adams and the management office.

Conrad stood for the ovation, but did not appear overly impressed with any of the night's performances.

After the intermission was announced, the royals were marched backstage for a reception, while the crowd broke for hot dogs. Backstage in a hospitality area, the prince and princess met the performers, managers and promoters. Members of the press were kept at a distance.

The prince shook hands with Adams and delivered the usual perfunctory compliments and an additional observation: Adams's music had vibrated his sternum, he said. When Diana got to Adams, the British papers reported, she greeted him with downcast eyes and a slight blush.

According to Adams, he and the princess discussed the weather and Charles's comment about vibrating sternums. "And she just said something to the effect that we were very popular in England, and that— what else did she say? I can't remember now. Oh, she asked me if I was married. That's the truth—she did ask me that."

With the reporters still out of earshot, she told another musician, as he fiddled with his cigarette package, that she, too, occasionally pined for a "fag."

The reception lasted just twenty minutes. As the audience settled back in their seats, the royal couple were paraded back to their royal box, the subject of four thousand uninterrupted stares.

Adams was paid $100,000 for his work. He donated his earnings to three charities: the Northern Lights For Africa Society, Greenpeace and the Variety Club (for a kids' aquatic playground in Vancouver's Stanley Park).

His next major project was geared to raise awareness, not money. Since the beginning of 1986, Adams had been actively campaigning for inclusion in an enormous, and enormously important, concert series being staged by the human-rights organization Amnesty International. Set for stadium-size venues around North America, it was a joint effort of Amnesty and megapromoter Bill Graham to bring attention to prisoners of conscience around the world. The two hottest bands of the decade, the Police and U2, had already signed up. It was expected to be the tour of the year, and it didn't pay a dime.

Adams was anxious to be a key part of the project, and he went after it with his usual vengeance. Bruce Allen was instructed to do whatever it took to make the business and logistics work, while Adams met with Amnesty's executive director John G. Healey. His efforts won him a coveted spot as one of a small core group of artists performing the entire tour.

The Conspiracy of Hope tour covered six cities, from San Francisco on June 4 to the grand finale at Giants Stadium in New Jersey June 15. Adams was one of seven artists to perform at all six shows. Tourmates included U2, the reunited Police, Peter Gabriel, Joan Baez, Lou Reed and the Neville Brothers. Numerous other artists joined in for one or more dates in the tour, which included stops in Los Angeles, Denver, Atlanta and Chicago. The finale, taped and rebroadcast by MTV, hosted a total of nineteen performers.

"It was an education for not only myself, but for my entire crew and band," said Adams after the tour. "Everyone learned a lot this tour, and we learned how to get on in a situation that was not necessarily our own. I think it was humbling for everyone, you know."

The Conspiracy of Hope experience was very different from Live Aid, he said: "Amnesty was a more personable thing. Live Aid was just like an amalgamation of every group that existed, whereas this was just more select.... There were no American groups or anything involved until the very last day. That's when everyone wanted to get in on it."

Bonnie Raitt joined Adams in Los Angeles for the second show, and the two sang "No Way to Treat a Lady," which he and Vallance had cowritten for her earlier in the decade but had only lately been released. He was introduced on stage by Madonna and Sean Penn, and caught a glimpse of what the highest level of celebrity life was like. Other performers at that L.A. show were Bob Dylan, Tom Petty, Dave Stewart, Bob Geldof, Joni Mitchell and Don Henley. Adams was in the thick of it.

Shows in Los Angeles, San Francisco and New York could have sold out four times over; the other centres drew respectable but not overflowing crowds. In Denver, though, ticket sales were lagging badly. Adams, U2's Bono and others made a last-minute appearance at a local radio station for an impromptu collective interview to muster more support.

Flying in to do the show at Giants Stadium also proved interesting. "We had a tire blow out on our airplane when we landed in New York just before the concert," recalled Adams. "The plane landed, and the tire blew. I thought the plane had hit the ground without the wheels. That's what it felt like. Yeah, and we weren't allowed to take pictures of it—so we went and took a picture of it."

Adams said he spent quality time with Bono and Peter Gabriel. "I found both of them to be very, very intellectual and very supportive of the whole Amnesty thing, which was great," said Adams. "Peter to me was just like a little boy. He just seemed so sweet, you know?" He said he and Bono related because they were coping with similar challenges of fame at the same age.

"Some of the highlights were singing onstage with everyone.... beating Sting at snooker. Giants Stadium was definitely the best night for us. I think it was my favourite performance of the tour, by far, because after the fifth show we finally figured out what songs we wanted to do and we were actually feeling confident again, because we hadn't toured for a few months.

"I was pretty tired by the end of it, it was really taxing, because there was too much time off between gigs."

Adams made the most of that time, alleviating boredom by flying to Toronto between concerts to copresent the Norris Trophy for best defenceman to New York Islander Denis Potvin at the National Hockey League Awards. He also staged a press conference to talk about the Amnesty cause and mixed the two Tina Turner songs he'd produced earlier that year.

The Amnesty tour was barely a wrap when Adams and the band were off to England to meet royalty for the third time. They were among the headliners at Wembley Stadium on June 20 for a charity concert in aid of the Prince of Wales Trust, a fund set up to give disadvantaged young people a leg up in business. Sharing the bill were Paul McCartney, George Michael, Sting, Mark Knopfler, Eric Clapton, Phil Collins, David Bowie, Mick Jagger, Howard Jones, Midge Ure, Rod

Stewart, Tina Turner, Level 42 and others. It ended with an all-star encore.

"I was sort of a spectator for most of that concert," Adams told *Rockline*, "until the end when Midge Ure came up to me and said, 'Are you going to play?' I said, 'I don't know, sure, O.K.' Then he just threw a guitar and said, 'Saw Her Standing There,' man, just follow us.' I just walked up there and it was pretty amazing at first, and then I started thinking I better learn the song here, so I was trying to follow everyone else's guitar chords. I think about thirty seconds into the song I noticed there was a free microphone, so I went and harmonized."

On the other side of the free microphone was Paul McCartney. Adams was harmonizing with a Beatle. "I don't think he was too impressed!" chuckled Adams. Earlier in the year, when asked by a fan magazine who he most wanted to meet, Adams had replied: "I'd like to meet Paul McCartney. I used to admire his songwriting. I don't any more."

Even singing face-to-face with McCartney didn't render Adams speechless. "I'd love to do something with McCartney," he told the *Record Mirror* after the show. "That would be a real one-off and I can't ever imagine it happening. I'd like to do a real rocker, bring him back to where his voice really stands out."

11

Into the Fire

"Tears Are Not Enough," said Adams, was a turning point in his career. He had cowritten the lyrics to a song that stood toe-to-toe with the best aid-for-Africa efforts. He had garnered the respect of his peers, the media and the public—people were visibly moved when they heard the song. It was a powerful feeling. It sowed the seeds for what would become the fifth Bryan Adams album, *Into the Fire*.

"It gave us confidence and it was a real challenge to write about an issue as sensitive as that one," Adams told journalist Tom Harrison. "The musicians who sang on the record liked the lyrics, too, which made Jim and I feel good. You feel honoured when Joni Mitchell says she likes your lyrics."

If his lack of stature at Live Aid was somewhat humbling, his participation in the core group of the Conspiracy of Hope tour for Amnesty International made up for it. Still, there was a mostly unspoken belief that maybe he shouldn't have been there. No one doubted his sincerity, but his appearance was musically awkward—he was the only mainstream rock act—and politically incorrect. The entire day was chock-full of statements fostering awareness of human-rights issues though speeches and song. Adams played right after Peter Gabriel and was followed by Sting and then U2. Gabriel provided one of the strongest moments of the concert when he closed his set with "Biko," a compelling tribute to the late

South African activist Steven Biko.

For Adams, whose signature song was "Kids Wanna Rock," it was a tough performance to follow. "Tears Are Not Enough," especially lacking the massive chorus heard on the recording, wasn't enough on its own to carry a whole set. The press, for the most part, respected his input; they were polite, if not enthusiastic. But not always. "When you're on the bill with U2, Sting and Peter Gabriel," wrote Los Angeles *Times* critic Chris Willman, "it's got to be a little embarrassing, peer pressure wise, when the most recent album you have to draw on was not only inconsequential by comparison but downright morally repugnant."

Adams had heard that kind of criticism for years, and responded to it in a 1985 interview with *Maclean's*: "Why do things have to be polluted with social issues all the time? I write about loneliness, which affects people more than nuclear war, more than starvation."

Adams and Vallance had turned their thoughts to a new album right after the *Reckless* tour wound down late in 1985. They had what Vallance described to *Rolling Stone*'s Steve Pond as their first-ever prealbum strategy session. "I guess we were really anxious not to do the obvious next record," Vallance told Pond, citing the progression of *Cuts Like a Knife* and *Reckless*. "We were using relationship scenarios to write lyrics, and we decided not to do that, which really narrowed the options. And yet we didn't want to tackle topics like Chernobyl and world hunger."

"We wanted to make a record that was still a good hard rocking LP," said Adams, "but with more depth lyrically. Like maybe what the Band was doing...songs that have stories and scenarios and writing in the third person."

Vallance joined Adams in England. "I just wanted to try writing in a different environment," said Adams. "But it was in January and it was just too cold—it's too damp."

When they first settled down to write what would become their fifth album, *Into the Fire*, the first few ideas came quickly. One of the first songs created was "Heat of the Night." They had taken a side trip to Berlin when the city was still part prison state. Said Adams: "That's why a lot of the energy on this record got to be quite dark—'Heat of the Night' particularly. It's the idea of being chased, a sort of paranoic feel, like The Third Man," he adds, citing the film noir classic from the 1940s, which starred Orson Welles.

Another speedily written number was "Another Day," which was partly Adams and Vallance responding to the pressures of fame, specifically the lack of privacy.

"Hearts On Fire" was left over from *Reckless*. "It could have been on the last LP," he told *Music Express*, "but we had to rewrite that song. The original lyrics were so different they would have stood out like a sore thumb. They would have fit on the last album, but not on this one. 'Got a girl/ She's all right/She said good to me every night.' Those were the original words."

Also included was "Rebel," the song recorded by Roger Daltrey. Adams and Vallance had reworked it into a slightly different version.

"That song was written for Roger," said Adams, "and no one is more qualified to sing about being a rebel than Roger Daltrey. That's why I sang it in the second person and he sang it in the first. We also added a third verse." Adams said he also had his grandfather in Plymouth, England, in mind when he wrote the song: "It comes from me visiting with him quite a bit—but I don't want to embarrass him, you know."

The subject of his family came up again in "Remembrance Day": "Both Jim and I had family that fought in wars," said Adams to Vancouver *Sun* reporter John Mackie. "So we wanted to write a song as a tribute to them. It's a tribute to our forefathers, but it's a romantic song too. It's about a guy sitting in the trenches realizing he's come to war and [he was] totally wrong about what it was going to be like. And he writes this letter home to his girl, saying don't forget me while I'm sitting here, and I'll be back for you. So it's a romantic song as much as it is a tribute."

The Adams/Vallance team had written "Only the Strong Survive" for a big-budget movie, but Bryan had pulled out when he learned that the film, *Top Gun*, was a glamorization of war, and not at all compatible with the philosophy of *Into the Fire*. The song was redirected onto the new album.

"There's a definite signature sound that happens between the two of us," Adams told the *Gavin Report* about his songwriting with Vallance. "Something like 'Only the Strong Survive' is more Jim, but then again, it was a true collaboration. 'Native Son' is more me."

"I had that title for about two years," Adams told a caller on the radio show "Rockline." "I never knew what to do with it until this record.... We painstaked over the lyrics quite a bit.... When doing research on Native Indians we came across an American Indian called Chief Joseph. He was a very eloquent and very thoughtful speech-maker who was a great inspiration. He wrote a speech of surrender, and that's where the famous line "from where I stand we will fight no more forever" comes from. He was so articulate—the speeches became the foundation for the lyric."

"Home Again" addressed at least one aspect of Adams's childhood, the nomadic life of a diplomat's family.

The hard-edged "Victim of Love" kept the album on the dark side. "I think there's almost too much darkness on the record," Vallance told Steve Pond in *Rolling Stone*. "But I like haunting melodies and haunting guitar lines. I love the despair, the emptiness, the feeling of love in vain."

As well as a different lyrical tack with *Into the Fire*, Adams said, there were a few musical changes: "The one thing about this record that's different from all my other albums is that each song on this record has an ending. They end. The song doesn't fade. Live, you can duplicate it."

Technology played a big part in the writing process for *Into the Fire*. Bryan was happy with the old method of "just playing away" with a guitar, a bass and a drum loop, but Jim was right up on all the latest synthesizers, emulators and samplers, and incorporated them into the process. Bryan was not as keen.

"It was fascinating working with the technology and trying different things," Adams told writer Larry LeBlanc, "but it was more difficult and more time consuming. There's a way of incorporating technology in writing which doesn't take away from the writing, but in my mind it always took away."

They worked on the songs until the summer, interrupted in May by the opening of Expo '86, and in June by the Amnesty International tour and the Prince's Trust concert in England. July was mostly spent working on his house, and on his new studio—which were one and the same.

Adams had bought state-of-the-art recording gear and had it installed in his new house. He christened it Cliffhanger Studios after his backyard terrain.

"The house was empty," he joked to rock journalist Lisa Robinson. "I didn't have any furniture in it at the time—so this was a way of filling up the house with something". The main inspiration, though, was the prospect of having unlimited access to his own facility. He had run into scheduling problems galore at both Little Mountain Sound and the Power Station, and he wasn't about to go through that again. He also wanted to be able to wake up, hit the studio—stopping only for a coffee and a croissant—and work until ready to drop conveniently into his own bed.

In August, the crews were frantically working on finishing the control room while Adams frantically gathered his band for rehearsals. Bob Clearmountain was due in Vancouver that month to start recording. Clearmountain's involvement in *Into the Fire* was not a foregone conclusion. With the different direction, and the difficulties in scheduling the producer's limited time, Adams had not ruled out other coproducers.

"'Heat of the Night' I wrote particularly for [Tears For Fears producer] Chris Hughes," Adams told the *Music Paper*. "I wrote the song thinking about his producing style, hoping he would be able to interject some influence on it. Unfortunately he didn't have the time to work with me. I wrote the song 'Somebody' thinking about Nile Rodgers, but I never asked him. But there's a great camaraderie between Clearmountain and me. I would hate to lose that."

Clearmountain had not reacted well to the fact that Adams

wanted him to come to his house to do the album. "At first," recalled Adams, "he thought I was nuts and I was kidding. Probably somewhere deep down he was waiting for it to fumble so we could move out of there, but it worked better than most studios because we had fine-tuned it so much. We were still plugging in cords until the day he arrived. He was mad at us."

Apart from "Rebel," the songs had never been road-tested, but Adams and the band spent enough time in rehearsals to well make up for it, and the songs had been demoed to the max. "When writing *Into the Fire*," said Adams, "there was a lot more thought to the arrangement of really tight bass and drums. That was all done on a computer, then I had a real drummer play it."

Pat Steward rehearsed and recorded with the band into the first few weeks of recording. His inexperience in the studio was somewhat of a problem for the persnickety, impatient Adams, and, more importantly, Hall and Oates had recently gone their separate ways, leaving Mickey Curry available full-time that summer for a price Adams was willing to pay. The drummer had been such a sought-after prize over the years—he was a trophy, Adams's own yardstick for success—that it was impossible for Adams to pass up the opportunity.

"It was kind of sad seeing Pat leave," said Adams at the time, "but it seemed like a logical thing to do, what with Mickey having participated on all the records the last few years. Pat played on a couple of tracks on the last record, and certainly he's a great friend and we're going to miss him a great deal, but it's a musical and personal choice for Mickey to be in the band. It just made a lot of sense.

"Mickey's done some great things this year—Stevie Winwood's album and a lot of other sessions. And he did that Tina track with us for 'Break Every Rule,' so this is definitely the band, the ultimate Bryan Adams band."

Adams's home "studio" was little more than the control room and unfinished workshop in the basement, and the normal upstairs living areas.

"I wanted to take us out of the environment of the studio and put us in somewhere where it isn't so expected," Adams told "Rockline." "You never know what you're going to get by recording in a bathroom or in a spare bedroom, or in a closet—which is where we recorded. We had microphone cables going up the chimney flue to get from the control room in the basement up to the living room. We recorded the organ in the bathroom, we recorded the bass guitar in the clothes closet. The final vocal tracks, I moved to a little workshop in the basement. I borrowed two portable Sony cameras and put one in the living room and one in the control booth so we could communicate."

The drums were recorded in the dining room, and that caused a couple of odd problems not usually encountered in a studio situation—one being waking up the neighbours. The drums could be heard throughout most of the block.

Mickey Curry pointed out another problem in a fan club newsletter: "If I'm really messing up when I'm recording, I'll get so aggravated that I just throw my sticks and say "F*@*!" "When we were recording 'Into the Fire' at Bryan's house, I ended up doing that a couple of times. He has this beautiful chandelier in the dining room, where my drums were set up. Luckily, I missed that, but I hit the ceiling, which was all plaster, a beautiful old ceiling. I said to myself, 'Oh God, what did I do?' But Bryan came in and he was laughing like crazy. I was so apologetic, but he said, 'Don't worry about it!' There was actually no real damage, but I'll never forget that sinking feeling."

The guitars were captured in the living room and the bedrooms, as ambience dictated. With *Into the Fire* a very guitar-oriented record, both Scott and Adams had chances to shine. "I think Keith Scott's playing on this record is colossal," said Adams in a 1987 interview, "the finest he ever played." But, added Adams, "people don't realize that the guitar on 'Heat of the Night' and 'Another Day' is me. It was my first sort of step out of the solo, and I haven't done that before, and my blues influence is sticking out. All I could ever play was Chuck Berry anyway."

Chris Ainscough would come by the house most nights and cook for Adams and the troops, everything from tandoori chicken to cheese sandwiches. He was also around to pick up ringing telephones and greet the neighbours when they came knocking on the door to complain about the noise. The tape rolling in the control room picked up some interesting extra sounds.

"We had a lot of fun," Adams told "Rockline." "And I really want to thank my neighbours because they were really patient through the summer of '86."

The album was actually recorded from the beginning of September to the end of November. Mixing the tracks—balancing all the recorded instruments together and tweaking the sounds—would prove to be a very slow process.

"The original rough mixes we did—we did all ten songs in one night—sounded better sometimes," said Adams when the album came out. "We couldn't get the sound back from those rough mixes. They were so interesting, just because they were so spontaneous and live. We eventually got them better, but it took a lot of work.

"It was mixed in London. We were there too long. I'll never do that again, that was a mistake. I still don't know why we did it in London.... it was really Bob's suggestion to do it there."

A number of events disrupted the recording and mixing of *Into the Fire*. Interruptions in September included Adams attending the MTV Awards and winning the MTV Best Live Performance award with Tina Turner for "It's Only Love," and taking the top pop songwriting honours with Jim Vallance at the P.R.O. Canada awards in Toronto. Without an album release in two years, his Juno nominations included "Diana" in the single category, Male Vocalist of the Year and Composer of the Year. The awards were staged on November 5—his 27th birthday.

He won Male Vocalist of the Year, but Vallance won out over Adams and three other nominees for the composer award, for his work with Adams and Glass Tiger.

Adams, when accepting his award, recalled that his father

used to say to him, "Boy! You've got a big mouth."

"Well, Dad," quipped Bryan. "You're right!"

By February 1987, Adams was satisfied with his new album. "I'm really pleased the way things turned out on this record," he said at the time. "Mind you, I've always been pleased with the way records have turned out. This would never have come out if it hadn't been just how I liked it."

"I want it to do really well," Adams later told Steve Pond, "but I know that these songs may not be as commercial as the last ones, and I'm willing to accept that responsibility.... Although I'm very excited about this record, I'm not gonna get too excited, because the letdown will be too big if it really did fail."

With his own record pretty much a wrap, Adams jumped from *Into the Fire* into the frying pan. In early February, he put on his producer's cap and travelled to New York's Power Station and recorded "It Should Have Been Me" for Carly Simon, a song written by Adams/Vallance. As with Turner, he again brought his own players—Keith and Dave, plus fellow Vancouverites Dave Pickell (who also played some keyboards on the new Adams album) and drummer Marc LaFrance.

"They were doing a song that Jim and I had written," Adams told the *Sun*'s John Mackie. "Instead of doing a butcher job on it, they asked me to [produce]."

This wasn't a successful Adams outing. "I would never go and produce an entire album, for anybody," Adams told Mackie a few weeks after his return. "That's just too much work, that's just a nasty job."

A flat "Fine" was Adams's reluctant response to the reporter's query about working with Carly Simon.

"What's she like?" prodded Mackie.

"Um, I don't know," Adams answered. "I don't really know her that well."

A few months later, Carly Simon herself had something to say about the experience. While on a press tour promoting the resulting album, *Coming Around Again*, she stated that the recording session with Adams had been one of the worst moments of her life; he had driven her to tears. "He felt compelled to teach me how to sing each syllable the way he'd have sung them," she complained to reporters. "He was something less than sensitive." (It also came out that she had never wanted to record other people's tunes in the first place; but the record company had forced her hand.)

Adding insult to injury, the next building over from the Bruce Allen headquarters housed an empty storefront that had its windows covered over with newspapers. One of them very prominently displayed the wire service story titled "'Bryan Adams Made Me Cry,' says Carly Simon."

Adams was stunned—little had been said by Simon at the time of the sessions. In his drive for perfection, he hadn't recognized the extent of her discomfort. He later acknowledged that the sessions had been difficult, and said the incident had terminated his career as a producer. "I don't enjoy it," he said with a grimace.

Adams made his first press trip for the album when he met the Japanese media in Hawaii at the end of February. *Into the Fire* was enjoying a huge international launch, courtesy of A & M, and a $250,000 promotional budget. Expenses included transporting several hundred broadcasters and retail representatives from across the country to a lavish reception in Toronto in March to preview the album.

According to David Farrell, editor of the weekly Canadian music industry tip sheet *The Record*, the Toronto bash wasn't "very rock and roll." It took place in an elegant dining room in a posh hotel. After a round of cognac, the lights were turned down and the album was played.

Neither Adams nor Allen, nor anybody else from the office, made the journey east to attend the event—being the only focal point of a large room full of media and radio executives was not the singer's idea of a good time. His nonappearance was a slap in the face to the media and to the record reps. Nobody took it well. Meanwhile, he was quite happily—and purposely—in Los Angeles, shooting a video for the first single, "In the Heat of the Night."

The video was filmed over two days in an abandoned Ford

plant in Long Beach, California, with cast and crew working from 7:00 p.m. to 7:00 a.m. The artsy black-and-white final result was a hot entry on the music television charts.

"Heat of the Night," backed with "Another Day," was shipped to radio as the crews completed the video. Later in the month, *Into the Fire* was delivered to record stores. It went to #1 in Canada in two weeks, and shipped platinum in the U.S. (a million copies)—and triple platinum (300,000) in Canada.

Adams was in Europe on a two-week promotion tour when his album hit the stores. He spent March 20 to April 3 in England, Italy, Holland and Germany. He returned home in time for a live satellite broadcast to two million Japanese viewers for Japan's "Night Hit Studio" show. (The band was beamed from Vancouver's 86 Street Music Hall at 5:00 a.m.)

The artist and his manager were lavishing attention on the foreign media, but offering little in the way of interview time to the North American press. Allen made the argument that he was going after a *Rolling Stone* cover and he was reluctant to overexpose Adams prior to the cover date.

The western media was given its shot towards the end of the month as the Adams camp announced an American tour scheduled to start in early May. The top syndicated rock radio show in North America, "Rockline", packed up its gear and crew and moved from their Los Angeles studio to CFOX-FM in Vancouver to interview Adams. He also finally talked to his hometown press.

"Did you know that you were going to write more than pop songs?" asked John Mackie.

"No, they are nothing more than pop songs," answered Adams. "Never mistake those for anything more than pop songs—that's all they are."

"It's better to remember that we're pop musicians, not politicians," he told the Vancouver *Province*, "and that that line should never be crossed. I think of *Into the Fire* as nothing more than a pop record.... I think Jim and I have really advanced in our music, and that's a personal satisfaction. I didn't write this for anybody else but us."

Into the Fire entered the *Billboard* chart at #36, cracked the Top 10 in four weeks, and by the start of the tour it was sitting at #7 with a bullet. The initial success of the record, which was expected—even demanded—after *Reckless*, unfortunately was not reflected by the ticket sales for the tour.

After more than the usual juggling of dates, the world tour kicked off May 6, 1987, in Shreveport, Louisiana. The first real hint of trouble was the cancellation of the third date of the tour in Birmingham, Alabama; only three thousand of fifteen thousand tickets had been sold when the promoter pulled the plug. The Birmingham newspapers were told the cancellation was because of sickness, but Adams told other media sources it was because he had to fly to New York to shoot a video.

The tour plans had been ambitious—five shows in a row scheduled at Madison Square Garden, two at the Forum in Montreal and two at Toronto's Maple Leaf Gardens, all in late June, and two hometown Vancouver shows in mid-August. The end result saw just two shows in New York, one each in Montreal and Toronto, and none at all in Vancouver.

Bruce Allen had wisely set up a bivouac system of touring. He'd check the band into one central hotel for several of the dates and have them commute back and forth to each show. Adams and the band were travelling in a small jet nicknamed "The Tubesteak" because of its resemblance to a large sausage.

The band played only about half of *Into the Fire* live. "One of the big things about this album," correctly observed Adams, "is that it's given the show a number of dynamics." The concert started with "Only the Strong Survive" and covered "Kids Wanna Rock," "Heat of the Night," "It's Only Love," "Cuts Like a Knife," and "Straight From the Heart" in the early stretch. Latter-half numbers included "Remembrance Day", "Heaven," "One Night Love Affair," "Somebody" and "Run to You." He'd usually do three encores—slow ticket sales or not, Adams always earned several—and included in the extended sets were "Into the Fire," "Summer of '69," "Victim of Love" and "She's Only Happy When

She's Dancing." Opening acts included Patty Smyth of Scandal, the Hooters and John Cafferty.

The reviews often mentioned the excellent sound quality at the shows, which translated to kudos for Jason Sound and mixer Jody Perpick. "[Adams] is travelling with a sophisticated, custom-designed, state-of-the-art sound system, utilizing over 150,000 watts of sound," said one magazine review. "Delivery [is] impeccable from every point in the house. Vocals are so clear you'd swear the band was playing in your living room."

Much of the excitement the first week of the tour was generated by the pending *Rolling Stone* cover story. "I've never been on the cover of Rolling Stone, it's important," Adams would answer when again kidded about his preoccupation with the event.

"I've got to prove myself," he told the *Atlanta Journal*. "No matter whether you're an artist, a singer, a songwriter, a welder or what, you've got to prove yourself."

Bruce Allen had been all over the magazine in typical Allen fashion—he wouldn't leave such a big project to the record company—from as early as the previous year, prior to the delay in recording and mixing the album. Writer Steve Pond flew over to England in January to interview Adams as he mixed *Into the Fire* with Bob Clearmountain, and talked to him one month later in Vancouver. A photo session took place the first week of the tour. Everything was happening but the record.

The article appeared in the September 10 issue of the magazine. He was not on the cover. Aside from that insult, it was quite flattering—Pond described Adams as "engaging, opinionated, open, wilful, guileless, cocky and likable." It was a revealing piece of journalism. Pond, following him through the streets of London, described how Adams got stubborn and argumentative when he couldn't get a cash advance on one of his credit cards; he noted that he signed all his papers by simply writing "Adams," and recounted how the rock star rode the bus almost unnoticed.

He described how in Vancouver Adams had called home to

warn Vicki Russell he was bringing a reporter by and not to leave his "underwear on the stairs." They arrived at the house—after Adams extracted a promise not to describe his home or furnishings—to find that Russell had neatly placed a pair of his grey jockey shorts on the bottom step.

Pond recalled in the article how rattled Adams got when referred to as a wealthy man. "If it wasn't for the fact that people were making up rumours about me," Adams told Pond, "I would have kept my private life completely to myself. I must tell you, I do feel really uncomfortable talking about my success.... And that's all I have to say about it."

The article also quoted Bruce Allen: "When Bryan Adams puts out a new album," said Allen, "it sells a quiet five or six million. When Sting puts out an album, it sells a loud million-and-a-half. This time, I want to sell a loud six million."

"Since its April release the album has sold a fairly quiet 1.5 million," pointed out Pond.

For the second year running, Adams was invited to perform at the star-studded Prince's Trust in London—his fourth royal audience. He broke from the American tour and arrived in London June 1 and rehearsed a version of Dion's "The Wanderer" with Dave Edmunds.

As a warm-up for Wembley, Adams made a surprise appearance at the four-hundred-seat Soho Marquis, and in spite of the short notice, fifteen hundred fans lined the streets and tied up traffic. It was an exceptionally hot set—literally. The small club lacked air-conditioning; it was a sweatbox. Within three songs, Adams and the band were soaked. The performance was kept to just ninety minutes, and the concert was taped.

At Wembley, Bryan did "Hearts on Fire," "Only the Strong Survive," "Run to You" and "Somebody." "We're boys from Canada," he told the screaming audience, many of whom were waving Canadian flags, "and we appreciate it very much."

The Prince's Trust concerts were taped for an HBO special. The highlights, said Adams, were when Elton John asked him up for a round of "Saturday Night's Alright For Fighting," and when he was onstage for the grand finale, singing "With a Little Help From My Friends" and "Stand by Me" with George Harrison, Ringo Starr, Eric Clapton, Phil Collins, Elton John, Boy George, Alison Moyet, Ben E. King, Curiosity Killed the Cat, Dave Edmunds and ELO's Jeff Lynne.

The crowning touch was when George Harrison asked him for an autograph for his son.

The Prince's Trust, of course, had been a freebie, but it was certainly more glamorous than most. Adams was showing his charitable side on a regular basis, or at least as much as his schedule allowed. He had thrown in a Christmas song— Chuck Berry's "Run Rudolph Run"—at his last-minute Marquis show, and although at the time Adams said it was a spur-of-the-moment thing, it was in fact recorded for a Christmas album benefitting the Special Olympics. Adams had been asked to contribute a track, along with Sting, Bruce Springsteen, Madonna and Bon Jovi among others.

When *Into the Fire* first came out, he had paid a quiet visit to an eight-year old boy just outside Vancouver who had just lost his leg to a noncancerous tumour. He chatted for two hours and gave the boy an electric guitar and one of his handmade cases. A couple of months later, Adams arranged for him to meet Bon Jovi—with no cameras or reporters allowed. He also showed up at several charity soccer events, and even dropped around to help producer Bruce Fairbairn coach his Little League soccer team.

He had aggressively—and successfully—put his dibs in for a planned Greenpeace "Rock the World" concert to be simultaneously staged in RFK Stadium in Washington, D.C., and in Lenin Stadium in Moscow, but the production was eventually cancelled.

After his London appearances, Adams immediately re-sumed touring the eastern states. He played only three cities in Canada—Toronto, where he received his triple-platinum award for *Into the Fire*, Montreal and Ottawa (the latter for the July 1 Canada Day celebration). He toured the western

U.S. in August, but skipped Western Canada. Bruce Allen was not about to confront a hometown crowd unless it was guaranteed one hundred percent successful. He still remembered a Loverboy homecoming show that had failed to sell out the local Pacific Coliseum at the peak of their career.

The video for the second single, "Hearts on Fire," was shot early in the tour at a Florida concert. Bryan shot the video for the third single, "Victim of Love," in mid-August in L.A., the day before he played a show at the Forum. Ex–Sex Pistol Steve Jones joined him onstage the next night for the usual "Hound Dog" and a couple of other Elvis Presley tunes. Jones then transported Adams on his Harley-Davidson to a postconcert party. Also joining Bryan backstage that night were actor Nicholas Cage, former Go-Gos Charlotte Caffey and Belinda Carlisle, the Bangles and Fergal Sharkey.

He did a few more shows the first week of September from Tennessee to New York, and finished the American arm in Allentown, Pennsylvania, September 6. The following week, he was back in Los Angeles, performing at the 1987 MTV Awards and taping a special version of "Top of the Pops"— his first appearance on the popular British TV show. After just a brief rest, the band arrived in Paris, France, October 6 for pretour promotional duties, and began their European tour October 14 in Newcastle, England.

Europe proved a more receptive market than America. Over the next three months they toured largely in England, Germany, Scandinavia, the Netherlands, France and Switzerland, and saw mostly sold-out concerts, including four full houses at Wembley Arena in London. A number of shows on the tour were taped, with the idea of a live album in mind.

Adams turned twenty-eight in Stuttgart, Germany—the entire audience sang "Happy Birthday" to him. A few days earlier he had accepted an early birthday present via a taped message from Leeds, England, as he won two more Juno Awards back home—Male Vocalist and a new category, Canadian Entertainer of the Year. The latter win was considered more of a coup by Adams—it was a public vote, not dictated by the music industry like the rest of the Junos.

The European leg of the *Into the Fire* tour finished in Dublin on December 19. The band headed back to Canada to enjoy the holidays, but Adams and Russell spent Christmas in England before returning home to spend the New Year with hometown family and friends.

The break was again a short one. A first-ever show was scheduled for Anchorage, Alaska, on January 22. Then it was across the Pacific to Japan for ten sold-out shows, including five at Tokyo's prestigious Budokan. Adams was platinum in Japan, and he received an award backstage for selling over 100,000 copies of *Into the Fire* in that market.

In Tokyo, he played "Light My Fire" by the Doors and "Heard It Through the Grapevine" by Marvin Gaye, and did an acoustic version of the song "Into the Fire" for the first time.

"I like playing it like that," Adams told his fan club. "People will remember that—all night long they've heard the band, and then to close the show with something that's completely different, it's a memorable thing to do. You've got to try new things—even if you fail miserably."

From Japan, Adams and the band flew directly to Calgary, Alberta, for a special concert at the Olympic Village on the University of Calgary campus. The concert was for Olympic athletes, coaches and officials only.

"It was an amazing experience," recalled Adams. "It was like doing a world tour in two hours. I guess this is what it would be like to play for the United Nations."

As his set wound down, in excess of two hundred athletes joined him onstage and danced around the band for the last three numbers. Adams was presented with a Canadian hockey team jacket by its coach, and after the show he met with team players.

Backstage, Adams flirted with the women, including downhill skier Laurie Graham and especially Katarina Witt, East Germany's figure skating gold medallist. The hot topic at the Olympics that year was Witt's sex appeal, which she displayed through provocative routines and costumes. She and

Adams hit it off extremely well.

The *Into the Fire* album had been greeted with mostly good reviews, although a few media types took shots at the album, using words like *insincere, contrived* and *trendy*. Several used the term *Hollywood* in their synopsis of the song "Native Son." Others wondered if Adams's recent exposure to the activist crowd had prompted him to jump on the human-rights bandwagon.

A *Music Express* reporter asked if his association with Sting had been instrumental: "I've known Sting since I toured with the Police in 1983," answered Adams. "It wasn't like because I know him, I have to write something relevant. The truth is that *Into the Fire* reflected what I was feeling at that time. Mutt [future producer Lange] says that if I'd put a couple of hit singles on it, the album would have done much better. But I wasn't thinking in those terms."

"*Into the Fire* wasn't full of Top 40 hits," he told the media, "but that was intentional. Six-minute songs don't get played on Top 40.... I'm happy to have a repertoire of songs that don't get lost in my pop hits. It makes things more interesting."

The album peaked at #4 in Europe, but that still wasn't the hot market they hoped for, although at the time Adams argued the point in *Music Express*. "*Into the Fire* has done very well in Europe," he contended, "but it is extremely difficult to gauge my popularity against record sales. I never have. All I can tell you is that this has been one of my most successful tours so far...without a current hit single, without a hitch."

Into the Fire sold two million copies—respectable, but a far cry from the more than eight million in sales generated by *Reckless*. According to his corporate taskmasters, social conscience be damned. Adams had lost six million customers.

"His teenage audience hasn't crossed over to the more ambitious material," noted *Canadian Musician* magazine. "Adams's more youthful fans may not be ready for or interested in songs about the plight of North American Indians.

And the more intellectual audience still perceives him as a teen artist."

"Over the next year I will be making the new album," Adams told his fan club. "I'm going to be recording it in Vancouver and I think that, well, for now, let's just say that I think the album is going to be more of a back-to-the-roots record. Lots of space."

12

Into the Void

Adams: "I've worked with Vallance for ten years now. He thinks that he deserves a medal. I think I deserve a gold watch."

It was early in 1988. *Into the Fire* was running its course. It was obviously not about to have the staying power of *Reckless*, and Adams and Vallance were turning their attention to a sixth album. Once Adams was back from Japan via the Olympics concert in Calgary, they began working steadily on new material.

In May, with more than a half dozen or so new songs under their belts, Adams asked Allen to put him on the road again. He had several reasons: He wanted to do some more exotic travelling—his previous European tour had been limited to a handful of countries, and there were a number of markets playing his records that remained uncovered; a tour would provide some substantial income not being generated by record sales; and, most importantly, he would have the chance to road-test and rearrange a few of the finished songs, while perhaps coming up with ideas for new ones.

The schedule was designed for Adams to travel at a leisurely pace—just a couple of shows a week—with particular attention to the Mediterranean, Israel and even East Berlin. Adams told the Canadian Press that he would continue working on the album when the tour ended in July, but there was no rush. He said the album would be out "when it's done."

Tommy Mandel was easily convinced by the money and the easy, exotic schedule to sign up as the keyboard player. He flew to Vancouver to rehearse with the band the third week in May. Adams wanted a live-rehearsal concert—the logical place was the 86 Street Music Hall, a thousand-seat nightclub partially owned by Allen. A charity was quickly rounded up—a commercial event at so small a venue would look pretty cheesy, and, in any case, this was the perfect opportunity to help out a worthy cause.

The selected recipient was the Leukemia Research Foundation. The inspiration was leukemia-stricken twelve-year old Chris Padwicki, the son of Bill Clark's nephew (Jane Clark was instrumental in making it all happen). Adams ripped through versions of "Walkin' after Midnight," "I Fought the Law," "I Heard It through the Grapevine" and "Doo Wah Diddy." Jon Bon Jovi, in town recording his next album, joined Adams on stage for "Johnny B. Goode" and "Born To Be Wild." Adams finished the night with a solo rendition of "Into the Fire."

He handed over a cheque for $20,000 in a short, emotional ceremony at the hospital the following morning. "Obviously this is a very small donation in comparison to what they probably need for research. I wanted to raise public awareness."

Adams accomplished his goal and made young Padwicki a media star in the process. Although the boy was too young to be allowed in the licensed nightclub, the event was the thrill of his young life—which sadly, in spite of the transplant, ended that December.

Two days after the 86 Street concert, Adams and the band flew to Athens, where Adams had sold out faster than any other North American artist in the venue's history.

The tour contained several "special events," including the June 11 Freedomfest at Wembley Stadium in London celebrating Nelson Mandela's seventieth birthday. The ten-hour concert also featured Phil Collins, Whitney Houston,

George Michael, Sting, Dire Straits, Peter Gabriel, Simple Minds, the Bee Gees, Eurythmics, Stevie Wonder and Whoopi Goldberg.

Adams and Scott chartered a plane and flew to London immediately following their show in Toulouse, France, and left again right after their performance (they did a version of "Somebody") to rejoin the band and crew in Spain.

A week later, the whole band participated in a three-day peace festival in East Berlin, headlining for a record 120,000 fans. The open-air concert kicked off the historic International Meeting For Nuclear Weapons Free Zones conference, and was hosted by Katarina Witt, Bryan's friend from the Olympics. The crowd was so large, sound mixer Jody Perpick couldn't find the mixing board, which was stationed in the middle of the audience.

Adams played a two-and-a-half-hour concert and went past the imposed midnight curfew; after three encores, he was advised to leave the stage by the East German authorities. Earlier in the day he had been granted permission to tour the historic bombed-out area of East Berlin. He also tried to meet soul godfather James Brown, who was staying at the same hotel, but it was not to be, as he explained to the *Toronto Star*. "Every time I asked one of his guys they would just shrug and say, 'James be upstairs.'"

Events also included five early July shows cobilled with Sting and INXS at open-air festivals in Denmark, Belgium and Italy.

Touring in foreign lands is always difficult, but Adams had requested cities very much off the beaten track, and hence there were some unusual settings and odd problems. In Israel he performed in an ancient Roman amphitheatre in Caesarea, then played the Sultan's Pool in Jerusalem. The dates in Italy and other centres were staged in large circus tents, often causing technical nightmares made worse by language barriers—they lost all the power at a show in France and ended up performing an acoustic set, and in Belgium saw the power go out twenty times.

They put thirty thousand tickets on sale in Lisbon before

the promoter cancelled because "people didn't really believe we were coming," Adams told the *Star*. "I phoned him, spoke to him myself, and said "'We're coming!'" When Adams arrived, he was given a police escort through the streets and made page one on every paper in Portugal. "By then," said Adams, "of course, the promoter had lost the football stadium. So we ended up playing a 200-seat club, with 10,000 people outside trying to get in." (He honoured the stadium dates three weeks later.)

The tour wrapped up July 10 in Locarno, Switzerland. Next on the list was ten days of record production in London with producer Steve Lillywhite. Adams had met with him the previous Christmas, and they had made arrangements to get together when Adams had some songs. Lillywhite had worked with U2, Talking Heads, the Rolling Stones and the Pretenders. Adams had tuned into him after hearing the results of his work with the Pogues.

"Steve has a good sense for capturing the band live," Adams told his fan club, "and I felt I needed someone that could really do that, but also help me work with my songs.... I was ready for a change with the last record producer-wise.... Bob and I will still probably work together mixing this album."

The album was expected to be completed late in the summer and released early in the New Year. The summer '88 issue of his fan club newsletter asked about the two-year gap between albums: "What is important is that it comes out," answered Adams. "Many people ask me for advice about their careers and I say the most important thing is to come up with good songs. If it takes you one year or four, you should wait. Whatever comes out, you are going to be judged by it and it's going to be your name on it, so don't put it out until you make sure it's as good as you can get it."

The sessions had continued in Vancouver in August, with Lillywhite working in Adams's home studio. According to Adams, Lillywhite "created a 'soulful' edge to the recordings." They produced eight songs. Adams played them for his friends, family and peers—his circle was much more select these days as his quest for feedback clashed with his quest for secrecy.

"Most of the feedback at first was 'Yeah, they're okay,'" recalled one coworker. "And then Adams would go, 'Oh, only okay?' And we'd go, 'They're fine, Adams!' But he was off and running with 'only okay.'"

Mickey Curry also used the term "okay." "They were better than most people's good stuff," Mickey told the fans, "but there was something missing."

That fall Adams threw four of the tracks out the window and got together with Vallance to do some more writing. "When the album was finished I decided I didn't want to release it," Adams told *Kerrang!*. "It was no reflection on Steve. I just realised the songs weren't right. A lot of them were too depressing."

"Steve was a trouper," Adams told *Music Express*. "His attitude was 'Let's go in, and if we can make a record, great. If not, at least we'll have some fun.' The truth is, my songs weren't even close to being ready. I was at least a year away from it. I think it was Steve who said so."

The next year did see frequent but sporadic work on new songs and rewrites of old songs. It was a busy time—Adams was off the charts, but certainly not out of the press. He was in the news when he donated the song "Remembrance Day" to a government-sponsored war-memorial video, and gave "Somebody" to Greenpeace for their *Rainbow Warriors* album, geared to fund the group's Soviet office. The album, the first major release of western music in the Soviet Union, also included U2, the Pretenders, Eurythmics, Dire Straits, John Cougar Mellencamp, Peter Gabriel, Bryan Ferry, Sting, Talking Heads and the Thompson Twins.

Adams even appeared in on the big screen after taking a bit role as a gas-station attendant in the Clint Eastwood film, *Pink Cadillac*.

"You're not supposed to mention that movie," Adams good naturedly told "Rockline." "Bruce Allen, my manager, is a huge Clint Eastwood fan—so am I, actually—and I was doing a song for the film [recorded by Dion]...and they said do you want to come on down and be a gas-station attendant in the movie? I said, 'Yeah, okay.' It was fun. I hung out with Clint for a day.... They wouldn't let me near [leading lady Bernadette Peters]."

Adams recorded backup vocals for Charlie Sexton's song "Don't Look Back" in his home studio, at the request of producer Bob Clearmountain, and in December he joined Joe Cocker in New York to record the Adams/Vallance/Diane Warren tune "When The Night Comes" for a pending Cocker album. They wrote another tune for, of all things, an album by the Irish folk group the Rovers, produced by rocker Bill Henderson. The song was "All Sing Together."

The main focus coming into the New Year was his first CBC-TV special, "Bryan Adams: Live in Belgium," which aired January 15, 1989. He had flown to Toronto in mid-December to oversee the production and tape a few interview segments to augment the sixty minute, ten-song show.

"We actually had two good tapes from Belgium, including one without the rain that might have been a better performance," he said in his newsletter, "but we chose the Werchter show because the weather created such an amazing vibe in the crowd. This one has a very strange atmosphere because it was raining so very, very hard. What's interesting is the crowd reaction and the interplay between the band and the audience, the whole thing heightened by the weather being so volatile.

"The curious thing is that in Belgium they'd never seen an album of mine on the charts. That concert is a prime example of us in a country where we haven't had hits, but people know the songs and respond to them without really knowing who we are. As a result of playing the concert, my albums went into the charts there for the first time since they were released. It's the best example of one show—unedited and unenhanced—that we've ever filmed. That's why after all these years, I decided we would do it. It's not a very glamorous example of what I do, but it's a very honest example."

He admitted that a few new songs had been performed at the concert, but that he would not include them in the special because they might prematurely shape the perception of the upcoming record.

He flew to Los Angeles in February to record Hall-of-Famer Dion's performance of the Adams/Vallance song "Drive All Night." At home in Vancouver, he contributed backing vocals on a new Mötley Crüe track titled "Sticky Sweet" with Steven Tyler of Aerosmith and Jack Blades of Night Ranger. Adams was in the news again that month when he lobbied civic authorities to save an old Vancouver medical building from the wrecker's ball. He attended several Greenpeace functions, and donated one of his favourite books to a charitable celebrity book auction—a first edition of *Klee Wyck* by Canadian painter Emily Carr.

In April, Adams and Keith Scott, along with Bruce Allen, flew to Glasnost-era Moscow to perform "Kids Wanna Rock" live with a Soviet backup band to an estimated 750 million viewers on the satellite-televised World Music Video Awards. It was Adams's first trip to the Soviet Union.

Adams was busy, but so was Jim Vallance. Vallance had followed his three Top 10 Billboard hits in 1986 (two by Glass Tiger, one by Heart) with a #1 hit on the Billboard country charts in 1987 courtesy of Anne Murray singing "Now and Forever," cowritten by Vallance, David Foster and another writer. Later that year, he made a big impression on the metal crowd when he cowrote four songs on the massively successful Aerosmith comeback album, *Permanent Vacation*, including the Top 20 hit "Rag Doll." He was on the charts again with Glass Tiger in 1988 with "Diamond Sun," the song that got him his second win in a row in the Composer of the Year category at the Juno Awards. Early 1989 saw Vallance again working with Aerosmith, who were writing and recording *Pump*. He was also an expectant father.

Relations between Adams and Vallance were strained. Vallance told William Deverell, researching an article for *Saturday Night* magazine, that Adams hated it when he worked with other bands. "Even when he was away touring for six or ten months," said Vallance, "I think he really expected me to just kind of sit around and wait for him to get back."

A rift that dated back to the *Into the Fire* tour was still separating the two writers. Vallance had carefully planned the recording sessions for the second Glass Tiger album to coincide with Adams's tour schedule, but with the response to the tour slower than anticipated, a number of dates were cancelled, and Adams had some unexpected free time.

"At the last minute," recalled Vallance, "Bryan asked me to postpone Glass Tiger so he and I could write. I had booked everything months in advance—studios, musicians, flights, rental cars. It would have been a nightmare to reschedule, and I told Bryan I couldn't move it. He was really angry, but the dirt didn't hit the fan until a few months later, when I asked Keith Scott to play guitar for me again like on the first [Glass Tiger] album. Keith called back and said he couldn't do it, Bruce wouldn't let him."

But it was Adams, not Allen, who had pulled Keith Scott, and Vallance knew it.

"I ended up getting Keith for two songs [after an argument]... I don't think my feelings towards Bryan were ever the same after that."

In July, Jim and Rachel became the parents of a baby boy, and Vallance took a sabbatical. In August of 1989, the Adams/Vallance partnership split up.

"I didn't like being part of the schedule," Adams told *Q* magazine. 'Y'know, "I can fit you in between Christmas and New Year. Well, thanks! I needed to work with someone who was committed to working with me, because it's easy to write songs, but it's hard to write good songs."

He told *Music Express*: "It was like a carton of food that has a best-before date stamped on it. I think we'd passed our sell-by date."

"We wrote the best when were surrounded by cat piss in a cold basement on an eight-track," Adams told MuchMusic's Terry David Mulligan. "When it got beyond that—money, technology, success, the phones ringing—things really changed."

Vallance, although deeply offended by any number of Adams's comments in the press, steamed quietly—he had little to say in return.

"I don't think there are two more opposite personalities than Bryan and I," Jim Vallance told Larry LeBlanc in 1990. "I don't know how we lasted as long as we did. The fact is every time we sat down we wrote a song. That's what kept us together."

But in 1992, Vallance vented his anger in a tirade to writer Deverell. Fumed Vallance: "I was really upset when I read the...interviews where Bryan claims I wasn't willing to put in the time, so he had to find someone else to write with. He makes it sound like he fired me, which is a load of crap. Bryan had to find someone else to write with because I quit."

Many of the problems, said Vallance, stemmed from the pressure that Adams was under to follow up the failed *Into the Fire* with a commercial success. He added that Adams was unhappy with his record deal, and especially with his publishing deal.

"He was carrying a lot of anger around. I was spending more time with him than anyone, and a lot of times I was on the receiving end of his frustration.

"He was pushing himself really hard, and he was extremely demanding of everyone around him. It got to the point, after a year or so on the *Neighbours* album, where the fun side of Bryan was showing up less and less. Some days he'd go out of his way to be unpleasant, just to see how far he could push you, to get a reaction.... People don't know Bryan, they just see the 'boy next door' image that he likes to portray—the kid with the infectious grin. I'm not saying that's not a part of Bryan's character, it's just that there's a darker side too, and when that darker side takes over, spending time with Bryan can be a real chore.

"We'd been writing songs for *Neighbours* almost every day for a year, and I felt we were starting to burn out, personally and creatively. I suggested we take a break, but Bryan refused. He was obsessed with getting the album finished. So we kept writing, eight and ten hours a day. It was like banging our heads against a wall, and the songs just got crappier and crappier, and the vibes got more and more intense.

"It got to the point where we desperately needed help with our writing. Bryan had been in touch with Mutt Lange on and off for a couple of years, and eventually he persuaded Mutt to help us out. It started with 'Depend on Me,' which Bryan and I thought was finished, but Mutt added this second chorus, and the song just took off. It was pretty exciting having him involved, and it finally seemed like we were on the right track, at least musically. Personally, though, things were still pretty tense between us."

Vallance said it didn't help matters when Adams called him about dividing the writing credits for "Depend on Me": "I thought it should be three ways between he and I and Mutt, but Bryan disagreed, he thought he'd written more than I had. We started to argue about it, something we'd never done in ten years of writing together, and finally I said, 'Why don't I call Mutt and see what he thinks?' I phoned him in England and explained about the argument. Mutt seemed genuinely surprised. He said "Bryan and I discussed it yesterday—I thought we were splitting the song three ways!". I called Bryan right back. I was really angry, but he laughed it off and said he just wanted to see what he could get out of me, like it was a game or something."

About a month later, Vallance and Adams were discussing the split on another song. Vallance had contributed some lyrics to a Lange/Adams composition, and suggested what he said was a modest percentage of the song, which Adams initially agreed to.

"Adams phoned back later and said I should take one half of one percent less. Half a percent! I really couldn't believe he'd haggle over pennies like that, and I refused to even discuss it with him.

"A few weeks later Bryan called and said, 'Let's get together and write,' as if nothing had happened, but I'd been giving it a lot of thought and had decided I couldn't carry on like that. I told him I didn't want to write with him again...."

It wasn't that difficult a decision, really. I could have fun writing with Aerosmith and the Scorpions, or I could have a knot in my stomach writing with Bryan.

"To be fair to Bryan, he called me two years later and offered to split all the songs equally. It was actually very generous of him—he didn't have to do that. In all the years I've known the guy, it's the closest I've seen him come to offering an apology or admitting a mistake. I think he knew he'd blown a good thing, and he was trying to make amends."

As time passed, Adams did become more charitable—and truthful-in his comments to the press: "The songs we wrote weren't good enough," Adams emphatically told Larry LeBlanc. "Jim didn't want to go back and write again. It was his choice. It wasn't my choice."

"I think if we could have taken a break and worked on it on a more casual basis, we'd still be together," Adams told Chris Dafoe of *The Globe and Mail*. "But because I'm very high-strung, I guess my seriousness about getting each project under way is a little too much to take. I'm a bit of a workaholic. Jim wanted to work with other people and he has his family and I didn't fit into that picture."

With the relationship with Vallance at an end, Adams checked out some other songwriters. Prism's Lindsay Mitchell was on the list. "He phoned me up one day," recalled Mitchell, "and said he'd been listening to an old tape of some tunes that he and I had been working on and he wanted to know if I was interested in coming over and giving it another shot. We just wanked around in his studio for a bit, but nothing happened."

Adams had been impressed by his dealings with Mutt Lange, and he sought to pursue that relationship. Lange was a notorious recluse. He was in demand but selective, and not one to overload his schedule. He had been a hot name as a producer since the mid-seventies. He worked with a number of pub rock and new wave bands like the Motors, Graham Parker and the Rumour, and the Boomtown Rats (led by Bob Geldof). His diversified résumé from that era also included the southern-rock band the Outlaws, British disco group Supercharge, and Clover, a roots-rock band that featured a young Huey Lewis. Yet it was with commercial hard rock that Lange really made his mark. In the late 1970s, he hooked up with Australia's AC/DC to produce such rock classics as *Back in Black* and *Highway to Hell*. In a slicker mode, he was at the controls for *Foreigner 4*, and he gave the Cars their most successful record ever with *Heartbreak City*. Lange's own biggest success was with Def Leppard's 14-million-selling *Hysteria* in 1987. That album in particular had piqued Adams's interest.

"Bryan had been wanting to work with me for a while," Lange told Larry LeBlanc in *Canadian Composer*. "He phoned one day to ask if I fancied writing a song. I happened to be free so we started writing together."

The first songs of their union had been "Thought I'd Died and Gone to Heaven," "Touch the Hand" and "If You Want to Leave Me." The second session saw the reworking of some of the Adams/Vallance songs, in particular "Depend on Me," and eventually "House Arrest," "Do I Have to Say the Words" and "There Will Never Be Another Tonight."

It was after that second meeting that the relationship gelled, recalled Adams. "There were about six songs altogether," he told Mulligan. "Mutt said, 'I think we have a real focus for this album now, let's write six more songs—by this time, I already had thirty songs.... The problem I had up until that point was that there was no focus for the record—even though I had written all these songs, there was no direction.... What Mutt was able to do with me was take all those ideas and contain them and say, 'We're going that way.'"

Adams booked time in London in June to write more material with Lange. Those in the know groaned. It was the teaming of the world's two most tenacious, nitpicking perfectionists.

In 1976, it had taken Lange just ten days to record the classic *Heat Treatment* for Graham Parker. Over the years, much like Adams, he had become such a perfectionist that the sixty-minute *Hysteria* took three years of studio work.

"I thought I was a stickler for getting it right but Mutt is even more so," laughed Adams to LeBlanc. "He came up with things I would never have thought of." And, said Adams, it was fun. "I remember one day we wrote three lyrics for three different songs, literally laughing with tears in our eyes, sitting over dinner. To me, that's the way to work."

"It was very natural for us to work together because we both write in the same way," confirmed Lange to LeBlanc. "However, I probably changed the songs more than he ever has before. I changed them a ton of times. We'd have a track recorded and, even if he had done the lead vocal, or if we'd done the lyrics three times, if we decided it wasn't good enough, we'd change the whole thing. I've always done that but it was very new to Bryan."

Adams told *Q* magazine: "[Lange] made me realize there really were no rules, and that a song just has to have something special, no matter what it is—that you have to come up with it, make it work, stretch it, rip it apart, strip it down, take its clothes off and see how it looks."

The two became kindred spirits through much more than just songwriting. "He improved my spiritual life," Adams told Bill Deverell in *Saturday Night*. "I'm not incredibly religious or spiritual, but I learned a lot of ways from him, the laws of karma. I read books on his path and it's very interesting."

With Lange's influence, Adams, already off red meat for health reasons, became a dedicated vegetarian. "I don't eat any fish or eggs," he told Deverell. "I don't know what tree a fish grows on.... People out there eating ten Twinkies a day; you've got migraine headaches, your eyes are red, you're scratching, teeth decaying: you're eating the wrong thing. Zap a hamburger in, go down to the game, slug a few beers and a hot dog in, and I'm fine, next thing you know you wake up a few weeks later with spots all over your forehead and you wonder, Jesus, where did *that* come from?"

They spent the month of June writing and demoing songs at Olympic Studios and at Mutt's home—dedicating themselves to the task at hand. The writing sessions would start with Lange and Adams on acoustic guitars and incorporate

Lange's Fairlight computer and a few other gadgets.

By early July, Adams had ten songs he felt were ready to go to tape. He was scheduled to participate in the Prince's Trust thirteenth birthday concerts in Birmingham July 18 and 19, but pulled out in favour of recording when both Little Mountain Sound and Bob Clearmountain became available at the same time. Adams, with apologies to the prince, left for Vancouver.

He spent the next few months recording the songs with Clearmountain and engineer Mike Fraser—the bed tracks at Little Mountain, the vocals at Cliffhanger, his home studio. "Then," Adams told LeBlanc, "Mutt and I had a little gathering and decided it would be better if we recorded together."

Most everyone else disagreed, knowing full well the lengthy process ahead. Mickey Curry, for one, also admitted to expecting a personality clash, or at least a clash of styles.

"At first I wondered how this whole connection was going to work for Bryan," he told the fan club. "I mean, Mutt sings, plays everything, and sings backup vocals.... I heard a couple of tracks off some [Adams song] demos and immediately I knew it was Mutt Lange stuff."

"I don't think I could have chosen a better person if I had to for a lot of reasons," Adams told *Music Express*. "His influence is evident throughout the record. He particularly helped with my vocals; he had some definite ideas on how I should sound. He pushed me to get more familiar with the songs, to inject my own personality into them. I could relate to this because I always sing better live once I've worked with the songs a lot."

"I've always perceived Bryan as a naughty kind of rocker having fun and that's how I insisted this album should go," Lange told LeBlanc. "This record is a slightly different style for him. It's a little more rock 'n' roll, a little harder-edged. To me, it's like taking Bryan's five biggest hits and expanding on them. Also we like Bad Company and Free...those classic bands that had Bryan's [type of] voice. It's harder than them, but it's that sort of thing."

Throughout the months of sessions, Adams maintained a

relatively high profile. A live acoustic video of "Into the Fire" from his performance at the Budokan was released worldwide, as was a three-song mini-CD with the acoustic version of "Into the Fire" and previously released versions of "Run to You" and "Diana."

While in England, Adams had taken part in an all-star session recutting the Deep Purple classic "Smoke on the Water" in aid of Armenian earthquake victims. In Victoria, B.C, Bryan and Keith had performed "Heaven" with David Foster at a fundraising banquet tied into the David Foster Celebrity Baseball Tournament. Adams didn't stick around to play ball.

He used his home studio to record background vocals for two projects of Bob Clearmountain's, Cindy Bullen's "Don't Let This Love Go Down" and Belinda Carlisle's "Whatever It Takes."

In October 1989 Adams performed two benefit concerts, "A Night for the Environment" at the 86 Street Music Hall in Vancouver. All 1,100 tickets sold out in just seven minutes. That night, a second show was announced for the following evening.

Bryan's thirtieth birthday, November 5, was a surprisingly elegant affair held at the Vancouver Art Gallery, organized by Bruce Allen's office. Waiters circulated through the crowd serving champagne and fancy trays of canapés and hors d'oeuvres; costumed chefs stood by buffet tables laden with caviar, smoked salmon, a baron of roast beef and international delicacies.

Members of the Vancouver Canucks hockey team dropped by to surprise Adams after their game and presented him with a team jersey. Adams was also presented with a life-size Fender guitar birthday cake. He finished off the night by taking a spin around the gallery on one of his many gifts—a new skateboard.

Adams travelled to London November 18 to meet with the Japanese press, to attend Tina Turner's fiftieth birthday party on the twenty-sixth and, of course, to continue working with Lange. Adams and the band were booked for a huge

New Year's party at the seventy-thousand-seat Tokyo Dome December 31 and January 1. It was billed as the New Year's party of the decade and also featured Huey Lewis, Don Henley, Michael Monroe and Steve Stevens. Also in Japan, the audio track of the "Live In Belgium" show, plus the acoustic version of the song "Into the Fire," were being released in the new year as a CD/cassette called *Live, Live, Live*.

Adams was back in Vancouver the first week of December and promptly rolled into the studio again with the band. He had Christmas with family and friends and left for the Japanese dates two days later. He was back in Vancouver—and back in the studio—the first week in January.

Mickey Curry told the fan-club newsletter that all the tracks were redone and that he had laid down eighteen to twenty new ones in a week and a half. Complained Curry: "Bryan would fly back to England to work with Mutt, and every time he came back we would end up recutting things.... It was tough trying to be the professional that I am supposed to be. Some of the songs were being recut for the fourth or fifth time. What we ended up doing was putting the original twenty-four-track demos up on one machine, and using another machine to record my parts. I played note for note over the Fairlight drums—we would go bar by bar, stop the tape, check it and then move on. If I missed one note, a high-hat beat or cymbal crashes, we'd recut it until they matched exactly what was played on the demos."

In a subsequent issue of *Modern Drummer* magazine, Curry admitted how little he had finally contributed to *Waking Up the Neighbours*. "Mutt did all the programming," he told writer Robyn Flans, "though much of the stuff came from my original ideas. A lot of the parts were played and then put into the [synthesizer]. The only *physical* thing I did was doubling all the cymbals track because the machine just sounded like shit."

By January, Bob Rock was engineering the sessions. "He's a nice guy who knows exactly when to take a break," said Curry. In the middle of the month, Adams returned to Lon-

don, this time for an extended (re)writing hiatus with Lange.
It was interrupted on February 21 when he and Keith Scott
flew to Los Angeles to take part in a pre-Grammies broadcast
called Grammy Week Live and, with the band, play a showcase for the Pollack Media convention of radio executives.
The performance took place at the legendary Charlie Chaplin
soundstage on the A & M Studios lot. Adams drew a standing-room-only crowd of six hundred and turned in a solid
ninety–minute set of hits, playing just one new song.

They returned to Vancouver to attend Bob Rock's February 24 wedding. The next morning Adams was again on a
plane for London. Although Lange was more prone to work
half days on a project, Adams spent time in the studio on his
own during the week—but not always on weekends. And
with Lange also on another project, Russell and Adams had
more than the usual leisure intervals over February and
March. Most weekends saw them on outings such as a visit
to the Imperial War Museum, various palaces around the
countryside including Gloucestershire, home of Prince
Charles, and a trip to Stonehenge (in the pouring rain). They
also took in a few stage plays like Oscar Wilde's *Salome* and
the elaborate hit musical *Miss Saigon*.

Adams was back in Canada March 18 for the Juno Awards.
He had kept organizers guessing, but he put in a surprise
appearance to hand out the final award of the night, Album
of the Year, won by Toronto's Alannah Myles. (Coinciden-
tally, Myles was suing Bruce Allen for comments he had
made at a Canadian music conference, including a reference
to "Alotta Miles.")

While in Toronto, Adams did a voice track for a twenty-
four-minute Canadian cartoon called *The Real Story of the
Three Little Kittens*. He played Hoodwink, a bounty-hunt-
ing, clumsy, boisterous "low-down, no-good, dirty rat."
Legendary Hollywood star Lauren Bacall provided the voice
of the evil ice queen, Freezelda.

A few days later he was back in London with Lange, ready
to make another stab at recording. Before settling into the
routine, he provided a background vocal for his song "Feels

Like Forever," being recorded by Eric Carmen, and he took a last minute sightseeing trip through France with Vicki and Andrew Catlin, Bryan's tour photographer since *Into the Fire* and his best buddy next to Beanbag. Catlin was his most constant companion in England next to Russell and Lange.

Adams came home only briefly in June, and at that point the term *home* was relative. He lived in a flat in London with Russell, and the home in Vancouver was still very much a working studio—virtually every area of the house had patch bays wiring them to the control room in the basement, and a select but steady stream of artists wandered through the rooms. While Adams was in London, Billy Joel recorded part of his album at the house, and on his June visit Adams added a vocal track to a David Foster tune, "River of Love." It was probably more homelike to Ron Obvious, the recording engineer and technician in charge of Cliffhanger, not to mention a seemingly endless parade of contractors and other workers tending to the house and studio, mostly under the watchful eye of Jane Clark.

When the traffic became too much, Adams took action. To reclaim his residence, he bought a heritage building in downtown Vancouver's old Gastown district and began extensive renovations for a new recording facility. The studio, to be called the Warehouse, would be state-of-the-art, and would eventually house all the gear from Cliffhanger, and then some. In typical Adams fashion, though, his perfectionism meant a multiyear project.

The summer of 1990 saw Adams and Allen put the band together for a handful of dates around Europe, including a three-day festival in Mifyns, Denmark, before a crowd of some seventy-five thousand with Alannah Myles and Bob Dylan. They also played the annual Rosskilde, Denmark, festival after the two headline acts, the Cure and Sinead O'Connor, cancelled out at the last minute. Little Feat and Canadian Jeff Healey were also on that bill.

Following those two dates, Adams promptly retreated once again to London, but returned to the stage in mid-July for one of the most momentous occasions of his career. He performed in *The Wall*, an elaborate Pink Floyd rock opera staged by exPink Floyd guitarist Roger Waters at the Potsdamer Platz in Berlin, a thirty-five-acre plot adjacent to the then-intact Berlin Wall.

"I'm one of the few guys who can say I played East, West and Middle Berlin," Adams joked to Keith Sharp in *Music Express*. Waters had called Adams personally and asked him to do the show. The live audience numbered two hundred thousand, and the concert was broadcast to an estimated one billion viewers in thirty countries. The $8 million production had been billed as the largest and most ambitious musical event ever staged.

Backdrops and props included a sixty-by-six-hundred-foot foam-brick wall strategically erected in front of the performers during the first two hours of the show by British, American, East and West German and Russian soldiers; projections of huge animated images on the completed structure; and the destruction of the wall amid a crescendo of music, fireworks, flamebursts and lasers at the end of the night. The performance also featured real bombers flying overhead; helicopters with searchlights sweeping the crowd; and six-storey-high inflated puppets floating through on cue.

Thomas Dolby, Joni Mitchell, Sinead O'Connor, Van Morrison, Cyndi Lauper, the Scorpions, the Chieftains, the Hooters and a myriad of international actors, dancers and orchestral musicians were among the other performers.

Backed by Roger Waters's band, Adams was scheduled to sing three songs: a solo performance of "Young Lust"; a duet with Waters titled "Empty Spaces"; and, with the rest of the cast, the finale, "Tide Is Turning." The day prior to the concert was spent in a full dress rehearsal.

"I was sensitive about being out of my element—which I feel I am when I don't know what's technically going on behind the scenes," Adams told Sharp, who attended the event. "Sure enough, my biggest nightmare occurred just fifteen minutes before I was due to go on. The PA blew up! I go running over to Bruce screaming, 'Bruce there's no PA!' He screams back, 'What the fuck do you want me to do?'

Luckily they had taped the night before at rehearsals so they ran the tape in sync. Then the PA came on but I had no monitors. I was rattled because I thought it would go again. I actually went into autopilot. I started off singing 'Empty Spaces,' and everyone in the crowd had these paper masks which they held in the air. I'm looking out at the audience and there's these 200,000 pink faces staring back at me. I don't know if I even sang the right words."

Although the house sound was nonexistent, the mikes had remained live for the broadcast feed, and so the video and audio recordings remained unscathed. The concert was released on a hot-selling double CD in August—the artists donated their royalties to a disaster relief fund—and "Young Lust" received decent airplay as one of the singles.

Adams went from the highs of *The Wall* to the woes of Live in the Park in Calgary, Alberta the following month. Adams and Allen had agreed to a rare Canadian appearance at an outdoor festival, Live in the Park, August 17, for what was rumoured to be very big money. The bill was also to include three other top Canadian artists, the Pursuit of Happiness, Blue Rodeo and the Tragically Hip. The local promoter needed crowds of at least twelve to fifteen thousand at the fifty-thousand-seat seat venue, but just a few days before showtime sales had only reached 5,500. With poor weather in the region, things were not expected to improve. The promoter was drastically underfinanced, and the show's future was in doubt.

Bruce Allen told the press that Adams did not want to see the show cancelled and had said: "Let's try to hold it together. I don't want to stiff Calgary." Whatever the reason, Allen and Adams made a concerted effort to keep the show alive.

"I think a little bit of it was guilt," observed one insider. "They felt bad because Adams couldn't sell tickets almost in their own backyard, and the promoter was going down the tubes—but I think they genuinely didn't want to stiff the city. They could have just pulled out, kept the deposit and blamed it on poor promotion, but they stuck with it and gave two hundred percent—they really worked hard."

Bruce Allen publicist Kim Blake told Jeff Bateman of *The Record* that it was Adams himself who insisted that the show go on. Said Blake: "When he heard the news, Bryan said 'wait a minute, I flew my band in from New York. I've got all my equipment here. Forget it, we're going to do this.' Bruce said that if it wasn't for Bryan pushing for this, we never would have stuck our neck out."

Adams and Allen turned the production into a free concert. Adams dropped his fee, as did the other acts that played—the Ontario bands didn't fly out—while Bruce Allen convinced both the production crew to work at cost and Labatt's brewery to cover the other expenses. Refunds were given to paying customers while the gates swung open for a nonpaying audience of twenty-seven thousand.

To add insult to injury, it rained—but only during the encore. Adams jumped right in and sang "Summer of '69" drenched to the skin, electric guitar and all.

The band had gathered in Vancouver for a quick rehearsal prior to the Calgary concert. The day before the show, Bruce and Bryan chartered a yachtlike pleasure boat and invited the band, Bryan's family and a few friends—including Andrew Catlin, visiting from England—for a late-afternoon harbour dinner cruise. The day following the concert, Adams and Catlin embarked on a driving tour across British Columbia in a touring car, making their way back to Vancouver via a meandering scenic route and dropping in on interesting towns and villages along the way. A book on British Columbia ghost towns was among their collection of maps and brochures, and the two tourists made a point of seeking out as many as possible.

When they returned to Vancouver, Catlin got to work on a photo shoot for the new album. It took place on the roof of the four-storey office building next to Bruce Allen's, and Adams and Allen spent the better part of the session throwing small rocks and pebbles at passers-by.

September proved an exciting month. For the first time, Adams broke down and sang the national anthem at a sporting event: His rendition of "O Canada" officially started the Molson Indy Car Races in Vancouver September 2. The event was a big thrill for Bruce Allen, one of the world's biggest racing fans and the co-owner of a NASCAR Winston Cup circuit stock-car racing team.

There was still life in the five-year-old *Reckless*, climbing the Dutch charts along with "Summer of '69." The album peaked at #10, the single at #4. And for the first time ever, Adams was booked to play South America. On September 28, he headlined "Rock in Chile," a three-day concert series at a fifty-five-thousand-seat stadium in Santiago. Ex–Rolling Stone Mick Taylor and his band opened the show.

Adams had been approached by the promoters just two weeks prior to the date in an attempt to boost lagging tickets sales. He had never played a South American date, and he had never sold any records in Chile (which was under the thumb of right-wing dictator General Augusto Pinochet), but he nonetheless accomplished their goal. He ended up outselling the combined ticket sales of both David Bowie and Eric Clapton—respectively the headliners the day before and the day after Adams.

The date had not been without a few problems, the main one being Tommy Mandel's refusal to do the concert. The show fell on a Jewish holiday, and Mandel elected to stay in New York with his family. Although Adams was able to call in an accommodating John Hannah at the last minute, he was obviously not happy with Mandel's priorities.

After South America, Adams returned to England to "rework some arrangements" for the new album. He was back in Canada October 24 at Ottawa's Government House for a ceremony marking his appointment as a Member of the Order of Canada, the highest honour for service or achievement that Canada can bestow upon its citizens. A month later, the Canadian Recording Industry Association honoured Adams as one of three Canadian Artists of the Decade at a gala charity dinner in Toronto. (The others were k.d. lang and Rush.)

Adams spent most of December in England, continuing to

work on the tracks. He returned to Vancouver for Christmas and managed to squeeze in a ski vacation in Whistler with brother Bruce and Beanbag.

By the first week of January 1991, Adams was again in London, but by now the end was in sight. He announced that the album was in the final stage of production.

13

Everything He Does

"It's been four years between albums. Aren't you afraid your fans will forget you?" queried his critics. "I think fans forget you faster if you put out a bad record," Adams responded.

It was January 6, 1991. Adams was on a plane back to England after not much more than a week in Canada. This was now the norm—he had spent not much more than a month of the whole previous year at his home in Vancouver.

The recording process was over—or so it was believed; Adams and Lange were about to do the "final" mixes. The release date for *Waking Up the Neighbours* was now April. Meanwhile, the European tour with ZZ Top had been announced for June. They worked through to the end of February; the going was slow—which came as no surprise to anyone involved. Adams spent the first week of March at A & M Studios in Los Angeles, mixing a few tunes with Bob Clearmountain. "I think we would still be there today if we hadn't brought Bob Clearmountain in to mix the tracks," Adams told *Music Express* publisher Keith Sharp. "He didn't stand for any nonsense. He'd say, 'You've got it. Try any more and you'll lose it!'"

Late in March, after a two-day photo session in New York, Adams returned immediately to London, with Keith Scott in tow. Scott had been spending much of his time recording guitar tracks in England, and Adams had another job for him. The fateful call had come from Michael Kamen—via his former A & M Records buddy, David Kershenbaum—and Adams was now at work with Lange on a song for the movie *Robin Hood: Prince of Thieves.*

Lange and Adams used Little Feat's Bill Payne on piano. It was a request from Morgan Creek—Payne and his band were signed to that label. Larry Klein (Joni Mitchell's husband) was credited on bass, Mickey Curry on drums, and of course Keith Scott on guitar.

Bob Clearmountain flew to London to do the mix; there was no time for the Adams/Lange perfectionism. When it was all over, Adams went to Vancouver for a few days, and took another brief ski holiday, in Whistler, British Columbia.

The lyrics were written in just a few hours. In a matter of a few weeks, "(Everything I Do) I Do It For You" was written, arranged, recorded, mixed, videoed and shipped off to the movie company. They shot the video of the song in Somerset, England, May 17 and 18. Keith Scott, Dave Taylor and Tommy Mandel took part in the filming, but Mickey Curry was unavailable, so a local drummer was used as a stand-in. The end of the month saw all the band and crew gathered in a rehearsal studio on the outskirts of London to spend a week preparing for the monthlong European tour.

At that point, the original twelve songs for the album had been completed, as well as the *Robin Hood* soundtrack song. Technically, *Waking Up the Neighbours* was finished. But Adams and Lange came up with two more songs. The inspiration was twofold: it carried on from the "I Do It For You" writing sessions, and Adams had broken up with Vicki Russell. The two songs were "Vanishing," originally written about the disappearing heritage sites, but ultimately another generic love song; and "Hey Honey, I'm Packin' You In," partially written with lyrics sent to Adams by Russell after he moved out of their shared flat to his own home in London.

"We had a great time together," he told the *Daily Express.* "She's really an open, straight-forward person, but we drifted apart. It was sad, but not bitter."

The song itself seems to shed some light on the situation.

"The lyric is a total piss-take on an argument Vicki and I had all the time," Adams told *Music Express*. "She'd say 'I'm packin' you in,' and I'd say 'No, I'm packin' you in.' So one day she wrote it down and I thought it was a good enough lyric for a song."

They both got in their shots—although Russell suggested the title and several lines of the song, much of it obviously came from Adams. The words tell of arguments over food (faddy diets), the car (smashing it up), razors (dull) and money (spent). The antagonist is accused of having a hand in the till, and told to forget about a wedding ring and to get on back to his/her next of kin. The song is reported to be more acrimonious than the breakup, however. Russell and Adams remained good friends.

Adams, Lange and Clearmountain were all hard at work writing, recording and mixing when the band arrived in London to rehearse. Tommy Mandel was asked to provide a Hammond organ track on a song late in May, and spent days on standby waiting for a call that never came. The first of June, it became obvious the session would not happen before the start of the ZZ Top tour.

A video for the first album single, "Can't Stop this Thing We Started," was scheduled between June 3 and 6. It was shot by Kevin Godley (ex–10 cc) at Pinewood Studios in London, using the same gyrating stage as in the film *The Poseidon Adventure*.

After just a few media interviews—MTV most notably—the tour kicked off June 8 at the Jubeck Festival in Germany. Adams headlined that date, but the rest of the tour was billed with ZZ Top. Most of the dates were outdoor festivals in Germany and France, but other stops included Denmark, Switzerland and England. Luckily for Adams, there were often two-to-three-day breaks between concerts, and that allowed him to return to London every few days to continue work on the album.

As Adams toured, Mutt Lange and Bob Clearmountain would set up a mix for a song back in London. Adams would fly in every few days to approve (and improve) their work.

"It was actually strange," Adams told "Rockline." "It was a bizarre way of working. I was on tour and every day off I had, I'd fly back to London to do mixes so it was back and forth, back and forth. It was a good thing to do because while we were mixing I was changing the songs around lyrically."

They had been on the road for only a few days when they saw "I Do It For You" take off in a big way. The crowds live were eating it up—and so were the record retailers. The song had advance orders for 350,000 copies.

The $67 million film premiered in over 2,800 theatres across North America June 14 and collected an incredible $26 million in box office receipts. It registered as having the eighth-best debut weekend in film history.

Along with the good news came some bad. Bryan's grandfather—Conrad's father—had died that month. Conrad came over for the funeral and spent some time with his son as the band toured Europe.

On June 17 in Baden-Baden, Germany, Adams performed a private show in an airplane hanger for more than three thousand service personnel just back from the Persian Gulf War. The military emphasis was fitting—Bryan met with a number of commanders and dignitaries and got a tour of the base that included a hands-on look at an F-18 jet. Onstage, he was presented with a plaque and a model of a fighter jet.

A stopover in London the day after the Baden-Baden show saw Tommy Mandel again on standby, ready to record an organ track. Again, it didn't happen.

The band returned to London early in July in preparation for their first outdoor performance ever in Britain, and the last date on the tour. Adams and the band played the Milton Keynes Bowl on July 6 with ZZ Top, Thunder and the Little Angels in front of sixty-five-thousand screaming fans. It was one of his best shows ever. He was well received by audience and reviewers alike. Backstage was schmoozer heaven. In attendance were Brian May, Paul Rodgers, Roger Waters and actor Robert Downey, Jr.

Mandel's sessions had been scheduled for just before the big festival, and this time he made it. They put the finishing keyboard touches on the two new songs just after the show. Adams and the band did a last-minute performance July 10 on "Top of the Pops" —performing "(Everything I Do) I Do It For You." The band headed home to North America, while Adams returned to the studio in London for a few more "finishing touches." They announced that the album would be released in September.

Adams met with the Japanese press in London August 5, then flew out to Vancouver. He and the band were booked for a concert in Revelstoke, British Columbia, on the tenth. It was an informal makeup date for his no-show at the Music 91 festival series and the Juno Awards. It would be his only North American appearance that year.

Revelstoke is a small community near the British Columbia/Alberta border, seven hours out of Vancouver by road, nestled on a lake in the mountains. Roughly twelve thousand tickets had been sold for the outdoor show. The site— Bryan's own choice—was along one of the scenic routes taken during his and Andrew Catlin's driving tour of B.C. Catlin was again on board with Adams, as was Andy Gill, a reporter for *Q* magazine, but this time, they took a six-seater jet.

Backstage between the afternoon sound check and the evening concert the adventurous Adams asked the locals about recreational activities in the area. His eyes lit up when he heard the words *white-water rafting* and he immediately put the wheels in motion for an expedition. Adams, Allen, Catlin, Gill and a photographer made the trek. The subsequent article in *Q* magazine was subtitled "The most fun you can have in a rubber suit."

The concert later that night opened with the *Reckless* rocker "She's Only Happy When She's Dancin'" and continued to feature all Adams's hits—many of the songs from *Reckless*, a few from *Cuts Like a Knife* and a couple from *Into the Fire*, and even "Diana." It also included a couple from the new album, *Waking Up the Neighbours*—"Can't Stop this Thing We Started" and, of course, "(Everything I Do) I Do It For You." The set closed with "Summer of '69."

"Bryan plays his Everyman role to the hilt," reviewed Gill, as he marvelled at the fact that Adams performed in the same sweatshirt and jeans he had worn that afternoon. He sported ordinary biker boots and played through two battered old Vox amplifiers.

After the concert, Bryan played Grizzly Adams. He and Catlin stayed for a few extra days in the Revelstoke area and camped, rode horseback and did some more white-water rafting. (Photos from the trip appeared in the *Waking Up the Neighbours* cassette and CD booklet).

On August 19, Adams and the band returned to London to shoot two more videos—"Thought I'd Died and Gone to Heaven" and "All I Want Is You," again with Kevin Godley at Pinewood Studios. In London, Adams was scheduled for a dozen or so back-to-back print, radio and TV interviews—a tiny fraction of the requests—and September 1 saw him in Paris, taping two more television shows. Then it was back to Canada to prepare for the September 24 album release.

By this point, Adams, on the basis of "(Everything I Do) I Do It For You," was about the biggest news in entertainment. It was the #1 song in fourteen countries, including the U.S., Australia, Japan, South Africa and all of Scandinavia. In the U.K., it was one week away from breaking the record for the most consecutive weeks in the top position, eclipsing Slim Whitman's "Rose Marie," which had lasted eleven weeks in 1955. For Adams, the thrill had come the previous week, when he passed Paul McCartney's "Mull of Kintyre"—which had gone nine weeks in 1977—and McCartney wished him luck in a U.K. newspaper. The single "Can't Stop this Thing We Started," released internationally on August 27, was also shooting up the charts.

His success in Britain had made Adams a top priority for the infamous British tabloids—a reporter and photographer from the *Sun* in London even hired a helicopter to fly over his house in Vancouver. They interviewed his old odd-job bosses, his neighbours, the local shopkeepers, and anyone else who would talk to them. When they started badgering his family, Adams finally consented to meet them for a beer in the Town

Pump, a club downstairs from Bruce Allen's office.

Adams, with Keith Scott, did a forty-five-minute in-store autograph session the day before the album release, but he refused interviews with almost all the North American media—especially print. It was another sign of his now almost nonexistent rapport with the press. Two weeks before the release date, A & M Records had let a small gathering of Vancouver music critics hear the album, and according to Tom Harrison in the Vancouver Province, "hell got a new name" when Adams and Allen got wind of it.

According to Harrison, Allen staged one of his famous "wig-outs" and was all over the A&M executives in Toronto, who in turn frantically called the attending press to ask them not to review the album. Neither of the city's two daily papers complied. Both reviews were thumbs-up, but the incident still widened the chasm between Adams and the media.

"The sign on [Bruce Allen publicist] Kim Blake's door should say Security, not Publicity," commented one source. "Adams doesn't want publicity—he does everything he can to avoid it."

The *Daily Mirror* reported with some surprise that Adams had topped a cover-star survey by appearing on 569,477 printed copies of music and teen magazine covers over a five-week span. "He lacks Marky Mark's teen appeal, Dannii Minogue's vibrancy and—most significantly—has rarely been available for photo shoots or interviews." They added that the record company only had one set of studio photographs.

Around the time of the release of *Waking Up the Neighbours*, another battle was brewing. Never one to respond well to authority, Adams already had a dim view of the Canadian government. He and Bruce Allen were constantly at odds with Canada Customs. Adams travelled with American lights, Canadian sound and a mixed bag of gear and personnel. Although he had no problem entering the States, his return to Canada to play a date meant the third degree and searches on top of duty charges, paperwork and, most annoyingly, the posting of a nonrefundable bond.

Allen took particular offence at the various regulations, grants and loans put in place with an eye to industry development. Such government programs hadn't existed when Allen was coming up in the ranks, but it was just as well— to Allen (and Adams) not making it on your own was cheating. Allen found the grants particularly irksome: He and his acts were paying more taxes, or so he thought, than the rest of the homegrown industry combined—thus the government was using *his* money to fund his competition.

One of the government programs that the two had often disdained was the protectionist Canadian content rulings for broadcasters. To make the FM stations more distinguishable from the AM and to protect the Canadian music industry, the FM licensees were heavily regulated. A song's musical style, the citizenship of the artist, producers and writers, and even the age of the song all dictated whether a radio station was allowed to play it, and if so, how often. The stations were closely monitored by the Canadian Radio and Television Commission.

Most rock stations were told to play between twenty and thirty percent Canadian material, and they were allowed to repeat Canadian songs more often than foreign ones. With a performance royalty paying the songwriters every time a song is broadcast, the Canadian acts had the opportunity to make quite a bit more money.

The CRTC judged a song's citizenship with a four-category "MAPL" system—Music, Artist, Production, Lyrics. The recording had to have at least two Canadian parts to qualify. Adams had full points as the artist, but only half points in the two songwriting categories. The way the rules worked, two halves were not allowed to be added up to a whole. Had Adams solely written music and Lange the lyrics, or vice versa, he would have been given status. Writing with Lange in both categories cancelled out the Canadian content in each. And with the vast majority of the album recorded and mixed in England, Adams also failed in the production section.

Waking Up the Neighbours was deemed not a Canadian record. Adams became the "Un-Canadian."

Ironically, at the same time, singles on the charts by British rocker Rod Stewart and U.S. singer Bonnie Raitt were given Canadian status. Both had been written by Toronto-based songwriters.

At first Allen said the CRTC ruling made no difference to him or to Adams, they had no plans to fight it, and they would not continue to comment. But, as it turned out, neither could keep quiet for long. The situation soon led to a small civil war.

"Try walking up to Bryan and say, 'Hey, guess what, Bryan? You've lived here all your life but you're not a Canadian artist.' That's how ridiculous it is," raged Allen to the press.

"To have it come from the Canadian government to me is disappointing really," Adams told "Rockline." "The country's caught up in all this bureaucracy and bureaucracy in the arts is a disaster.... Get the government out of the music business, man!"

Allen had booked a tour of Europe for the rest of the fall, and had scheduled a cross-Canada run for the New Year. Adams wanted plenty of rehearsal time—the band gathered in Vancouver well in advance of the October 24 start date. On October 6, Adams and the band played their now-customary pretour warm-up benefit, this one a last-minute call to help out Vancouver musician Brian MacLeod, a veteran of top Canadian bands Chilliwack and the Headpins, who had just checked into an expensive Houston medical clinic to fight a rare form of cancer. Allen and business partner Sam Feldman—who managed MacLeod—put together a show in a forty-eight-hour period featuring Adams, Colin James, MacLeod protégée Chrissy Steele, a reunited Loverboy and Chilliwack's Bill Henderson.

Adams and the band ran through most of the new tunes, threw in a few older favourites, and then ended the show by trotting out all the night's performers for a loose jam on "Let's Spend the Night Together," "Louie Louie" and "Stand by Me." They raised over $50,000.

The world tour kicked off on October 24 in Belfast, Northern Ireland with all the dates in Europe—thirty-five shows in sixteen countries—completely sold out well in advance.

They shot the video for "There Will Never Be Another Night," during the Sheffield performances on November 1 and 2, and that song was released as the third single the following week as they played three back-to-back shows at Wembley Arena.

The Wembley concerts were used as the big showcase dates. England had become Adams's strongest market. It had previously been among his weakest—he had never had a Top 10 hit in Britain before, and the advance orders for "(Everything I Do) I Do It For You" had been for a mere twelve thousand copies. Now Adams was well past the record for the most consecutive weeks at #1 in the U.K. "Rose Marie" had stayed eleven weeks; at showtime, "(Everything I Do) I Do It For You" was going into its sixteenth week in the top spot.

Press from all areas of the world descended on Wembley, as did a large Canadian contingent of promoters, agents, staff—the Bruce Allen office was there in its entirety—and family, including, of course, Jane and Bill Clark.

The Wembley show's repertoire was representative of the rest of the tour. A capacity crowd of 12,800 was on hand; the opening act was Australia's Baby Animals. On the first of the Wembley nights, Adams and the band opened with "House Arrest" then followed with "Kids Wanna Rock," "Hey Honey I'm Packin' You In," and "Can't Stop this Thing We Started." They went into "It's Only Love," followed by "Cuts Like a Knife," "Take Me Back" and "Thought I'd Died and Gone to Heaven." In an unusual move, Adams performed an acoustic solo rendition of "When the Night Comes," the tune originally penned for Joe Cocker, and then the band played "Heat of the Night".

Adams, A & M Records and Bruce Allen had made the show a special event by flying Slim Whitman in from Jacksonville, Florida. Adams introduced the sixty-six-year-old country singer who came out on the stage dressed in a rhinestone-studded white tuxedo, carrying an equally ornate acoustic guitar. He warbled "Rose Marie," backed by the Adams band. Adams took over on a few choruses, then joined in at the end to finish with a duet.

After Whitman left the stage, Adams swung into "(Everything I Do) I Do It For You" to a strong ovation, then drew an equally strong reaction for "Run to You." He teased the crowd with the opening bars of "Summer of '69," but closed the set with "Somebody." The first encore included "One Night Love Affair," "Long Gone" and "There Will Never Be Another Tonight." The second time they were called back they played Eddie Cochrane's "Come On Everybody," Heaven" and "Summer of '69." Adams had left the stage and the crowd was filtering out when he pulled a surprise finale. The band pulled Adams through a hidden hole behind the drum kit and carried him to the front of the stage to sing a final number, "She's Only Happy When She's Dancing."

In a backstage hospitality room, according to Vancouver *Province* writer Tom Harrison, Slim Whitman and his "taller, slimmer son Byron" Whitman mingled with the "cowboy-hatted, bolero-tied" Bill Clark and other guests munching the British version of sushi—pickled herring, smoked salmon and crab stick on rice. Adams and his personal guests—Mutt Lange, Kevin Godley, Roger Daltrey, Belinda Carlisle and Chrissie Hynde—stayed cloistered in Bryan's private dressing room. (George Harrison, Eric Clapton and Elton John were no-shows).

The next day, 1,500 fans packed a giant record store for an autograph-signing session. Later in the day, Adams was interviewed live on a British talk show and performed "There Will Never Be Another Tonight."

Backstage after the last night at Wembley, Adams was presented with a plaque from the publishers of *The Guinness Book of World Records* marking his chart-breaking feat. The entourage then gathered at Brown's—one of London's more prestigious nightclubs—as A & M Records hosted a belated birthday party for Adams and six hundred guests.

Meanwhile back in North America, the Bruce Allen office had received word that former Klu Klux Klan leader David Duke was using "(Everything I Do) I Do It For You" in his campaign for Governor of Louisiana. The song was being played during a slide show at political rallies. It featured pastoral scenes of Louisiana, and Duke with his young daughters.

Adams instructed Allen to get the legal department on the case to stop Duke from using the song, and then issued a statement to the press from Rotterdam. Said Adams: "Everything I am about and everything I stand for is diametrically opposed to David Duke. The use of 'Everything I Do' in his campaign is a complete and intentional corruption of the message and intent of my song."

He also asked the state's radio stations not to play the song until the election was over so that listeners wouldn't be subliminally influenced to vote for the man.

Well into the tour of Europe, one of the odder performances was a special "in-home" appearance by Adams and the band—a fully amplified concert at an MTV contest winner's home in Bartelsdorf, Germany, on November 23. The prize had been Adams's own idea, and it worked brilliantly—or at least would have, had the winner not had a flat the size of a postage stamp. After an afternoon of scrambling, an alternate location in the form of a small pub was found, and Adams and the band performed a set for the woman and 124 of her closest friends.

The last stop on the tour was December, 18, with two first-ever shows in Reykjavik, Iceland.

Adams was home in Vancouver for Christmas; he and his brother, Bruce, took some vacation time and went sailing and scuba diving at an undisclosed location.

Bruce Allen, meanwhile, spent the season planning the next year's touring schedule: New Zealand February 8, then Australia for six shows, followed by Japan for a dozen shows through to March 7. The United States was scheduled for the spring, then back to Europe and the U.K. for stadium and festival dates. But first, Adams was going to tour Canada.

The Canadian leg of the Waking Up the World tour was scheduled to begin January 13 in Sydney, Nova Scotia, and wrap up in Vancouver on the thirty-first. After his time off, and a few days before the start of the tour, Adams had flown directly to New York City to attend a Grammy Awards announcement. Adams was nominated for six awards—the most ever for a Canadian. "(Everything I Do) I Do It For You" was up for Record of the Year, Song of the Year, Best Pop Vocal Performance (Male) and Best Song Written Specifically for a Motion Picture. "Can't Stop this Thing We Started" was nominated for Best Rock Vocal Performance Solo and Best Rock Song.

Over the next few weeks, announcements would also be made that Adams was up for an Academy Award and an unprecedented seven Juno Awards. By this point, the *Robin Hood* song had made it to the #1 position in twenty-one countries, and sales were climbing to the eight-million mark. *Waking Up the Neighbours* was peaking at #6 in Billboard.

To pacify the Canadian media, who were clamouring for interviews, Adams spoke at a large press conference the day prior to the first show in Sydney. But instead of resulting in fewer requests, the event generated even more. With Adams refusing to comment on the Canadian-content ruling when it was first delivered in late September, the initial media response had been a small flurry of activity that passed quickly. At the January conference, a reporter asked Adams to express his views on the Canadian content rulings, and he did just that. He gave honest answers, delivered coldly but evenly, and they added up to quite a tirade against the Canadian government. He was again on the front page of every newspaper in the country, and he remained close to the front for weeks. His position was the ongoing subject of editorials, letters, statements and rebuttals.

The press, by this point, were insatiable—the Canadian media, according to Bruce Allen, were "lined up at the trough," and, of course, the U.K. tabs were having their own feast.

With Adams virtually incommunicado, they turned their

attention to his family. Even quiet brother Bruce was in the limelight as reporters rang him up and cameras appeared in his office. Bruce, a successful denturist, lived near Bryan in North Vancouver and had his office in the suburb of Coquitlam. Caught off guard, and likely a little pleased with the attention, he did give a few interviews—much to Bryan's chagrin, even though the younger brother only repeated the public comments Bryan had already made.

The worst, though, was yet to come. The London *Sun* reporters, still on an "information at all costs" crusade, were back in Vancouver that January, appearing on Jane's doorstep, and also at Conrad's house, near Victoria, B.C, on Vancouver Island, a ferry ride away from Vancouver. Conrad was semiretired and living in the suburb of Colwood. He was still a fighter. He had successfully run for alderman of the borough, but had argued incessantly with his colleagues and quit in a huff. He went on to form the B.C. Property Tax Reform Committee.

Sun reporter Peter Willis played Conrad against Jane, and vice versa, obviously taking advantage of both their tempers, and and came up with some strong words supplied by both parties. The clincher would come a few weeks later, when the paper unearthed their divorce documents in the official records office in Ottawa.

The media were already in a feeding frenzy, snapping up the few tidbits of information that fell their way. Adams's relations with the press were at an all-time low. He had been ignoring ninety-percent of his European interview requests, ninety-five percent of the American ones, and ninety-nine percent of the Canadian ones. Adams toyed with them when he could—he responded to the European press's questions about his rustic Canadian roots by launching into a description of a daily trek across the water in his canoe, fetching groceries to cook on his wood-burning stove. He carried it on to America, and came out dressed like a lumberjack on the David Letterman show.

At least one writer poked fun back at Adams—Liam Fey of Dublin's *Hot Press* wrote of the lunch interview that saw the reporter dodging flying particles of partially chewed food as Adams ranted, spat and swore his way through a variety of topics. Fey left Adams's four-letter words intact and offered a vivid blow-by-blow description of his subject's table manners—or lack thereof—in the article. Adams failed to see the humour. The city's largest paper, the Vancouver *Sun*, reran the hated *Hot Press* story on the eve of his hometown concert. Adams was livid.

He continued to deny nearly all media requests. The day of his homecoming show, at least one TV station took their cameras to West Vancouver to film his house (address intact on the door) and to chat up his neighbours.

Backstage at the Pacific Coliseum that night, a small group of approved news photographers waited impatiently as Adams took the stage. The usual procedure was for the press to take pictures during the first three songs of a concert, but they were kept waiting long after the start of the set. When someone finally did appear to usher them out front, the photographers were told they would be restricted to just one song. As they filed into the pit in front of the stage, Adams, in midsong, acknowledged their presence with an ever-so-slight smile and a nod, then pointedly turned away. Adams spent the entire song with his back to the cameras. The message was obvious.

As much as he disdained the press, Adams appreciated the rest of the audience, and he and the band worked hard to entertain. As usual, it was a show devoid of effects and gimmicks—it was just the singer, his band, his songs and the crowd. It was another 'on' night; the trademark Adams voice was in top form; the band was tight and the fans were responsive—his rapport with the fifteen thousand in attendance likened the coliseum to a living room.

He loved and respected his fans. They loved and respected him back.

Herein lies the key to Bryan Adams. Success to Adams is respect. That's what it's all about, a lifelong search for respect. And, as one of the most successful artists in the world today, Bryan can rest assured that he has that respect from millions.

Whether his career will surpass the success of "(Everything I Do) I Do It For You," or whether he will be remembered as the singer, cowriter and coproducer of one of the biggest songs in music history, Adams has made his mark in life, just as he was determined to do. He is already the most successful Canadian musician ever—you don't get much bigger than that—but it's a sure bet he will continue in his quest to conquer the rest of the world.

14

So far . . . so good

When Bryan Adams started his long, hard climb to the top
in the early 1980s, he jokingly likened the non-stop slog of
touring and recording to "digging the highway".

Yet by the time 1994 rolled round, the diplomat's son
from Kingston, Ontario, had dug a rock and roll highway
that stretched round the world three times over. Along the
way he'd clawed his way into rock's Hall of Fame: one of
that select band of artists whose album sales are measured
in tens of millions and whose names are household words.

All he'd ever wanted was respect—both as a singer and a
songwriter. And he'd earned it the hard way. It was a fitting
triumph for a rock and roller who has consistently shunned
the limelight and always preferred to let his music do the
talking.

When Bryan Adams the new superstar played his final
show of the 'Waking Up The World'/'So Far So Good' tour
in Salzburg, Austria, on August 14 it was the climax of over
850 days of gruelling, non-stop touring. Over three years
which saw Adams and his band perform 500 shows to an
estimated audience of 3.5 million fans around the globe.

Yet in the midst of the touring mayhem, the loyalty of
Bryan Adams's British fans was not forgotten. Interrupting
his European dates, Adams and his band flew into the UK
on July 14 for a rapturously received outdoor concert at the
Gateshead International Stadium.

Meanwhile the album which launched Adams into the rock and roll stratosphere continued to cause a sensation. And Adams—born on Guy Fawkes Day—is always ready with more musical fireworks to keep his fans happy. Almost unbelievably *Waking Up The Neighbours* was first released way back in July 1991. Over three years later it has notched up sales of over 12 million copies worldwide and topped the album charts in no fewer than fourteen different countries.

To cater for a seemingly insatiable demand for new Adams' material, a greatest hits album was released towards the end of the epic world tour. *So Far So Good* hit the Christmas market at the tail end of 1993. To date it has sold over 12 million copies worldwide, reaching the top selling album slot in nineteen different countries.

And while Adams may have sung 'Please Forgive Me' on the platinum hit single from 'So Far So Good' (a chart topper in ten countries), his millions of fans didn't need to hear any more excuses. No sooner had 'So Far So Good' taken up residence in the album charts, than Bryan was ready with a new hit single, 'All For Love'; the theme song from Disney's 'The Three Musketeers' continued a success-ful association with the movie world. But it was Adams's choice of fellow singers that made everyone really sit up and take notice.

Recording with fellow rock stars Sting and Rod Stewart was just another measure of how far Bryan Adams had travelled since his glam rocking days with Sweeney Todd. The single, a chart topper in fifteen different countries, was nominated for the prestigious MTV Movie Awards, as the 'Best Song of 1994'.

As a live artist too, Bryan Adams had established himself as a legend to rank alongside the all-time greats—from the Rolling Stones through to Bon Jovi, from his teenage heroes Bachman Turner Overdrive through to contemporary stad-ium fillers like U2 and Def Leppard.

And fittingly it was the Rolling Stones—the legendary Glimmer Twins, Mick Jagger and Keith Richards them-selves—who provided an intriguing new chapter of the

Bryan Adams story in the autumn of 1994. The first time Bryan met Jagger, at the infamous Bottomline Club in Los Angeles in 1982, the venerable Stone simply introduced himself as 'Dad'. Then, in October 1994, Bryan Adams was invited to make a guest appearance alongside the Stones during their sell-out tour of the States.

Adams made his first appearance as 'an honorary Rolling Stone' at the monumental New Orleans Superdome on October 10. Over ten years on, the rock and roll wheel had turned full circle. Only a month earlier, Bryan had come up with an even bigger surprise, duetting with italian opera maestro Luciano Pavarotti during a televised concert in Modena, Italy, on September 13!

Back home in Canada, Bryan Adams's greatest ever year was touchingly celebrated at a top-level meeting of record company executives. Shortly before the close of the Poly-gram Managing Directors Conference in Bryan's home town, the star was presented with a custom platinum Fender Stratocaster guitar to signify career sales of over 40 million albums worldwide—one of only a handful of artists to do so.

Then, as Bryan began to wind down and consider new studio projects that would take him well into 1995, A&M released the album that encapsulated the history—and the best—of their reluctant hero.

Of course there will be a new studio album to look forward to next year. As for tour dates, videos, movies even . . . Bryan Adams is as cagey as he's ever been. He's never been prepared to compromise, and no amount of accolades is going to change his character.

Just for a minute, consider the plaudits that spring to mind when you're noting the qualities of the typical rock star. It isn't likely that 'modest', 'workaholic' or 'very unglamorous' would appear on anyone's checklist. Yet each of these terms has been used time and time again in describing Bryan Adams—most often by the artist himself.

With Bryan Adams, what you see is what you get. And that quality alone will ensure that his concert tours will be sell-outs for years to come. He may have hit quadruple platinum, but he's not about to throw it all away.

Instead Bryan Adams ended a meteoric decade in anyone's language by quietly returning to his own roots in Vancouver. Meanwhile we were left with the memories and a long-awaited album to sum up the legend.

Just as it had so many times before, the music was left to do the talking. *Live! Live! Live!*—recorded during the summer of 1988 in Werchler, Belgium, and previously only available in Japan—delivered seventeen red-hot tracks from Adams and the band at their best. Straight, unadorned—and played from the heart.

"All I ever wanted to was play rock and roll," said Bryan Adams. It was his motto when he started. It's still his motto now.

Appendix

BRYAN ADAMS ALBUM LISTINGS

BRYAN ADAMS

Side One

Hiding From Love*
Win Some, Lose Some
Wait And See
Give Me Your Love*
Wasting Time

Side Two

Don't Ya Say It
Remember* (video single)
State Of Mind
Try To See It My Way

Released 1980
Status: Gold (Canada)

———

YOU WANT IT, YOU GOT IT

Side One

Lonely Nights*
One Good Reason*
Don't Look Now
Coming Home*
Fits Ya Good*

Side Two

Jealousy
Tonight
You Want It, You Got It
Last Chance
No One Makes It Right

Released 1981
Status: Platinum (Canada)

———

CUTS LIKE A KNIFE

Side One

The Only One
Take Me Back
This Time*
Straight From The Heart*
Cuts Like A Knife*

Side Two

I'm Ready
What's It Gonna Be
Don't Leave Me Lonely
Let Him Know
The Best Was Yet To Come*

Released 1983
Status: Quadruple Platinum
(Canada);Platinum (US)

———

RECKLESS

Side One

One Night Love Affair*
She's Only Happy When She's
  Dancin'
Run To You*
Heaven*
Somebody*

Side Two

Summer Of '69*
Kids Wanna Rock
It's Only Love* (with Tina Turner)
Long Gone
Ain't Gonna Cry

Released 1984
Status: Diamond and One Plati-
num (Canada); Quadruple Plati-
num (US)

———

INTO THE FIRE

Side One
Heat Of The Night*
Into The Fire
Victim Of Love*
Another Day
Native Son
Side Two
Only The Strong Survive**
Rebel
Remembrance Day
Hearts On Fire*
Home Again

Released 1987
Status: Triple Platinum (Canada)
Platinum (US)

___

*LIVE, LIVE, LIVE ***

She's Only Happy When She's
    Dancin'
It's Only Love
Cuts Like A Knife
Kids Wanna Rock
Hearts On Fire
Take Me Back
The Best Was Yet To Come
Heaven
Heat Of The Night
Run To You
One Night Love Affair*
Long Gone
Summer of '69*
Somebody
Walking After Midnight
I Fought The Law
Into The Fire

Released 1989

___

WAKING UP THE NEIGHBOURS

Is Your Mama Gonna Miss Ya?
Hey Honey, I'm Packin' You In!
Can't Stop This Thing We Started*
Thought I'd Died And Gone To
    Heaven*
Not Guilty
Vanishing
House Arrest
Do I Have To Say The Words?*
There Will Never Be Another
    Tonight*
All I Want Is You*
Depend On Me
(Everything I Do) I Do It For You*
If You Wanna Leave Me (Can I
    Come Too?)
Touch The Hand*
Don't Drop That Bomb On Me

Released 1991

___

SO FAR SO GOOD: GREATEST HITS

Summer of '69
Straight From The Heart
It's Only Love (with Tina Turner)
Can't Stop This Thing We Started
Do I Have To Say The Words?
This Time
Run To You
Heaven
Cuts Like A Knife
(Everything I Do) I Do It For You
Somebody
Kids Wanna Rock
Heat Of The Night
Please Forgive Me

Released 1993

___

BRYAN ADAMS
COMPLETE UK DISCOGRAPHY

SINGLES

Cat. No.	Title
AMS 7460	Let Me Take You Dancing/Don't Turn Me Away (7/79)
AMSP 7460	Let Me Take You Dancing (extended)/Don't Turn Me Away (12″, 7/79)
AMS 7520	Hidin' From Love/Wait And See (3/80)
AMS 8183	Lonely Nights/Don't Look Now (11/81)
AM 103	Straight From The Heart/Lonely Nights (3/83)
AMX 103	Straight From The Heart/Lonely Nights (12″, 3/83)
AM 129	Cuts Like A Knife/Fits Ya Good (7/83)
AMP 129	Cuts Like A Knife/Fits Ya Good/Hidin' From Love ?)(12″, 7/83)
AM 170	One Good Reason (1/84; apparently withdrawn)
AM 224	Run To You/I'm Ready (12/84)
AM 224	Run To You/I'm Ready/Cuts Like A Knife/Lonely Nights (double-pack, 12/84)
AMY 224	Run To You/I'm Ready/Cuts Like A Knife (12″, some in poster sleeve, 12/84)
AM 236	Somebody/Long Gone (2/85)
AMP 236	Somebody/Long Gone (picture disc, 3/85)
AMY 236	Somebody/Long Gone (12″, 2/85)
AM 256	Heaven/Diana (5/85)
AM 256	Heaven/Diana/Straight From The Heart/You Want It, You Got It (double-pack, 5/85)
AMY 256	Heaven/Diana/Fits Ya Good (12″, 5/85)
AM 287	Summer of '69/Kids Wanna Rock (live) (7/85)
AM 267	Summer of '69/Kids Wanna Rock (live)/The Bryan Adamix (12″, 7/85)
AM 285	It's Only Love (with Tina Turner)/The Best Was Yet To Come (11/85)
AM 285	It's Only Love (with Tina Turner)/The Best Was Yet To Come/Somebody Long Gone (double-pack, 11/85)
AMY 285	It's Only Love (with Tina Turner)/The Best Was Yet To Come (12″, 11/85)
AM 297	Christmas Time/Reggae Christmas (12/85)
AMY 297	Christmas Time/Reggae Christmas (12″, 12/85)
AM 295	This Time/I'm Ready (2/86)
AMY 295	This Time/I'm Ready/Lonely Nights (12″, 2/86)
AM 322	Straight From The Heart/Fits Ya Good (6/86)
AMS 322	Straight From The Heart/Fits Ya Good/Run To You/Somebody (double-pack, 6/86)
AMY 322	Straight From The Heart/Fits Ya Good/Straight From The Heart (live) (12″, 6/86)
ADAM 2	Heat Of The Night/Another Day (3/87)
ADAM 212	Heat Of The Night (extended remix)/Heat Of The Night/Another Day (12″, 3/87)
ADAM 3	Hearts On Fire/Run To You (5/87)

ADAMC 312   Hearts On Fire/Run To You (cassette, 5/87)
ADAM 312   Hearts On Fire/Run To You/Native Sun (12″, 5/87)
AM 407   Victim Of Love/Heat Of The Night (live) (9/87)
AMF 407   Victim of Love/Heat Of The Night (live) (7″ box set with
             postcards and patch, 9/87)
AMC 407   Victim Of Love/Heat Of The Night (live) (cassette, 9/87)
AMY 407   Victim Of Love/Heat Of The Night (live)/Victim of Love (live)
             (12″, 9/87)
AM 769   (Everything I Do) I Do It For You/She's Only Happy When
             She's Dancing (live)(6/91)
AMMC 789   (Everything I Do) I Do It For You/She's Only Happy When
             She's Dancing (live) (cassette, 6/91)
AMY 789   (Everything I Do) I Do It For You (extended version)/(Every-
             thing I Do) I Do It For You/She's Only Happy When She's
             Dancing (live)/Cuts Like A Knife (live) (12″, 6/91).
AMCD 789   (Everything I Do) I Do It For You (extended version)/(Every-
             thing I Do) I Do It For You/She's Only Happy When She's
             Dancing (live)/Cuts Like A Knife (live) (CD, 6/91)
AM 812   Can't Stop This Thing We Started/It's Only Love (live) (8/91)
AMMC 812   Can't Stop This Thing We Started/It's Only Love (live) (cas-
             sette, 8/91)
AMY 812   Can't Stop This Thing We Started/It's Only Love (live)/Hearts
             On Fire (12″, one side etched, 8/91)
AMCD 812   Can't Stop This Thing We Started/It's Only Love (live)/Hearts
             On Fire (CD, 8/91)
AM 838   There Will Never Be Another Tonight/Into The Fire (live)
             (11/91)
AMC 838   There Will Never Be Another Tonight/Into The Fire (live)
             (cassette, 11/91)
AMY 838   There Will Never Be Another Tonight/Into The Fire (live)/One
             Night Love Affair (live) (12″, one side etched, 11/91)
AMCD 838   There Will Never Be Another Tonight/Into The Fire (live)/One
             Night Love Affair (live) (picture CD, digipak, 11/91)
AM 848   Thought I'd Died And Gone To Heaven/Somebody (live) (2/92)
AMY 848   Thought I'd Died And Gone To Heaven/Somebody (live)/
             Everything I Do) I Do It For You (12″ gatefold 'silver disc'
             sleeve, 2/92)
AMCD 848   Thought I'd Died And Gone To Heaven/Somebody (live)/Heat
             Of The Night (live) (CD picture disc, 2/92)
AM 879   All I Want Is You/Run To You (live) (7″, 7/92)
AMY 879   All I Want Is You/Long Gone (live)/Run To You (live) (12″
             includes free poster, 7/92)
AMCD 879   All I Want Is You/Long Gone (live)/Run To You (live) (CD
             single, 9/92)
AM 68   Do I Have To Say The Words?/Summer of '69 (live) (9/92)
AMCD 68   Do I Have To Say The Words?/Summer of '69 (live)/Kids
             Wanna Rock (live)/Can't Stop This Thing We Started (live)
             (CD single, 9/92)
AMCDR68   Do I Have To Say The Words?/Summer of '69 (live)/Kids
             Wanna Rock/Can't Stop This Thing We Started (live) (CD
             single, 9/92)

580422	Please Forgive Me/Can't Stop This Thing We Started (live) (10/93)
580423	Please Forgive Me/Can't Stop This Thing We Started (live)/ There Will Never Be Another Tonight (live)/C'mon Everybody (live) (10/93)
580441	Please Forgive Me/House Arrest (live)/(Everything I Do) I Do It For You (live)/Can't Stop This Thing We Started (live) (alt CD version, 11/93)
580476-7	All For Love/All For Love (instr.) (features Sting and Rod Stewart, 12/93)
580477-2	All For Love/All For Love (instr.)/Straight From the Heart (live): Bryan Adams/Love Is Stronger Than Justice (The Munificent Seven): Sting/If Only: Rod Stewart (special 5-track CD edition, 12/93)

ALBUMS

AMLH 64800	Bryan Adams (3/81)
AMLH 64864	You Want It, You Got It (4/82, relaunched 8/85)
AMLH 64919	Cuts Like A Knife (3/83)
AMA 5013	Reckless (2/85)
AMLH 64919	Cuts Like A Knife (reissue in new sleeve, 3/86)
AMA 3907	Into The Fire (3/87)
397164-1	Waking Up The Neighbours (8/91)
54157-1	So Far So Good: Greatest Hits (11/93)
397094-4	Live! Live! Live! (7/94)

IMPORTANT CASSETTE

AMC 24101	Cuts Like A Knife/Reckless (reissue, 5/90)

CDs

CDA 4919	Cuts Like A Knife (3/83, reissued 3/86)
CDA 5013	Reckless (2/85)
CDA 3154	You Want It, You Got It (8/85)
CDA 3100	Bryan Adams (1/87)
CDA 3907	Into The Fire (3/87)
CDMID 100	Bryan Adams (mid-price reissue, 1988)
CDMID 101	You Want It, You Got It (mid-price reissue, 1988)
CDMID 102	Cuts Like A Knife (mid-price reissue, 1988)
397164-2	Waking Up The Neighbours (8/91)
CD 540157-2	So Far So Good: Greatest Hits (11/93)
397094-2	Live! Live! Live! (7/94)

All the above releases are on A&M

with thanks to *Record Collector* and Justin Brown

BRYAN ADAMS: CANADIAN HERO

The Juno Awards are the annual Canadian Music Awards presented by the Canadian Academy of Recording Arts and Sciences as voted by its membership.

   - Denotes Nomination
   * Denotes Award

1979
- Most Promising Male Vocalist of the Year

1980
- Most Promising Male Vocalist of the Year

1982
* Male Vocalist of the Year

1983
* Album of the Year—*Cuts Like a Knife*
* Male Vocalist of the Year
* Composer of the Year—"Cuts Like a Knife"
* Producer of the Year—*Cuts Like a Knife*
- Composer of the Year—"Straight From the Heart"
- Single of the Year—"Cuts Like a Knife"
- Single of the Year—"Straight From the Heart"

1985
* Album of the Year—*Reckless*
* Male Vocalist of the Year
* Composer of the Year
- Producer of the Year—*Reckless*
- Single of the Year—"Run To You"

1986
* Male Vocalist of the Year
- Single of the Year—"Diana"
- Composer of the Year

1987
* Canadian Entertainer of the Year
* Male Vocalist of the Year
- Album of the Year—*Into the Fire*
- Single of the Year—"Heat of the Night"
- Producer of the Year—"Heat of the Night"
- Composer of the Year

1989
- Canadian Entertainer of the Year

1992
* Canadian Entertainer of the Year
* Producer of the Year

- Album of the Year—*Waking Up The Neighbours*
- Single of the Year—"Can't Stop This Thing We Started"
- Single of the Year—"(Everything I Do) I Do It For You"
- Songwriter of the Year

1993
- Canadian Entertainer of the Year

BRYAN ADAMS: WORLD AWARDS AND HONOURS

1982
Yamaha Music Festival (Japan)—"Let Him Know" nominated for Pop Song of the Year

1983
National Association of Record Merchandisers (NARM)—Best
Selling New Artist
Album Network—#2 Male AOR Artist
Radio and Records—#3 Most Played AOR Album

1984
Canadian Association of Recording Arts and Sciences (CARAS-BC)—4th
Annual Tribute to West Coast Music—
Special International Achievement Award
Music Express Magazine Reader's Poll Gold Microphone Awards —Best
Artist, Album, Single, Male Vocalist and Video.

1985
City of Los Angeles—February 1st, 1985, proclaimed "Bryan Adams Day"
MTV Video Awards—Nominated for:
- "Run To You"—Special Effects, Art Direction, Editing, Cinematography, Direction and Most Experimental.
- "Heaven #2"—Cinematography and Most Experimental.
Performing Rights Organization of Canada Ltd. (PROCan)—William Harold
Moon Award for International Achievement
Canadian Recording Industry Association (CRIA)—Diamond Award —Presented for Canadian sales of over 1 million for "Reckless"
Billboard—named #1 Top Male Pop Singles Artist, #3 Top Male Pop Album
Artist and #5 Top Pop Artist.

1986
Grammy Awards—Nominated for Best Male Rock Performance for "Reckless"
and Best Rock Performance by a Duo or Group for "It's Only Love" with Tina
Turner.
Rock Express Magazine's Reader's Poll Awards—Top Male Vocalist Award
and the Bob Geldof Humanitarian Award for his work with Northern Lights,
Amnesty International, the Prince's Trust and other charity projects.
MTV Video Awards—Best Stage Performance in a Video for "It's Only Love"
with Tina Turner.

1987
Performing Rights Organization of Canada (PROCan)—Crystal Award —to commemorate radio airplay of over 100,000 times for "Straight From the Heart".
Canadian Music Publishers' Association (CMPA)—Rock Song of the Year— "In the Heat of the Night."
Canadian Association of Recording Arts and Sciences (CARAS-BC)—International Achievement Award.

1988
Rock Express Magazine Reader's Poll Awards—Top Male Vocalist and Single of the Year for "Victim of Love."

1990
Order of British Columbia—for outstanding citizenship
Maple Ridge Hospital Foundation—Humanitarian of the Year Award
Order of Canada—for outstanding achievement as a Canadian citizen.
Canadian Recording Industry Association—Best Male Artist of the Decade

1991
Guinness Book of World Records—longest standing #1 single (16 weeks) in the history of the British Charts for "(Everything I Do) I Do It For You"
Popcorn Magazine (Germany)—Golden Elvis Award for Top Male Vocalist
Bravo Magazine—Golden Otto Award—Top Male Vocalist
Pop Rocky Magazine—Best Male Vocalist
Australian Music Awards—Most Popular International Male, Most Popular International Song (for "(Everything I Do) I Do It For You") and Most Popular International Album (for "Waking Up The Neighbours") at the Australian Music Awards.
Big Magazine (UK)—Best Male Singer, Best Pop Video
West Coast Music Awards (CARAS-BC)—International Achievement Award
Billboard Magazine Awards—Hot 100 Single, #1 World Single and Hot AC (Adult Contemporary) Single for "(Everything I Do) I Do It For You."
Radio & Records—#1 Contemporary Hit Radio Song for "(Everything I Do) I Do It For You."
National Association of Record Merchandisers Award—Best Selling Single for "(Everything I Do) I Do It For You"
ASCAP (Association of Song Composers, Authors and Publishers) —Most Performed Song of the Year for "(Everything I Do) I Do It For You."

1992
Grammy Nominations and Awards (*) for:
- Record of the Year—"(Everything I Do) I Do It For You"
- Song of the Year—"(Everything I Do) I Do It For You"
- Best Pop Vocal Performance Male—"(Everything I Do) I Do It For You"
* Best Song Written Specifically for a Motion Picture or Television — "(Everything I Do) I Do It For You"
- Best Rock Vocal Performance Solo—"Can't Stop This Thing We Started"
- Best Rock Song—"Can't Stop This Thing We Started"
Academy of Motion Picture Arts & Sciences—Nominated for an Academy

Award for Special Achievement In Music (Original Music) for "(Everything I Do) I Do It For You."

American Music Awards—Nominations for Best Pop/Rock Male Vocalist and Song of the Year for "(Everything I Do) I Do It For You."

American Paper Institute—Environmental Grammy Award—for using recycled material in packaging his 1991 CD "Waking Up The Neighbours."

American Top 40—#1 Song of the Year for "(Everything I Do) I Do It For You."

Canadian Academy of Recording Arts & Sciences—Special Recognition Award for Unprecedented Global Success for "(Everything I Do) I Do It For You."

Irish Record Awards—Best International Male Artist

Billboard Magazine—International Achievement Award

Golden Penguin Award (Australia)—Singer of the Year

Ivor Novello Award (Britain)—Songwriting Award for "(Everything I Do) I Do It For You."

MTV Movie Awards—Best Song From A Movie—"(Everything I Do) I Do It For You."

Playboy Magazine Music Poll—Best Video Award—"(Everything I Do) I Do It For You."

MuchMusic Canadian Music Awards—Special Recognition Award

125th Anniversary of the Confederation of Canada—medal for a significant contribution to the compatriots, community and to Canada.

Good Rockin' Tonight Video Teddy Awards—Best Video ("Thought I'd Died and Gone to Heaven"); Best Canadian Male Performer; Best International Male Performer.

Australian Performing Rights Association Awards—Most Performed Foreign Work for "(Everything I Do) I Do It For You."

Daily Mail News / Capital Radio #1, the Top 500 of all time for "(Everything I Do) I Do It For You." (Also, three other songs listed).

The Record magazine—Top Retail Album for "Waking Up The Neighbours."

1993

American Music Awards—nomination for Favourite Pop/Rock Male Artist

Grammy Awards—nomination for Best Rock Male Vocalist for "There Will Never Be Another Tonight."

BRYAN ADAMS: Factfile
Twenty Things You Didn't Know

* Bryan Adams celebrated his thirty-fifth birthday—and his most successful year ever in 1994. He ended the year with live guest appearances with Luciano Pavarotti (in Italy) and the Rolling Stones (in New Orleans)

* He was born in Kingston, Ontario, Canada on November 5 1959. Fittingly enough, his middle name is Guy.

* Bryan received a guitar for his tenth birthday in 1969. His treasured first 'real' guitar was a white Stratocaster, purchased in the 1970s . . .

* . . . over twenty years later his record company presented him with a custom platinum Stratocaster—to honour career sales of 40 million albums

* His first ever singing engagement was with Canadian bar band Shock. At the age of sixteen, he joined pop and rock band Sweeney Todd, for whom he wrote his first ever song, 'Until I Find You'

* Seventeen years later, in 1991, Bryan Adams claimed his place in British chart history as the singer, cowriter and coproducer of '(Everything I Do) I Do It For You'—a chart topper for sixteen straight weeks, it is still the longest running number one single of all time

* Bryan Adams has earned a reputation as one of rock's most hard working live performers. He has toured the world virtually non-stop since the early 1980s—playing over 500 live gigs to an estimated audience of 3.5 million people

* Meanwhile Adams achieved worldwide fame with the extraordinary success of his *Waking Up The Neighbours* album, released in 1991. Writing, recording and producing his masterpiece took over eighteen months

* *Waking Up The Neighbours*, released in July 1991, has to date sold over 13 million copies worldwide and has topped the charts in fourteen countries. It

also includes the single '(Everything I Do) I Do It For You'—a number one chart topper in no less than 20 countries

* Incredibly, *Waking Up The Neighbours* is Bryan Adams' only new studio album of the 1990s. Meanwhile all of the artists' back catalogue is still available on A&M Records—and work continues on a new studio album hopefully scheduled for some time in 1995 . . .

* A dedicated live performer, Bryan Adams has always welcomed the chance to help others through his music. He appeared at the 'Live Aid' concert in Philadelphia in 1985 (and also wrote the Canadian charity record 'Tears Are Not Enough' for Ethiopia) and followed this with a two-week, six-date American tour for Amnesty International along with Sting, U2, Peter Gabriel and Lou Reed in 1986 . . .

* . . . he also sang on Rock Aid Armenia's version of Deep Purple's 'Smoke On The Water' in 1989

* Other famous musicians and performers Bryan Adams has worked with include: Tina Turner (on the hit single 'It's Only Love' in 1985), Rod Stewart and Sting (on the 'All For Love' single and video in 1994), Motley Crue, Belinda Carlisle, Paul Rodgers (backing vocals) and Joe Cocker (he wrote and played on Cocker's American hit 'When The Night Comes In' . . .

* . . . he also made an acclaimed appearance at the elaborate Berlin Wall side staging of Roger Waters' *The Wall* in 1991

* Does the superstar have a pet hate? If he does, it's probably publicity. Bryan Adams has consistently shunned any attempts to pry into his personal life, summing up his success with the comment: 'I'm just a guy that's lucky to be there . . .

* So what's Bryan the songwriter's all-time favourite lyric? 'I got my first real six-string/bought it at the five and dime/played it till my fingers bled/it was the summer of '69' (from 'Summer of '69). "A great lyric," said Adams. "Probably the best I've ever written . . ."'

* Highest UK chart debut: 'Please Forgive Me' which entered the UK charts at number three in November 1993

* Bryan Adams completed a movie soundtrack No 1 hat trick in 1993 with 'All For Love' from Disney's *The Three Musketeers*. Previous chart toppers were 'Heaven' (from the movie *A Night In Heaven*, a US No 1 in 1985), and of course '(Everything I Do) I Do It For You' from *Robin Hood: Prince of Thieves*

* Most collectable Bryan Adams single: The 'Heaven' 7″ double pack from 1985

* Most unusual Bryan Adams single: 'Let Me Take You Dancing'—a disco hit in 1979, Bryan bought his first car on the proceeds